THE CUCKOO'S LEA

THE CUCKOO'S LEA

The Forgotten History of Birds and Place

Michael J. Warren

BLOOMSBURY WILDLIFE

LONDON · OXFORD · NEW YORK · NEW DELHI · SYDNEY

BLOOMSBURY WILDLIFE
Bloomsbury Publishing Plc
50 Bedford Square, London, WC1B 3DP, UK
Bloomsbury Publishing Ireland Limited,
29 Earlsfort Terrace, Dublin 2, D02 AY28, Ireland

BLOOMSBURY WILDLIFE and the Diana logo are trademarks of Bloomsbury
Publishing Plc

First published in the United Kingdom 2025

For legal purposes, the Author Acknowledgements on p. 270 and the Permissions on
p. 278 constitute an extension of this copyright page.

Bloomsbury Publishing Plc does not have any control over, or responsibility for, any
third-party websites referred to or in this book. All internet addresses given in this
book were correct at the time of going to press. The author and publisher regret any
inconvenience caused if addresses have changed or sites have ceased to exist, but can
accept no responsibility for any such changes

A catalogue record for this book is available from the British Library

Library of Congress Cataloguing-in-Publication data has been applied for

ISBN: HB: 978-1-3994-1207-0; Audiobook: 978-1-3994-1208-7;
ePub: 978-1-3994-1205-6; ePDF: 978-1-3994-1204-9

2 4 6 8 10 9 7 5 3 1

Typeset in Deanta Global Publishing Services, Chennai, India
Printed and bound in Great Britain by CPI Group (UK) Ltd, Croydon, CR0 4YY

MIX
Paper | Supporting
responsible forestry
FSC
www.fsc.org   FSC® C013604

To find out more about our authors and books visit www.bloomsbury.com
and sign up for our newsletters

For product safety related questions contact productsafety@bloomsbury.com

*To my late father, also Michael John Warren (1940–2020),
who loved Kent and spent the final decade of his life there.
This book is dedicated to the years we spent living four miles
apart in our bird-named towns, Cranbrook and Hawkhurst.
He knew I was writing this book.*

Contents

Prologue   9

Chapter one: An Antiquity of Cranes   19

Chapter two: The Cuckoo's Lea   41

Chapter three: Pathless Ways   63

Chapter four: Charterlands   87

Chapter five: An Owl's Cry   111

Chapter six: Marsh Dwellers   133

Chapter seven: The Gull's Home   157

Chapter eight: Everywhere and Nowhere   183

Chapter nine: Hawk in the Wood   207

Chapter ten: Crow Hill   233

Epilogue   259
Acknowledgements   270
Birds in English Place Names: A Glossary   273
Permissions   278
Notes   280
Further Reading and References   290
Index   299

Places of *The Cuckoo's Lea*

North Sea

DAL RIATA
PICTS

Rubhna na Faoileige and Rubha nan Sgarbh
Islay

Insula Farne
Inner Farnes

NORTHUMBRIA

Roudecliva
Rockcliffe Marshes

Solway Firth

Ravenstandale
Ravenstonedale

Rochebi
Rookby

Caberg
Kaber

Crakepot
Crackpot

Irish Sea

0   50   100 miles

N

Olleie
Ulley

Wizebi
Whisby

Hikelinga
Hickling Broad

BRITONS

MERCIA

Castre
Castor Hanglands

EAST

Snitefeld
Snitterfield

Geakeslea
Yaxley

Cranewisse
Cranwich

ANGLIA

Werochestan
Wroxton

Clife
Bishop's Cleeve

ESSEX

Purlea
Purleigh

Walfliet
Wallasea

Brin Eos
near Heol-y-Cyw

Frilesham and Borgedeberie
Frilsham and Bucklebury

Uulacumb
Ulcombe

Hedekaruna
Headcorn

KENT

Slapeford
Lapford

WESSEX

Cranebroca
Cranbrook

Ulaham
lost village

Yekesburn
Exbourne

Swealewanclif
Swallowcliffe

Bedinges
Upper Beeding

SUSSEX

Hauochesten
Hawkhurst

BRITONS

Earnaleach and Bosanhamm
Earnley and Bosham

La Bataile
Battle

Hulecombe
Owlacombe

English Channel

Prologue

Glydwish, East Sussex

The place was nothing much. A slip of woods on private land, accessible by a duck-and-cut under barbed wire and a push through bramble. It was mostly coppiced sweet chestnut, no tree older than the twentieth century, no understorey except for a mat of autumn leaves. I struggled for the right word; wood felt too grand, thicket or copse too small. A spinney, perhaps. I arrived quickly and moved quicker. Stooped under daybreak murk, I made a brisk pace of it from one side to the other, pausing only once because I thought a vehicle on the treeline might be waiting to confront me. Busted, before six o'clock in the morning. The wood, it turned out, was so small that from inside the boundaries I was momentarily confused. The car was my own, parked on the treeline just minutes ago, still ticking under a hot bonnet.

The place, I say, was nothing much. If the thrill of trespass was my aim, there were far better places, and the intrusion was so momentary it could hardly be said to count. Nor was this the place for a leisurely, distracted Sunday stroll with the possibility of losing your way. If it weren't for the name, it would have been disappointing. If it weren't for the name, I would never have found it.

Glydwish is the surviving fragment of something considerably older, hard though it may be to imagine now. There are ghost stories attached to the place: the tormented soul of an innocent farm labourer, hanged in 1825 for murder. His wails still haunt the wood, it is said (the wails of an innocent fox, more likely). It's a place that

obscures its history in accumulating human changes, like
the layers of centuries, only just revealing its secret in the
letters of its name, which have altered over time as slowly
as the land itself. I happened upon it when scanning the
antique map that has hung on a wall in every house I've
lived in since I first moved to Kent 16 years ago. This
splinter of trees doesn't show on anything less than the
minutiae of an Ordnance Survey map. Mine is an inch-
per-mile edition of the whole Kentish Weald, and the
wood is conveniently located in the far bottom left-hand
corner, south of Burwash and Etchingham, not far from
the Sussex–Kent border.

Glydwish. Beneath what seems like small-place
insignificance, there is moment and happening, though
the name, like the wood, masks it well. Traces of an ancient
landscape, birds and people echo faintly to anyone with
care and patience enough to discover the signs. To speak
the name is to speak the past. *Glydwish*. The two parts of
the name derive from Old English. *Wisc* means 'marsh or
damp meadow'. It's still there, the *wisc*, where the land is
wet and soft between the Rother and Dudwell rivers,
marshy with reed and sedge as it must have once been
extensively in this little Sussex spot. Aged thorn bushes
with bearded lichens create dense, gnarled boundaries,
and alder or willow grow where it is dampest. A winter
walk here demands a reliable pair of wellies through the
plashy clods where tributaries of the Rother intersect and
flood the meadows.

But what of the other half of the name, the first half? It
sounds no less strange than *wisc* to our ears, but you might
just guess that it bears some sort of relation to our modern
word 'glide'. And you'd be right. *Glida* comes directly
from the verb *glidan*, 'to glide'. It is an old word for kite.
The red kite.

The 'glider' is a bird of my childhood, a bird of particular place. It was probably the first bird to give me some half-understood intimation that birds *could* affect my feelings for a place, like the shifting light of day. Seeing red kites now is always freighted with some misplaced desire for exoticism, as though red kites do not belong outside the locations and memories of my childhood holidays. Those were days when it was still necessary to visit central Wales if you wanted to see these resplendent birds. We did, year after year, making the long trip in a clapped-out green Astra that wheezed under the weight of suitcases, my brothers and I wedged in between whatever luggage wouldn't fit anywhere else. The red kite was an important bird to me very early on for that reason: the anticipation, the searching, the hard-won elation; the sense that this was a bird for the distinguished occasion of the annual family holiday when my brothers and I roamed young and easy under the Welsh hills. Such was the impact of those experiences that it is impossible for me to detach red kites from that time and place, wherever I might see them. They are, for me, dearly and perpetually, a bird of Wales, of one remote Cambrian valley where the River Towy flows down past the tiny village of Rhandirmwyn. The tension in those hills raised by the possibility of kites still impels the thrill of seeing them now.

The kites of Glydwish are different. They are a reminder that these birds, before the persecutions and egg collectors that very nearly did for them, were once widespread all over the British landscape, including in Sussex, as, thankfully, they are again today. I have seen them here. *Everywhere* was home to the red kite then, not just the Welsh uplands that became their last refuge for most of the twentieth century. Place names can tell us that sort of thing – the distributions and populations of species long ago. They remind us of how things have changed.

But what seized me about Glydwish was something even more powerful. It was the story I could half-read, squinting through obscurity, like viewing a long-hidden painting through whitewash on a church wall. A story connecting me across centuries to others who knew a place by its kites, by the fork-tailed sky-wheelers figuring the marsh-damp air. Those people enshrined that bond of bird and place in a name that has endured for a millennium and more, even, perhaps most poignantly, when the birds did not. Speak it now and you summon those old relationships and identities again, the name still pulsing with the force of that first moment when a person looked and saw and spoke.

This is a book about places such as Glydwish and its kites, about how and why birds inspire our sense of place in such profound and enduring ways. It is about my own relationships with places through birds – places that matter to me and us now in the twenty-first century. Some I discover for the first time, while others, well known and much loved, have formed deep impressions upon me for years. Not all of these places have bird names, but birds have defined and transformed all these places. This book, however, is also about the world that places like Glydwish transport us to, the imaginations we can enter through the secrets of place names all around us to know the forgotten relationships at the heart of dwelling and belonging.

That world is ancient Britain, specifically England at the time of its origins. A 'Dark Age' England, as it has wrongly been called for so long, before the Norman Conquest; an England of Celtic Britons, Anglo-Saxon settlements and kingdoms, of Viking invasions and yet more settlements. If we speak of the whole Middle Ages (spanning some 1,000 years from AD 450–1500), it is no exaggeration to say that in Britain we have been 'medieval' for most of our recorded history. It is an age of beginnings: the age when our language, our literature, our nationhood, first come into being, and when most of our places – our hamlets, villages, towns and cities – get their names, and the forms and features of our varied landscapes acquire their vocabularies. And hidden in those names are the earliest tantalising glimpses into what early English people knew, thought, even felt, about nature, long before anything like modern scientific understandings came about. In a way then, and along the way, what follows is also a sort of untold origin tale of our natural history.

We live in medieval places. Quite literally. Nearly all English places and their names are very old.[1] Some probably go back to the fifth- and sixth-century migrations of Germanic-speaking peoples to these shores – traditionally identified as Jutes, Angles, Saxons and Frisians – whose languages evolved into what we now call Old English, the first phase of a long development that eventually produced modern English. Alongside these place names, there are also many derived from Old Norse, in more northerly and easterly parts of the country where Viking influence was dominant from the ninth century. Some (though few by comparison) are far older, such as the Celtic or even pre-Celtic place names of most of our rivers (Derwent, Ouse, Wye, Thames, Avon and so on).

A little bit of knowledge about place names can get you a long way. Begin with the suffixes, learn your *ings* ('the people or descendants of') and *tons* and *hams* (both variously referring to settlements, from where we get 'town' and 'home'), and you've already begun to map out early England, to visualise how this world looked, to what extent it might still exist today, and where you require a little imagination to see back through urban expansion or agricultural clearance. Some names are straightforward, but others, seemingly obvious in modern English, will trip you up. So, while Mudford, Wetwood and, believe it or not, Shitterton will give you no trouble, you'd be unlikely to correctly guess the original meanings of places such as Braintree, Bitchfield, Scratchbury or Frostenden.[2]

Many names mention the individuals or people who owned or settled territories, Our places, in this respect, are a repository of obsolete but marvellous medieval names: Beorma (Birmingham), Cippa (Cippemore), Dudda (Doddington), Gunnhild (Gunthorpe), Mucel (Muckleford), Nunna (Nunton), Ormr (Ormskirk), Poca (Pockley), Reada (Reading), Snotta (Nottingham), Wassa (Washington). Names of this kind are, unsurprisingly, often linked to human-made sites (forts, towns, villages, manors, estates and so on), but a huge number of other names are associated with landscapes and habitats: open land (*feld*), hills (*hyll*), valleys (*dene*), rivers (*ea*), estuaries (*fleot*), woodlands (*leah*), marshes (*mersc*), flood plains (*wæsse*). The language of landscape, in this sense, was one of the first topics in English culture, and as the great place name scholar Margaret Gelling states, the old words 'were rarely, perhaps never, synonyms'. Sometimes, these land features stand alone in place names with no attachment to any one or thing, the land itself being the point of interest, as in the case of Caldy in Cheshire, which in its original form, *Calders*, literally means 'cold arse'. It refers to a 'buttock' of exposed coastal hillside, but you can detect, I like to think, a wry local humour – some poor soul's complaint on the bitter cold.

Take a walk, a cycle, a drive almost anywhere in this country and you confront this inventory of Old English toponyms (place names derived from the land's physical features) in almost every signpost you pass. Get your eye in and you can navigate, not by road numbers and remembered directions, not by the network of tarmacked surfaces, but according to the lay of the land, allowing the names of each place you pass to reveal underlying existence and form, reading their meanings like contours, conceiving the whole as a map of ancient thought and emotion, of connection to the land. You can learn to visualise these hidden histories as excavations down through boggy *wisc*, where the imbrications of each seeping layer bleed versions of place names into one another across centuries as they change, preserving and obscuring at once.

And then there are those names, a great many of them, that look to the creatures inhabiting the land. These names, to my mind, are the most enthralling of all, because they reveal a world in which *we* are not so apparent or dominant. They describe places that are inhabited and owned by other lives – trees, flowers, and all kinds of animals: the gnat's valley, the fox's town, the bramble's corner. To be in some of these places now feels as though the medieval world has survived fully intact in another dimension parallel to our own. As often as not though, you have to discover that same past differently. How strange it is today to imagine the ash tree by a river ford that gave its existence to what is now a large town in Kent, sprawling outwards into retail parks and industrial estates. Was it a single, majestic ash or a distinctive ash grove, I wonder? There is a dizzying shift in scale across the centuries implied in locations like Ashford. This was a time in which the localised was so central and entire to people's existences that a place could be identified or characterised by a single tree species growing by a ford.

Among all this toponymic flora and fauna, birds feature best of all wild creatures as vitalising elements and forces in medieval places. There are those you might expect – crows, hawks, ducks, swans and geese – and those you wouldn't be surprised to find in an earlier historical age, such as eagles and cranes. But there are many others – owls, woodpeckers, swallows and cuckoos – including those you probably wouldn't expect: who would imagine, for instance, the mulch-and-mud snipe probing the wormhouse, reedbed bitterns, or dunnocks and buntings as spirits of place? There is almost certainly a town or village, a farm, house or lane near to you, wherever you live, with an avian origin. The identity of bird reverberated again and again in people's attachments to place.

Of course, England is but one country in the British and Irish archipelago. In the earliest medieval centuries, there was no 'England', only competing kingdoms that were eventually unified in the tenth century. The peoples of our Isles included Celtic populations, speaking various languages, all of whom had made Britain and Ireland home long before the arrival of Germanic settlers who conventionally mark the historical beginning of what we term the Middle Ages.[3] Undoubtedly, these peoples had their own complex relationships with the natural world, as assured and sophisticated as the field systems they created, which, in many cases, we now know to be the prehistoric patterns of agricultural landscapes surviving to this day. In short, associations of birds with places are not unique to England and the English language, and consequently you will find examples from other countries and languages in the chapters that follow. However, early origins of Britain and Ireland's places are best evidenced in the names of England,[4] and the vast majority of these – among them those recording birds in an impressive variety and number – are indeed Old English. While, therefore, our relationships with nature clearly long predate the English Middle Ages, this is the story of how birds enchanted us and our homes in the beginnings of a language that became English, in the lands that became England.

What is it about birds that caught people's imaginations and made them such vivifying spirits and shapers of place? The journeys in this book seek answers to that question; journeys made and told in search of the origins of our relationships with birds and place that still matter, poignantly and profoundly, in our love of both today. What does it mean for our sense of these places if the creatures and habitats that once defined them are no longer there, when only names remain, creaking in the wind like pub signs whose buildings have long since closed or fallen into ruin? These are questions that echo soberly in present times when we are all too aware of how dramatically and devastatingly our spaces – wild or otherwise – are changing or disappearing. Sometimes the birds are still there, but many are gone, and the physical locations themselves unrecognisably changed. Sometimes, even the places themselves are gone. Entirely and long vanished. Ghosts of birds in the ghosts of places.

Always, I am guided by the names. Or rather, the birds in the names; secret, hidden, but all around us. In the end, all are inseparable to me. Birds and places and names, past and present. All become entwined with my connections to the places I explore to know them now, and to imagine them as they once were, to discover birds like the Glydwish kites in places we have long known, loved, made, transformed, celebrated and, sadly too often, destroyed.

1

An Antiquity of Cranes

Cranbrook, Kent ~ Hickling Broad, Norfolk

We lived in Cranbrook for 12 years. Not so very long perhaps, but long enough to know the magic of a place, its conjurations upon the heart. It is the place where I've lived for longer than anywhere else in my adult life. My wife's connections are older still. She attended the centuries-old grammar school where we both now work, and where we met. The house we lived in for our final few years in the town is one of the oldest dwellings on the High Street, and probably all of Cranbrook. We chose it for this very reason; we like to live close to the past. It was once part of an old coaching inn, and the carriage archway passed directly underneath what was our daughters' bedroom. Inside is all warped wood and crumbling plaster. Some of the beams are thick as masts, knotted, twisted and nowhere straight, as though the house had been built around a mighty tree never cut to rectilinear form, but which remained standing, the bole and branches growing into gnarled age with the dwelling. Its natural imperfections are mirrored in the low lintels and ship-sloping floors. The oldest beams have their histories marked, cut and bored into their woody heft: mortise and dowel holes from prior uses, candle holder brackets, the crevices of age and stress, craftsmen's graffiti, the tunnels and pocks of woodworms.

We love this about Cranbrook. Cranbrook's history is rich and evident in buildings that span 700 years of human residence and industry, right back to its lucrative wool and cloth days in the time of Chaucer. St Dunstan's Church, built in lustrous sandstone on the highest ground in town and visible from nearly all directions, is the splendid testament to Cranbrook's flourishing late medieval trade. But the name, and the town, is older. And older still, much older, is the brook itself. It is an ancient latitude through this place. Everything begins with the brook.

For most, it passes unnoticed and ignored. It is a river-runt, a feeble litter-leak. What attraction could it have to anyone? It would never have been large. Old English *broc* refers to small waterways, carrying much the same sense as modern 'brook'. But its flow was once fast and strong enough to power mills and supply the fulling ponds essential for the production of wool. Things have changed. For large parts of its town passage, the brook now runs under concreted ground, and where it runs parallel to the High Street it trickles slow and murky as sewage through a culvert (a state partly created by centuries of industry). Plastic bottles, crisps packets and drinks cans litter its ditches. Its most frequent and loyal visitors are small gangs of teenagers who come to the adjacent children's playground to puff on vapes, chat, and be away from small-town attention. This is the Crane Valley, a name that implies something rather more impressive than the reality (rocky declivities, burbling riffles, wildflower dingles). But follow the Crane out of town, beyond where most bother or even think to venture, and the story is different.

Downstream, eastwards, past where the course runs under a car park, where it resurfaces south of the school, the waterway is grown over with briar and holly and, in summer, great forests of nettles, hogweed and hemlock water dropwort. The going is impenetrable in places, but further east still the brook turns wide and clear, with high, steep banks that shimmer with bluebells and pungent wild garlic in spring. One hot April I waded a length just like this through private land, barefoot, ducking under and climbing over branches that had fallen long ago and never been cleared.

In the other direction, west of town, the brook is equally secretive. Where the town's youths and the debris gather, it runs to the south of a small nature reserve managed by a team of local volunteers – a hectare water meadow with native wetland flowers and a smart wooden walkway, all within sight of the supermarket car park and its chain-link fences. Then, in one corner of the reserve, it disappears into thicker undergrowth. There is a track of sorts, beyond a leaning stile and into the bramble. It's on no map; you must find it yourself. It is my way out to the old Weald and into Cranbrook's deeper past. From the brambles onwards, it is harder work through an overgrown belt of wood, and then no right-of-way. But ignore that. Take the brook as your guide and make your own path.

Across private land and up to its source, the brook runs in its own valley. Down here you cannot see over the ridge into fields on either side, and all the way along trees grow up the banks, concealing you in a wooded tunnel. Even in winter the growth is dense enough that you are well hidden from any landowners who might be walking or working their fields along the tree lines (I've evaded one or two this way).

These strips of woodland guarding the brook may not look like much, but they are long-lived. There are huge, hoary field maples, and in spring the presence of flowers such as wood anemones also indicate the habitat's ancestry. These are gill woods – woodland along 'gills', stream-valleys. This part of the Weald is riven with a gill network, little green ravines hidden away in the farmland between towns. They are rarely explored today (most are private) and have survived precisely because of their topography: claggy Wealden clay on steep inclines, too bothersome to farm, is best left to the trees, which at various times in the last 2,000 years have provided charcoal for the Wealden iron industry. The damp micro-climates in the brook-carved valleys are ideal for a rich variety of ferns, mosses and liverworts (recently, they've even been identified as surviving examples of temperate rainforest, akin to the better-known vestiges on the west Atlantic coasts of Britain and Ireland). If you follow the gills south into the hills you discover larger remnants that have likely been continuously wooded since the medieval period, and in some cases perhaps since the last Ice Age, when the brooks themselves began life.

These gill landscapes are my Cranbrook. As much as their beauty, I love their secrecy; these places need seeking, as all the best places do. They are a glimpse into Cranbrook's likely origin: a wood pasture by running water, reached through the lanes that once led into the great medieval Weald. Drovers came in autumn from their estates on the forest fringes, or further out on the coasts, to fatten their beasts on acorns and beech mast by the good water, driving them home again for slaughter that coming winter, until one autumn, one year, someone thought it might not be a bad idea to stay put. And so a place comes to be. And a place's people. The brook people.

There comes a time, though, when the brook is not all. There are birds too. And these birds enter the people's consciousness, become part of their attachment to the land. And at some point – some tantalisingly irrecoverable moment – these birds have made such an impression that they are no less important than the brook itself in the identity of this place. How long ago that moment was is impossible to say. The earliest written reference to Cranbrook is from the eleventh century, in a manuscript associated with the Domesday Book surveys – William the Conqueror's ambitious, grand censuses of his newly acquired lands in 1086, 20 years after his invasion, and the most vital evidence we have for the early existence of England's places and their names. There are very few details there about Cranbrook's size and status in those early times, but the name is unmistakeable. *Cranebroca* (pronounced '*Craahhn-uh-braw-cuh*'). By the eleventh century, and for some time before, probably centuries before, this was the cranes' brook.

Cranes are good to start with. For much of human history they have been 'good to eat' and 'good to think with', as anthropologist Claude Lévi-Strauss said of non-human species generally in his famous adage.[1] But cranes – elegant, beautifully plumed and coloured, large and loud – are very good to start with too. They have always been, it seems, birds *par excellence*. Such is their appeal that the family Gruidae (cranes) have long been, and still are, emblem birds in almost any country worldwide in which they are found.[2] In early European art and literature, the crane is one of the very earliest represented birds: in Homer's famous description of the Greek army as vast crane flocks on the Bronze-Age Trojan plains, for instance, or on Neolithic Çatalhöyük's stucco walls, in what is now modern Turkey. People living in the northern hemisphere where most crane species live (and breed, in the far north) celebrate and revere their presence, from North America to Sweden to India to Japan, in some places gathering annually to greet returning birds in spring. Depending on

where one is in the world, there are different species with
different symbolic values that are locally important to
different nations, but the extent of their appeal implies an
underlying quality that has made cranes compelling birds
to us for a very long time.

This was no exception in the cultures of medieval
Europe. The common crane's status already had a
considerable pedigree – as suggested by the fact that
even the word pedigree is connected with cranes,
deriving from the Anglo-Norman term, *pé de grue*,
meaning 'foot of the crane', because this image suggested
the lines of lineage now better known as a family tree.
The most familiar instances of crane mania are largely
from the later Middle Ages and go hand in hand with
the aristocratic obsession for falconry and other
ostentatious displays of status. The common crane was a
highly desirable quarry at which to fly peregrines or
gyrfalcons, and its size and splendour made it popular
on the banquet table (sometimes in staggering numbers).
The bird also appears frequently in the illustrated
margins of illuminated manuscripts – it is probably, in
fact, the most depicted of all species in these exquisite
books. Before all this though, cranes made their mark
upon our places.

There are more cranes in our place names than any
other bird species. Type straight Old English *cran* into
Google Maps – or better still, do it the old-fashioned way,
pick up a road atlas of Britain and scan through the index
– and you'll see what I mean: Cranbourne, Cranford,
Cranmore, Cranleigh, Cranfield, Cranham … some 26
names or so. But there is also a huge number of so-called
'minor' names that you won't find listed: Cranmere,
Crankland, Cornhill, Cansiron …. If we add in Old Norse
trani too (the related Viking origin of crane-named places

in northern counties), there are hundreds of crane places all over England.[3]

To go by the names, these birds were apparently everywhere, a fact that seems inconceivable to us now. Some names are thrillingly obscure, their secrets hidden like fossils between the stratified layers of time's pressures upon the names into strange, modern forms. Who now would recognise the 'crane island' in Cornheyte (Oxfordshire) or the 'crane's strip of ploughland' in Cheshire's Cronkebuttis, both of which no longer exist? The spirits of cranes haunt the oil refinery on the Mersey dockside at Tranmere and the flyover conurbations of west London's Cranford, where the River Crane still runs (I've followed it under the thundering M4 overpass down to the boundary of Heathrow Airport). Other names make more sense, such as Cranborne in Dorset, where watery meadows line the River Crane out west of the village, or Cranwell (the cranes' spring) in Lincolnshire, and Cranmore (the cranes' pool) in Somerset, neither situated far from former or surviving wetlands.

Others still epitomise the unsolved mystery of cranes in Britain's past. Not because certain places are so modernised that it's hard to visualise cranes in long-gone habitats, but because in some places it's puzzling how cranes ever existed *at all*. Cranbrook is a case in point: cranes in the wooded High Weald? Did early drovers see and hear these birds each autumn in noisy, migrating flocks over woodland clearings? Did cranes touch down in these pastures to feed or rest? Was the land here between trees temptingly boggy (*brook* in Kent and Sussex can also mean 'swampy land')? Did cranes appear just once – a momentous and auspicious occasion – or were they seen regularly? The truth is we don't know. Cranbrook's cranes, as with nearly everything about the cranes of pre-modern

Britain, are both within our grasp and irretrievably lost. This is the crane's intriguing mystery in modern Britain. They have long vanished from our folk memories.

Because it seems just too remarkable that cranes were once widespread across England, it has often been suggested that Old English *cran* must also have referred to other big, long-legged water birds, such as the grey heron (for which there was, incidentally, a separate Old English name: *hragra*). Even with this possibility, the sheer wealth of crane places hints at something more, something intrinsically special about cranes that went to the heart of people's experiences of places. What was it that made cranes such appealing totems? Were our earliest place-namers drawn to an unmistakeable and unmissable sight and sound they and their ancestors knew well from back across the seas, where the seasons turned on the cranes' wheeling flights? Or, even earlier, when cranes were just one species in the abundance of life on the wetland plains now known as Doggerland – the bridge of land that joined Britain to the continent until it was flooded by rising sea levels about 6,000 years ago? Perhaps cranes somehow created and evoked for earlier peoples the same necessary bonds to their pasts as their beloved epics and sagas. For certain, the act of observing cranes is ancient.

That feeling for an antiquity of cranes has struck a chord with more than one modern writer trying to articulate why these birds matter to us. It is, in the words of American conservationist Aldo Leopold, part of their 'peculiar distinction'. In his beautiful and moving essay 'Marshland Elegy', Leopold evokes a profound sense of deep crane-time:

> *Our appreciation of the crane grows with the slow unraveling of earthly history. His tribe, we now know, stems out of the remote*

*Eocene. The other members of the fauna in which he originated
are long since entombed within the hills. When we hear his call
we hear no mere bird. We hear the trumpet in the orchestra of
evolution. He is the symbol of our untamable past, of that
incredible sweep of millennia which underlies and conditions the
daily affairs of birds and men.*

This is no hyperbole; cranes really do descend back that
far. One of the oldest indisputable sandhill crane fossils,
unearthed in Nebraska where this species still gathers in
tremendous numbers on migration, dates back 2.5 million
years (another crane fossil of unidentifiable species from
the same region is 10 million years old). It is one of the
earliest records we have of any modern bird species on
earth, and certainly older than us *sapiens*. For Leopold,
even at a moment when he feared their imminent
extinction, it is these staggering 'wider reaches of
evolutionary time' that underpin how cranes manifest a
sense of place: 'Amid the endless mediocrity of the
commonplace, a crane marsh holds a paleontological
patent of nobility, won in the march of aeons.' These
places where cranes are found are places in their fullest
and truest sense *because* of cranes.

Leopold was writing about sandhill cranes in North
America, but common cranes must have conferred upon
our Eurasian ancestors the same powerful feelings of time
and place, with no less fervency than Leopold's birds on a
Wisconsin marsh in 1937. For early English people, all of
that crane past was embedded in the very word itself.
Cran is one of a number of Old English bird names (we'll
encounter others) that has remained almost unaltered in
thousands of years. *Cran*, from Old Saxon *krano*, descends
back to the Indo-European beginnings of our language
somewhere around the Black Sea. *Ger.* It was a simple

word for 'noise' or noisemaking itself. *Ger* called across the Pontic steppes of our Neolithic ancestors. Strange though it might sound, that word already contained the distinctive consonants that cry 'crane' to us, shifting and clustering in different forms around a bugling vowel, the initial consonant transmuting over time as the name echoed down through the emerging proto languages of Europe and refined its mimicry of the crane's orotund notes. The descendants of *ger* – *geranos, grus, garan, krano, trani* – thronged in Homer's epic simile, resounded in the Celtic tongues and the marshland gutturals of the North Sea coasts.

The long procession of crane-time marches on. It gathers in its slow and stately step the smallness of human centuries, which are nonetheless to us the gradual making and history of our places. I feel its mysterious progress in my affections for Cranbrook: a stirring awareness of its force, which carries with it the wisdom of *cran* and flows through the ancient gill woods. When I follow the brook's ways out of town I follow the crane's ways too. They are as old as each other – the passage of brook and migration of bird formed when ice retreated 11,000 years ago.

The secrets of the town's brook, for me, are inseparable from the mystique of its cranes. I learned to love the allure of simply not knowing. All the same, I couldn't help wondering what it might be to know a place alive and loud, not through the inherited memory or myth or abstracted elemental of crane, but because of the birds themselves. I didn't know, but I knew a man who did.

Naturalist and writer Nick Acheson has crane on his garden list. For that matter, he also has white-tailed eagle, white stork, barn owl, marsh harrier, hobby, cuckoo and peregrine. You will consider that unsurprising when you learn that Nick lives in North Norfolk – widely regarded as one of the best regions in the whole country for its wildlife, particularly along its north coast. Nick, though, does his watching from home beside a duck pond in a tiny village, where he shares his flint cottage with a hybrid pheasant-chicken and a series of orphaned ducklings.

Nick does most things from home. He spent more than 20 years travelling and living all over the world working in conservation and wildlife tourism, but after much agonising gave it all up in 2019 on environmental grounds. Now he keeps to his vicinity, wherever possible getting around on bike or foot (in 2020 he travelled more than 1,000 miles on his mother's 42-year-old bicycle following the famous Norfolk herds of pink-footed geese, though that species too is on his garden list).

Nick's attachment to the local did not begin when he gave up flying. His cottage is a short walk from the River Wensum, near to where Nick spent the first seven years of his life, and just a few miles north-east is the village of Little Snoring, the other location of Nick's childhood, by the River Stiffkey. The Wensum most of all, the 'river of my life', as he calls it, is a compass and touchstone to Nick, the winding course (Wensum comes from Old English for exactly that) by which he orients and measures his own journeys, and every nook of which he identifies with childhood memories: his mother's lost purse, his father showing him his first dabchick by the millpond, catching crayfish with his brother. Nick's long associations with this little wedge of Norfolk combine memory and history with an extraordinary here-and-now alertness to the natural world's daily happenings. His nature knowledge, as wide ranging as his former travelling, is lent a paradoxical intensity under these conditions: it transforms the minutiae of local existence into a whole world whose bounds and biodiversity cannot be fully fathomed or mapped, even in a lifetime of trying.

I experienced all this for myself the first time I visited Nick's home for a self-invited saunter around his Wensum patch. We spent a morning in early August walking the parish: the common, the cock dump (where people offload unwanted chickens – Nick has rescued a few from here in his time), hummocky remains of the original medieval village, the meadow on the site of the former priory where a corncrake sang in 2020 and 2021. But mostly we took the way of the Wensum, and I thought of the times I have followed the brook out of Cranbrook. We talked of wilding and writing and our respective homescapes, and every turn in the conversation was punctuated by Nick attending to flowers and grasses and trees, hoverflies, dragonflies, butterflies, birds, bees, naming each one quietly and momentarily as if this litany of wild things were not a digression, but always and simply a natural immanence in any and every topic. Occasionally, when he spotted something more unusual, Nick paused for longer, descending to a flower or insect's height. At these moments he has a habit of speaking to these fellow parishioners like close friends or lovers – 'Hello my darling, what are you doing here?' – softly, sincerely, without the slightest hint of affectedness.

Cranes featured very little on that first visit. I was distracted by everything else. It was only when Nick pointed out a verge-side cranesbill flower that I remembered to ask him about the birds at all.

Growing up during the 1970s, the decade in which cranes returned to the UK, Nick knows what it's like to have local cranes, if not quite in your backyard (except when they fly over your garden), then at least on your stomping grounds. He has grown up with cranes and watched them stage a comeback in the Norfolk Broads landscape, where he learned and honed his love of natural history.

'Cranes go to my soul. I totally get why someone living in one of those old crane places hundreds of years ago would have seen them as a special part of something, even if the birds only turned up once or twice a year at migration time. They have such an impact. Their arrival anywhere is an announcement. They just own a place.'

Nick's words reminded me of that wonderful habit many of our old names have of making non-human species, no less than humans, the keepers of place: the cranes' brook, the cranes' ford, the cranes' field. They own place.

'Have you seen our cranes?'

I admitted that I had not. I'd not seen cranes in Britain at all.

'You have to see them. In winter. Come back in the winter.'

The village of Cranwich – it is apparently a village – is so small you'd miss it unless you were looking for it. I was looking for it, and I still missed it. Twice. The second time I was *in* Cranwich, and it still took me a short while to realise that its single street, which I mistook for a layby off the road out of Mundford, was, in fact, it. None of the handful of houses along Cranwich's street looked old, but the place is so small that it felt old – a sense that the place hasn't changed all that much since 1086 when the Domesday census recorded 36 households.

The church is equally hidden, just south of the village, down a track off another track behind a line of trees. It's a

medieval gem; a flint and limestone round-tower beauty
with a thatched roof. The tower, dating to the eleventh
century, is one of the oldest in East Anglia (most round-
tower churches in the country are in Norfolk). Not all
that many of our churches have such conspicuous and
extensive surviving Anglo-Saxon architecture, but a great
number are built on the site of former early medieval
foundations, or have early structures embedded in later
additions. Most of our churches are medieval in origin in
one way or another, and nearly every town and village
across the land has one. When visiting new places, I often
gravitate to the church as a starting point for exploration:
they are, though we take them for granted, immediate,
stone-solid contacts with the long past. To feel such
impressive endurance in their immense walls is to be
transported. More often than not, too, you'll have them all
to yourself.

I had to be on my way; there was much to do in a short
winter's day and I had some distance to travel yet across
Norfolk to reach the Broads. Brief as my visit was,
Cranwich at sunrise – even a blustery and cold sunrise in
February – was a pleasant discovery. A well-kept secret
serendipitously in keeping with the mystery I'd come to
associate with cranes.

Cranwich is one of very few crane-named sites in
Norfolk (another, Cranworth, is 19 miles east, and there
is Cranmer at Fakenham). It is nowhere near the Broads,
but if you didn't know you might well guess that
Norfolk's famous wetlands are the likely location of this
place meaning the 'cranes' marshy meadow'. There is no
problem imagining cranes in a boggy description like
that, though now all you'll find is miles of bare earth
and regimented lines of corrugated pig huts on the land
opposite the village. The Broads – as the scattering of

meres and pools in this region of East Anglia are known
– have always, in one way or another, been wet.
Centuries before these lakes which the Victorians made
so famous for leisure boating – they are the product of
flooded medieval peat and clay excavations – locals of
the region would have known blanket peat bogs where
cranes may well have bred (as they do in such habitats
elsewhere in northern Europe today). Cranes were
surely present on the medieval Broads right up to the
time of their extinction as breeding birds: written
records concerning the species from the sixteenth and
seventeenth centuries (when cranes finally disappeared
from Britain) relate to Norfolk and fens in surrounding
counties. The Broads may conceivably have been the
cranes' last stronghold.

I collected Nick and coffee supplies from his cottage by
mid-morning. Gale-force storms were forecast across
the country in the following 24 hours and I was nervous
that sortie gusts of wind might pick up early. That
wouldn't do. We got down to crane talk immediately,
discussing Nick's childhood memories of the birds in
the 1980s and the pair that first turned up at Hickling
in 1979.

'They're legendary now, and they were borderline
mythical back then because it was kept so quiet, but those
birds have been in my life from the start. Cranes can be
long-lived, so some of the offspring born to the early
generations at Horsey are still around now – the birds I
was watching in my teens.'

I envied Nick this. No one now living in any place in
England named after cranes of old can talk of the real

thing in their love of home turf, but being brought up on these Norfolk birds was surely the next best thing. There are other places in twenty-first-century Britain where you can find cranes, but these are mostly reintroduced birds (on the Somerset Levels, for instance). The Broadland birds returned themselves to the landscape where they were last recorded in England, as if they were pointedly emphasising their own revenant status. I was born in the year the pioneer pair reared their first female chick. There have been British breeding cranes all my life. It's possible that someone told me as a child that there were cranes in a place called Norfolk but, for all the chance I had of visiting them, they might as well have been in a foreign country.

'I found out about them at school,' Nick continued. 'I was friends with two brothers whose family owned land near Horsey, and one of them told me he'd seen cranes on their farm. He even showed me a photo to prove it. I just didn't believe it though, so I went to find my biology teacher, Dave Horsley, who was a huge influence on me at the time, still is, and said what I'd heard, fully expecting him to scoff as much as I had. He said it was true! There were cranes, actual wild cranes, breeding in the Upper Thurne valley!'

Hickling Broad, a Norfolk Wildlife Trust reserve, is now the most famous British site for cranes. The pair in 1979 had first been seen in Hickling fields, but had settled to breed, sensibly enough, on private land further east on the Horsey estate. In the late 1980s, some years after the first breeding occurred, cranes began to roost regularly in the marshes between Hickling and Horsey, and eventually a pair bred on the reserve (though not until 2007). Now, winter-roosting flocks at Hickling can number 50 birds or so, viewable, when they put in an appearance, from

Stubb Mill, an isolated spot at the far north-east of the reserve looking out towards Horsey.

Nick marched me to the Stubb viewpoint by the empty mill with a stride set by the lengthening shadows and withering winter light. There were hours to go before dusk yet, but cranes might come in any time. We set up and sat down, hugging ourselves against a wind that made everything a lot colder.

Nick knows the Hickling reserve intimately. It is another coordinate on his internal atlas, etched in repeated pencil lines; the first scratchy markings drawn as a boy on trips with Dave Horsley or with family, then subsequent lines, thicker, laid down as an adult working as an employee or ambassador for the Norfolk Wildlife Trust. Everything and everyone at Hickling are part of Nick's great and fond attachment to the place. He has written so often about the Trust's history and work that he speaks of its founders and archives as good friends, with the same affection that I remember him addressing plants along the Wensum the previous summer.

'We shout about the cranes now of course – they're a flagship bird. And people come from all over to see them. But to me they're still shrouded in the secrecy they had in my childhood, the secrecy of this exact spot where we're sitting now. Stubb Mill was where I saw my first cranes, and where I've been returning ever since. It was nothing back then, no viewpoint or anything, just a place where you sat in the grass and waited. It was exciting though; no one came here then, or barely anyone. And the birds were like classified information. News got around eventually, of course, but you'd think a bird as big and extravagant as that would be easier to see. They stand as tall as some of us and have a bigger wingspan than any other bird in Britain, and you can hear them from literally miles away! But these birds can really hide when they want to.'

I'd already got some idea of that. We'd spent time before arriving at Hickling driving and walking the broadland roads in hopes of a few grazing birds in fields or dykes. As Nick had said, I'd expected to find them easily enough – their leggy, long-necked heights perpendicular to the distinct horizontality of their landscape. With a little local knowledge from a contact of Nick's, we did locate a flock of 12 birds on ploughed land near Clippesby, which immediately flew off the minute we'd clapped eyes on them. We re-found them, eventually, viewed precariously from a busy roadside, down on marshland beside the River Bure. These were my first British cranes. Distant and hazy, even in my telescope, but my first nonetheless. They were curiously out of place and in place all at once.

Now, in the fading day at Stubb Mill, I was hoping for more and better views. A group of four birds had put in an exasperatingly brief and distant appearance shortly after we'd arrived, rising and dipping quickly below horizon trees. We waited on.

I reflected on what Nick had said about secrecy. It was, after all, the hallmark of my own associations with cranes, though for very different reasons: the cryptic allure of absence and precious little evidence, rather than the whispered, in-on-the-secret excitement about actual birds that Nick had known as a boy, and which clearly still seeped into this place for him now. Nonetheless, Nick's secrecy was, I thought, akin to that I knew by those brooks I trespassed out of town into the Weald. We are bonded in that because secrecy is the crane's way in modern Britain. Everything about cranes for us – evidence for past populations, whether they migrated or were resident, whether or not they bred, why there are so many crane place names, exactly when they became extinct, their surreptitious return in 1979, the gradual success of their breeding attempts on the hidden Horsey marshes, the extent to which they will populate Britain from hereon – is mysterious, unknown, unpredictable. The secrecy that thrills us is all about their extinction and their return; a return, triumphant and celebrated though it is, which is unavoidably touched by the sad fact of their extinction to begin with. Our anxiety to prevent loss or recover the lost shapes how many of us feel generally about the concept of 'the wild', and so it is no surprise that cranes and wilderness are often thought of together, each evoking the other. Cranes, highly wary of human interference, seek isolated, unpeopled locations, and in so doing make wildness of themselves, signposting to us those places that might validly be deemed wild by a perspective other than our own.

This realisation marks a major difference between modern sensibilities and those of our early ancestors. For them, where cranes were found, there was no sense of such places being 'humbled, adrift in history', as Leopold wrote of the North American bogs where cranes had already disappeared in his time. That is a modern idea, born of our conscious and sensitive awareness to ecological destruction, and our ensuing guilt. Perhaps they did connect secrecy and wildness with cranes, but not for the reasons that we do. For the people of pre-modern Britain, the names of crane places were not meaningful because of the poignant way in which they denoted what was not there, but because of what *was* there. Because these were indeed the cranes' places.

This difference was why I had travelled to Hickling that day. I wanted to see what I knew *was* there, to see how the place had become the cranes' place again after centuries 'adrift', because of the cranes themselves. I wanted to see cranes because to do so would be to feel the heartbeat of this landscape; to grasp Leopold's 'wildness incarnate'; to appreciate why naturalist and writer Richard Mabey, upon uprooting from his lifelong home in the Chilterns to Norfolk, sought dancing cranes – the 'epitome of wild places' – in the initiating days of his 'edgy baptism' in new territory. I wanted to know something of that wildness in the land for myself.

Nick pointed east with one hand, his other holding up binoculars. 'There.'

I couldn't see them. I kept checking Nick's direction of gaze. And then the big dark bird heading straight for us on the horizon, the one I'd scanned past quickly, became four birds as they changed direction and flew north across the marsh, multiplying themselves like a child's cut out string of concertinaed angels. Another three joined them, seven in total coming in to roost. Now they were unmistakeable: all leg and neck, everything stretched to its furthest reach as if invisibly pulled from each end. They flew so closely together that it looked to me as though they were all one, beak to feet to beak, a single crane thread sewing a seam in the sky. These huge birds had appeared without me even noticing, but they were impossible to ignore now. Just seven birds, but with each wingbeat they conveyed such ceremony. It was a moment of declaration, a grand incoming, a homecoming. As Nick had put it to me the summer before, they know how to own a place. They went to ground as one too, as elegantly timed and performed as their slow flight.

'In the spring, when they fly over each other's nests, they send up this wave of crane sound – unison calls. You can hear it reverberate as birds on the ground yell to birds passing overhead. It's about defending their territories, but when you hear that, right across the broad, it's like a crane dance in song.' Nick smiled. 'You'll have to come back in spring.'

I thought of the thread of birds in flight, and the chain of time along which cranes have existed; those millennia and aeons perpetuating like the spring songs of cranes across the broads. Cranes suggest antiquity like no other bird: their outsized magnificence; prehistoric, lithic legs and bill; a call at once as desolate as heartache and triumphant as victory, so resonant it's like the cry of time itself. To encounter cranes is to be connected to all that, to feel yourself small and humbled in and by time, especially so at Hickling where the birds' future impresses upon you too. I like to think our ancestors felt the same, stirred to nostalgia by old *cran* about old lives in old lands.

2

The Cuckoo's Lea

Exbourne, Devon ~ Yaxley, Cambridgeshire

In Exbourne's village church, displayed in its full tremendous size on the south wall, is an early nineteenth-century map of the parish. 'Surveyed & Mapped by Hans W. Allen, Oct 1840' is autographed in looping copperplate script by the tithe commissioner. The paper is yellow with age, but the cartographic detail retains its rich inky colours. My attention is drawn to the right of the map, where the village peters into farmland. The precise configurations of the fields have altered since then, but the boundaries are broadly the same, creating a pendulous, lung-shaped group of rough pastures. And there, between field numbers 543 and 544, is the spot I'm after.

I leave the church, Allen's map in my head, and set off for the eastern boundary where the sun is just rising. The village has not yet stirred. It soothes to woodpigeons' dawn songs and loop-the-loop claps. I walk to where habitation stops short and the high Devon hedges narrow the road to a tiny sheep-width track. And there it is, hidden beneath leafy hazel sprays. Another stream, but this one a burn (Old English *burna*) – stony-bottomed, rather than the silt-bedded brook I know back home. It is Exbourne's beginning, as the brook is Cranbrook's. But unlike Cranbrook, whose modern name has barely altered from the original Old English, Exbourne defiantly masks the first part of its name. You might reasonably assume that it has something to do with the great Exe river that runs through the county's capital. The truth, though, is much better.

Echeburne. It's easy enough to see how we end up at 'Exbourne' from here, but other records of the village make it clear that this Domesday Book version is an approximation, or that by 1086 the original form of the name was already being abbreviated for ease's sake. In the thirteenth century, the place is recorded more than once as *yekesbourne*. For the medieval community who lived in this settlement by a tributary of the River Okement, what they knew – saw, heard, felt – is water, steady and eternal, clear over dark stone. But they also knew an unmistakeable song. It is passing, here and heard for just a few months in a year; not the eternal purl of the brook, but so affecting that it is deeply associated with that place-defining water, resounding all year through. This is the cuckoo's stream.

In Old English, a cuckoo was a *geac*. *Se geac*. The cuckoo. You can get a much better feel for the old name in other cuckoo places around the country. Yaxham in Norfolk. Or the Yaxleys in Suffolk and Cambridgeshire. The modern spelling of these nicely indicates how to pronounce Old English *geac*: the *g* is a *y*, then skip lightly over the *e* so that it elides immediately into the short *a*, almost as one letter.[1] The *x* reminds us that in Old English this particular piece of land was said to belong to the cuckoo: as in modern English with all nouns, many nouns in Old English added *es* to show possession, and *es* after *ac* makes an *x* sound: *geaces*.

The Norse word *gaukr* was very similar, sharing a common ancestral route with the Old English name.

Where Danes settled in more northerly parts of the country, arriving from where some of those earlier Germanic tribes had arrived centuries before, their cuckoo word settled too (as in Goxhill and Gokewell in Lincolnshire), and still survives in *gowk*, a northern and Scottish dialect term for the bird. It's the root of modern Scandinavian cuckoo names for the bird too. To those of us so familiarised to cuckoos a-cuckooing, *geac* and *gaukr* are strange. They seem so … un-cuckoo-like. To modern English ears, it is perfectly and unquestionably obvious that 'cuckoo' is what the bird sings. But in early England cuckoos didn't 'cuckoo'; they 'yakked'. What did people hear in this sound? What did the word mean to them when they spoke it? Does *geac* also mimic the cuckoo's song, heard differently to other ears, or does it represent something else entirely?

One possibility is that *geac* should remind us to heed cultural differences. The root of modern English 'cuckoo', from Old French *cucu*, is Latin *cuculus*, which itself derives from an older word that is the root of cuckoo names in a great many Eurasian languages.[2] In Greek, French and Polish, for instance, or Spanish, Russian, German, Lithuanian, Dutch and Italian, in Persian, Kashmiri and Sanskrit, or in many non-Indo-European languages too, such as Hungarian and Finnish, speakers hear and pronounce versions of the same thing; vigorous, plosive 'k's surrounding cooing open vowels. But with others, including early English, perhaps the cuckoo's familiar notes are heard and translated differently, in the way that some languages do with a dog's 'woof' or a cockerel's 'cock-a-doodle-do'.[3] Perhaps single-syllable *geac* and *gaukr*, Swedish *gök*, Danish *gøg* and Norwegian *gjøk*, or Welsh *cog* via the Celtic languages, are simply different ways of hearing a cuckoo.

That's one thought. But what, I wonder, if *geac* was never 'cuckoo'? After all, the male's disyllabic song, distinctive and easily heard as it is, is only one of a number of calls the species makes. The female utters a snickering trill that sounds like devious laughter, and both sexes when excited or territorial give a hacking hiccough that is often transcribed in field guides as 'goch', or even 'gowk'. Is this what *geac* cries out? Perhaps it was not only the male's unmissable song that struck the ears of early listeners, but also the sexed-up birds' strange and guttural grunts. Both names are Indo-European, so perhaps there was a time when both names existed simultaneously, describing different cuckoo sounds. *Cuc-koo, cuc-koo. Yeac! Yeac! Yeac-c-c-c-c-c-c! Cuc-koo. Cuc-koo.*[4]

This place at Exbourne's burn is green with spring. The new season swells to the mild sun and bulges over Dartmoor's ridge to the south, though the air is still cautiously cool. Frost is still on the ground some mornings. But the young day grows now to the vigour of a blackbird's song and a thorn's gentle blossom. It feels good for cuckoos. It *feels* as if I *ought* to hear them in such a spring-green place. A cuckoo here would set the clock ticking, the year's machinery turning, and there'd be no going back.

I hear none. There are teasing signs: pink cuckoo flowers on the verges, sweet and flushing, lots of them. Cuckoo-pints too, erect with vernal excitement, their barely sheathed spadices ribald as a cuckoo's laugh. Various British flora have the cuckoo's name; in some cases because they bloom at the same time as the cuckoo arrives on our shores, and in others because they are humorously

associated with the lubricious antics we have levelled at
the bird: everything about a cuckoo-pint is phallic ('pint'
is an abbreviation of 'pintle', meaning penis), and this was
apparently quite enough to indict the poor cuckoo's lewd
influence.

All these other 'cuckoo species' are testament to the
bird's immense popularity in our culture. There can be few
other birds in Europe that have obtained such a broad and
deep folkloric status, or which are simultaneously maligned
and celebrated, condemned and welcomed. One of the
more eccentric traditions concerns a 'Cuckoo Bush' in
Gotham, Nottinghamshire (search for the term online and
you'll be directed to a pub here bearing the name – the
modern vestige of an ancient lore). The 'bush' in question
refers to a Neolithic barrow that became the alleged hill
on which the medieval Wise Men of Gotham attempted
to fence in the cuckoo. As the legend goes, the men sought
to keep the cuckoo eternally on their little piece of ground
so that summer would never leave, and warm weather and
fat crops would grace Gotham's people for all days to
come. This lovely piece of folklore encouraged similar
cuckoo rituals elsewhere, so there are numerous cuckoo
pens and cuckoo pounds round the country where people
performed cuckoo-capturing rituals.

At the root of the Gotham legend is the powerful
conviction that a cuckoo's disembodied voice, suddenly
sounding to our great anticipation one April day from the
back-end of winter, and just as suddenly ceasing in
midsummer, is somehow spring itself. It is the genesis of
the season, and the breath of its invocation calls forth
warm and generous life.

As if to demonstrate this profound effect of the cuckoo's
affirmative song in our lives, the earliest surviving example
of part music with English words is all about this

phenomenon: *Sumer is icumen in, Lhude* ('Loudly') *sing, cuccu!* The song has become almost as famous as the bird itself. Recorded in just one manuscript associated with Reading Abbey and dating from the mid-thirteenth century, it depicts rustic images of lusty, cavorting farm animals to the intoning notes of the cuckoo in the *pes* or 'foot' – the repeated ground bass that underpins the cascading melody. This little canon with its command to the cuckoo echoes the sentiment of cuckoo-pen rituals: the bird, as the last line of the song goes, must *Ne swik thu naver* 'never ever stop', and it does not for the entire song. The singer enjoins as insistently as the cuckoo calls, and the closing notes of the melody's refrain mimic the cuckoo's paired descending thirds. *Cuccu, cuccu.* Summer in the song is not in the process of arriving, not 'a–coming' as most people think – it *has* arrived (*icumen* is past tense), and the cuckoo's presence triumphantly confirms this fact.

'Sumer is icumen in' is very likely older than its manuscript. You sense in the song's vernacular vitality that people have been singing it for as long as *cuccu* has been in the language, and perhaps other ditties by the name of *geac* for centuries before that, even. Despite the cloistered context of the song's manuscript, 'Sumer' is emphatically a song for outdoors, the fields, a song for people to hail the season and its bird. Whatever its origins, and despite its famous status, 'Sumer' is not the first time that someone writing in English expressed their wonder at cuckoos. That occurred some 300 years earlier, somewhere not all that far away from Exbourne.

In 1072, six years after the Norman Conquest, Bishop Leofric of Exeter died. It is one of the few things known about the man, and even this fact may have suffered complete obscurity were it not for Leofric's fondness for books: this being the case, he bequeathed to his cathedral library several volumes for posterity. One of these, so the contemporary record states, was *an mycel Englisc boc be gehwilcum þingum on leoðwisan geworht* 'one great English book on various things written in verse'. Almost certainly, this *boc* is what is now known simply as the 'Exeter Book'. I have seen it once. It is 'great' indeed: a hefty volume containing 131 sheets of vellum (which produces a book considerably thicker than the equivalent pages in a book today). We know even less about its origins than we do about Leofric, other than that it was compiled in the last half of the tenth century by one scribe in one place, that Leofric came by it at some point and it was definitely at Exeter cathedral by 1072, and that it has remained there ever since. Its survival into the modern world has tremendous significance – a fact grandly acknowledged when UNESCO recently awarded it official status as one of 'the world's principal artefacts'. It is one of just four manuscripts that collectively contain very nearly all we have left of Old English poetry, most of which appears in the Exeter Book. In short, if this manuscript had fallen victim to fire or Henry VIII's dissolution of the monasteries (the fate of many medieval manuscripts), we would have lost an immeasurable contribution to English literature. And so, too, would we have lost what might be the earliest ever poem written in English about a cuckoo.

In these days my father and mother
left me for dead. There was no life in me yet,
no spirit within. Then someone started –
a very loyal kinswoman – to cover me with clothes,
held and kept me, wrapped me with a protective cloak,

quite as kindly as for her own kin,
until under that covering – as is my nature –
I was ensouled with spirit among unrelated kin.
Then the fair woman fed me
until I grew up and could depart
on greater journeys. She had fewer dear
sons and daughters because she did so.

Appropriately enough, this cuckoo is disguised. It is cloaked in metaphor: a family drama in which a human mother adopts an abandoned child (the cuckoo), wilfully and tenderly nurturing it as her own. Underneath the personification, though, the cuckoo chick accurately depicts the stages of its own genesis: 'abandoned' in the host nest, the egg is accepted and incubated by the new mother who treats it like one of her own, hatching the imposter among her own doomed offspring and feeding it until it has fully grown, at which point it leaves the nest to travel far.

All the hiding behind metaphor is pertinent for another very particular reason: this cuckoo poem is, in fact, a riddle – one of nearly a hundred riddles that form one of the largest parts of the Exeter Book. The presence of these riddles isn't unusual in itself – riddling, in Latin, was a popular medieval monkish exercise. But these particular riddles are as unique as the book in which they appear, the only surviving set of riddles in Old English, and perhaps the only set ever written down in Old English. There is a compelling immediacy to them that modern readers may find surprising, an abrupt plain-speaking from the riddle subjects who describe themselves in a series of clever contradictions and demand that we reveal their identities: *Saga hwæt ic hatte* – 'Say what I am called' – the voices often say. This directness comes with a vivid ordinariness in other ways too, a feeling of homespun knowledge and earthy realism, which suggests that at least some of them were derived from old oral traditions. The subject matter is largely everyday items, such as a plough, a badger, a weathercock, bellows, a key, a cockerel and hens. Some are surprisingly rude (like the onion that grows tall in a bed, grabbed to a stiffness by a tearful woman; or the swelling loaf of bread that has a similar effect). Among all these, the cuckoo is made to seem commonplace too – a feature of medieval English life as familiar as a rake, a moth or beer.

One of the central aims of the Exeter riddles is to make readers marvel at this mundanity, to repeatedly imbue the ordinary with extraordinary qualities. Wonder is always present in the riddles. In fact, the Exeter Book is a book of wonder. Quite literally. The word, Old English *wundor*, is everywhere in it. And so are *wundorlica wihta*, 'wondrous creatures'. Wonder, a sense of wonder, is never far in much modern writing about nature, but just as today 'experiences of wonder can jolt us into the realisation of how remarkable ... all existence actually is', to borrow Michael McCarthy's words, so it was for people living millennia ago. In the Exeter Book, you could say, we find the original 'wonder' texts in English writing.

Whoever the cuckoo riddler was, it was not the bird's song that caught their wonder, as was clearly the case for whomever composed 'Sumer is icumen in'. It was that other fundamental trait that has endured in cuckoo lore no less powerfully to this day – the species' infamous parasitism and foolery. Infamous indeed, but it is scientifically true that trickery is what cuckoos do best. Some of these tricks have only become known or confirmed in modern times, but much about the bird's parasitism was already a well-known story in the Middle

Ages, and clearly the cuckoo riddle poet knew they could rely on a certain degree of audience knowledge (how else could you ever be expected to guess the answer otherwise?). Medieval ornithology was steeped in classical learning as well as ordinary experience, so monks scratching their heads over this riddle could have read about the cuckoo's devious habits in Pliny the Elder's *Natural History* (a standard text on any monastic library shelf), just as they might have come across the tale from native folklore too.

The cuckoo's essence is all deceit – 'a cheat in various guises', as world expert Professor Nick Davies describes the bird. The common cuckoo fools its hosts by producing an impostor egg designed to mimic almost exactly the colour and pattern of its specific host species (except in the case of the dunnock), whose chick, once hatched, dispatches all competition by heaving the other eggs or naked, blind 'siblings' over the side of the nest, and then calls for food incessantly with a voice that mimics an entire brood of chicks. Within two weeks the cuckoo chick will usually be about three times heavier than its foster parent, bulging grotesquely on the tiny nest, and yet the parents still feed it as their own. This is the wonder of the cuckoo, no less than its spring-bringing song. For Nick Davies the call of the cuckoo is 'not only a harbinger of spring. It's an invitation to solve an enduring puzzle: how does the cuckoo get away with such outrageous behaviour?' The cuckoo riddler may not have looked to solve that puzzle, but the riddle is certainly an invitation to marvel at that outrageous behaviour.

When you think about it, what better subject for a riddle could there be than a creature that is a kind of riddle itself? Cuckoo and riddle both grow through a series of feints, pretending honesty, transforming and disguising themselves. The Exeter riddle cleverly mimics the mimicker because its central metaphor (bird as fostered child) adds another layer of misleading deceit to the cuckoo's already impressive armoury of tricks. For most of the poem, the cuckoo's sleights are presented benignly, as though the grateful chick is oblivious to its own species' habits. It is the final sentence, laced with a psychopath's sinister indifference, that deals the blow: the cuckoo chick is a killer. The fact is delivered with such adroit and wry understatement that you'd be forgiven for missing it. There is no outright horror: simply, the mother had fewer children. In a stroke, the cuckoo's thankful humility is exposed as a sham. The cuckoo has tricked its earnest mother. What's more, it has tricked us.

As it turns out, the riddle itself has one more trick to play on us. Once you think you've correctly guessed the solution, you will, of course, want to turn to the answers to confirm how clever you've been. But this is where you will hit another problem. Because there are no answers. These are riddles with no ends. Every solution we have for these riddles has been deduced and defended by philologists and literary scholars over the last hundred or so years. Most of the riddles have very well-established, firmly accepted answers now (including the cuckoo), but there are some that are still debated, more than 1,000 years after the riddles were first written down. Through intent or accident, the fact that the Exeter Book provides no answers to its riddles only increases the mystery. Our wonder at these strange speaking creatures and objects is all the more because we must accept mystery. The cuckoo and its riddle have had the last laugh.

There is a sad irony to all this. Exbourne and Exeter with their cuckoo secrets, one a former cuckoo home, the other the home of our earliest surviving English cuckoo

poem, are on the doorstep of one of the last cuckoo
strongholds. Dartmoor is now one of the few places left in
England to find decent numbers of cuckoos. Almost
everywhere else the species has disappeared or sharply
declined in numbers. As Benedict Macdonald solemnly
reports in *Rebirding*, his vision for restoring Britain's wildlife,
only in remaining sites such as 'the moth-rich landscape of
Dartmoor's wooded margins can the cuckoos of Devon
now survive'. The Exbourne dwellers of old and the Exeter
cuckoo riddler could never have imagined or believed it.

It was a similar story where I went later that same year.
In this case, though, even the landscape I sought has
vanished. Once it would have thronged to cuckoos' songs;
it is silent now except for in a few isolated pockets where
the birds manage to return each spring and sing on. Never
stop now. *Ne swik thu naver nu.*

Yaxley in north Cambridgeshire, a short way south of
Peterborough, just off the A1, is easy to get to. Its name is
signposted alongside the more famed village of Stilton,
suspended big and clear on motorway blue. You'll have
been past Yaxley, probably even registered the name as a
momentary distraction from tarmac boredom on journeys
up and down this well-used route that ghosts the medieval
Great North Road and Roman Ermine Street. It's the
most central cuckoo place in England, but the one, I
suspect, you'd be least likely to visit. The road into Yaxley
is not a through-road to another town beyond. Besides
the church, there are no especially historic sites, tourist
attractions or vital service facilities. If curiosity or the
possibility of old-world charm drew you off the A1 for a
fleeting detour, you'd pass through the high street until

you reached the industrial estate at the far end of town, at which point, you'd turn around and carry on your way.

Yaxley's big expansion into the village it is today occurred in the middle of the last century. It paralleled Peterborough's rapid growth, as though the great city spawned little selves in its fast and sprawling orbit. As railways closed down all over the country (Yaxley's included) and motor cars quickly became the dominant mode of transport, Yaxley entered the modern world and never looked back. In fact, it seems to exist in a state of perpetual renewal. It is boldly modern, the product of decades of continuous development, which has produced, let it be said, a very impressive exhibition of twentieth-century housing styles. These frequently abut each other in the same road, as though generations of zealous builders have squeezed in new properties wherever they can to plug the gaps.

I wound up in Yaxley on a cold and wet November day when cuckoos are least in anyone's thoughts. I drove past the one and only cuckoo I would see all year (a very serious-looking bird painted above an escutcheon and between frisky fallow bucks on the village's signpost), parked in a residential street full of bungalows, waited out a torrential downpour, and then walked through another back onto Broadway, the village's main thoroughfare.

The past of Yaxley felt teasingly hidden. There is the old village, right on the southern edge, as though it sloped downhill in a sulk. In Main Street ('main' no more), you'll find evidence of an older Yaxley, but even here the sprawl of modernity dominates, wedged in and tagged on wherever there is a just little more space to do so. Back up on Broadway, I spied a few late-Victorian terraces playing hide-and-seek behind pebbledash and render, the old brickwork peeping with a wink here and

there, or crudely incongruous where it is literally grafted
onto brand-new builds.

When I grew bored of pacing up and down the high
street, I browsed kitschy window displays in the 1960s
shopping centre to kill time, bought chips from Wong's to
kill some more, then sat on a graffitied bench, struggling
to get a purchase on the place at all, on a past so seemingly
well past that it felt impossible to resurrect the world
suggested by the name. I knew that somewhere in Yaxley,
perhaps even right beneath the very spot where I now sat,
there were once trees (not far, in fact, from one of
England's big early medieval woodlands; Bruneswald,
'Brun's wood', which formed a boundary along the high
ground west of the Fens where the A1 now runs). Among
those trees there was a clearing, and in that clearing there
were once cuckoos. And so, someone, once upon a time,
called this place Yaxley, 'the cuckoo's lea'. The name
effortlessly brings to mind a hawthorn, frothing white in
warm, glade-dappled May, and there a male cuckoo
proclaiming itself each spring from the thorny top. *Sing
cuccu. Sing cuccu.* But at that moment, sat in a concrete
arcade between the bookies and a greasy spoon in cold
November rain, eking out my last few chips from a
polystyrene box, all that seemed pretty ridiculous – as
ludicrous as contemplating or finding a cuckoo in a
service station toilet cubicle. *Sing cuccu. Sing cuccu.*

In this respect, Yaxley has become a symbol to me of
the wider landscape that surrounds it. Finding a sense of
the past is difficult everywhere here. It can feel invisible,
obliterated, grubbed up like hedgerows. But this difficulty,
quite against my expectations, has become part of the
fascination – it is the reason I have come to love this part
of England, where nothing feels easy to love at first. Time
spent in places such as Yaxley breeds a strange exhilaration;

in large part, I think, because what remains stands in such contrast to what glitters darkly now only in the surviving names. Our vision of a past world in these places appears in such astonishing relief to what we see in front of us that its force on our senses is somehow all the more mesmerising.

On the face of it, the face is all there is. A floor of agricultural plains that sweeps out east of Yaxley; field after field after field converted and devoted to nothing but crops, eternally renewed by the yearly workings of intensive farming. This is England's arable heartland, otherwise known as the Fens. They are not pretty, striking, or appealing by any conventional standards. Like many non-Fenlanders, when I first came here some 20 years ago (to visit family who had moved into the area), I was immediately and heavily underwhelmed by a landscape which, as Graham Swift describes in his novel *Waterland*, really amounts to 'Nothing'. These endless, rectilinear prairies failed to raise any delight in me. Suitably enough, I thought, for such flatness. Depending on my mood and the occasion, all that monotonous flatness can feel either distinctly ahistorical, or, quite to the contrary, the embodiment of *all* history: the endless horizontal stretching like time's continuum in each direction.

Whatever one's perspective, this strange landscape *is* wonderfully rich in history. And Yaxley is an ideal place from which to contemplate that past because it sits prominently right on the Fens' western edge, located on the border between uplands, which sweep out north and west to limestone peaks and wolds, and the lowlands, which sink down into the immense basin that describes a wide, parallel arc around the gaping maw of the Wash on England's east coast. It is surrounded by important archaeological sites that tell of a long and productive

human occupation of this region since at least the Bronze
Age – millennia of ancient Britons, Romans, and then
medieval populations, dwelling in these edgelands where
the low floodlands and dry higher grounds created
adjacent, double possibilities for amphibious living and
farming. We know now that the traditional perception of
the Fens as an unpopulated, impenetrable wilderness is
entirely wrong; it is indisputable that these waterlands
have been inhabited, managed and cultivated since way
back into prehistory. In all probability, a settlement has
existed on this site since long before anyone speaking the
Old English tongue thought to call it Yaxley.

Later that afternoon, a good way out of town and all
out of cuckoo thoughts, I found a gap in a roadside
hedgerow that allowed a grand view eastward over the
flatlands as far as I could see. I'd glimpsed it between
bricks and slates from the heights of south-sloping streets
in central Yaxley (streets with names such as 'Mere View'),
but now I was literally on the Great Fen edge, looking
down from an escarpment. Down there was where fen
began – neat, straight drills in neat, straight fields that
stretch flatness taut over some 1,300 square miles of the
UK's lowest land, from here all the way east to Norfolk,
south to Cambridge and Suffolk, and north up into
Lincolnshire.

If I'd been stood here 1,000 years ago or more, the
view would have looked very different. I, and Yaxley itself,
would have been poised on the drop off to one of Britain's
biggest wetlands; indeed, one of Europe's biggest wetlands.
Like the cuckoo's parasitism, it's a well-known story, told
so often that it has achieved the status of myth: this was
the great wild place we modern Brits will never know.
Created by rising sea levels after the last Ice Age and the
slow deposition of peat and silt, the Fen once teemed

with life of all kinds, in numbers we can barely imagine, but was drained intensively and successively from the seventeenth century onwards to convert it to arable land, and is now the most productive farming soil around.

The clue to the land's past is in the word itself. Fen. It's as old as our language, unchanged in thousands of years, a medieval word that has its damp roots in a mire of Germanic terms for land that is indisputably *not dry*. The word is immanently fenny. A stern syllable that conveys a stubborn flatness. The word's fetid swampiness seeps through the earliest English description we have of the Fens – a translation of an eighth-century Latin saint's life by a monk called Felix about the most famous Fenlander of them all, Guthlac, who lived as a hermit on the isle of Crowland, 13 miles from Yaxley. The anonymous Old English writer describes a *fenn* of 'immense vastness', reaching from *Granteceaster* (what was to become Cambridge) to the *norðsæ* 'north sea'. There are 'enormous moors, sometimes dark stagnant pools, sometimes foul streams flowing, and also many islands, and reeds, and barrows, and carrs'.

From where I stood, the tantalising Fen vision described by medieval hagiographers felt like an impossibility. It didn't feel as though it really could have existed. Two hundred years ago, in the early nineteenth century, it would have been just possible still to stand here and see some of that medieval-style fenland. The first Ordnance Survey maps show marshy ground immediately east of Yaxley, surrounding what would have been even more magnificent to witness – Whittlesey Mere; once the biggest lake in lowland England (six miles across), and the last of the great fen meres to be drained. This Victorian view was still only remnants, but it is possible to travel a little further back in in time yet.

Remarkably, there are surviving seventeenth-century maps predating the final, extensive drainage efforts of the 'Adventurers' – the Dutch engineers hired to finish off the job. Cartographic engravings such as Jan Jansson's 'General plot and description of the Fennes' seem like illustrations from the endpapers of some fantasy fiction novel. There it is, the 'immense vastness', stretching just as Felix said from Cambridge to the North Sea. Land reclamation has clearly begun (there are large areas of dry land in the Holland region of Lincolnshire just below the Wash), but the Fens are still there for the most part. There is Peterborough, right on the marshy edge, and Deeping in big type (literally 'the deep place'), and all those places ending in an 'ey' sound – Thorney, Ramsey, Whittlesey, Ely – we're told were once islands really *were* islands (in the sense of a shallow hump of land above surrounding marsh just high enough to constitute dry land). No one in the last 400 years has observed the great Fen for real, but these astonishing maps get us just a little closer.

I tried to superimpose these impressions onto what I saw below me, to lay fen back down over field, or, in reverse, exhume the old, flooded world like the loam-black bulk of a bog oak (those famous pre-Ice Age relics that are turned up in these parts by farmers ploughing their soil). My thoughts had wandered far from cuckoos that afternoon, but suddenly, there they were again, brought to mind by the oaks. I thought of Yaxley's glade, imagined the place's trees preserved under concrete sprawl like the fenny giants; and its cuckoos too, recovered by archaeologists, tiny, fragile bones, but with all the majesty of an auroch's skull.

As tangential as all my fen thinking seemed, I saw that the opposite was true – each thought further east and deeper into Fenland in fact brought me closer back to Yaxley and its cuckoos. It occurred to me now, looking down to all that land rolling away to the long east: what if the cuckoos weren't so much *up here*, but *down there*? What if folk on this western brim of the Fens, generation after generation, lived their summers to the sound of cuckoos from across the wetlands?[5] The 'wandering Voice' that calls 'At once far off, and near', as Wordsworth put it, more than a thousand years after the first Yaxley dwellers would have understood exactly what he described. And not just one wandering voice, but many voices.

If one of the last remaining fragments of old peat fen, Wicken Fen, is anything to go by, this is a distinct possibility. For its size (not even two square miles), it's up there with Dartmoor as a lifeline for cuckoos, one of just a handful of tiny spots of old, true wetland, tirelessly kept wet, suspended in time by careful human intervention, rather than natural processes such as flooding, which would have done this work in the past. It is the home of Nick Davies' decades-long, famed study of cuckoos; quite literally the origin place, therefore, of so much of what has been discovered and proven about the wonder of cuckoos and their trickery in modern times. Wicken Fen, and others like it, such as Woodwalton Fen or Holme Fen, close by Yaxley itself, are vital sanctuaries. Vital, but also sad inversions of Guthlac's 'immense vastness': swamp islands in the drained land, where once scattered islands of dry land existed in the swamp.

Nonetheless, Wicken today is just about the most biodiverse single site in the whole of Britain. Literally thousands (more than 9,000 to date) of plant, fungus, insect and other animal species have been recorded there. It constitutes less than 0.1 per cent of remaining fenland, but it can still give us some idea of the rich life that once

existed right across the Fens. It provides just the right
habitat for the particular 'host race' of *Cuculus canorus* that
you find here and would have found all over the old Fens:
a wet, reed-dense place full of reed warblers, the
unsuspecting 'host' species.[6] In early summer, cuckoo
song must have been one of the most insistent and
distinctive sounds of the marshes, just as it still is in other
parts of Europe where big wetlands have survived, such as
the Danube Delta or Poland's Biebrza Marshes.

This is how I tried to imagine the place I saw below
me: a summer fen-cuckoo-land, viewed through a hedge
on an out-of-town road in cold, wet November. The land,
to be sure, was as sopping as me today, as though it lay
open and bare to a blessing, returned itself to an old
deliquescence. Were I magically granted the impossibility
of transporting myself back in time, this place in early
medieval England would certainly be on my wish list. To
stand at Yaxley and see the true Fens stretching to the
vanishing horizon, beyond which, I knew, there was only
more fen, and more beyond that; to hear amidst the din of
life down there, warblers scratching their voices on the
summer air from reedbeds and ditches and carrs, and
above that, softer, like a burden to the warblers' rattling,
rollicking folk tune, the airy notes of cuckoos.

A place like that, animated by the strong song of life,
helps to explain the power of so many old bird names that
are related to sound, such as the cuckoo's, the crane's and
many others we've yet to meet. It wasn't just the sounds
themselves that mattered, very often mimicked in the
names, but the places in which these sounds were heard
too. Sound reified and situated place. It's an idea we'll
encounter repeatedly. Few of us now perceive place in
bioacoustic terms, such is our hankering for the visual
above all, but our ancestors did, and not even that long

ago. As recently as the early twentieth century, for instance, naturalist Richard Jefferies wrote in *Nature Near London* of seeing from a train carriage window a 'ploughed field ... alive with small birds ... whose voices were audible across the field. ... There must have been thousands; they continually flew up, swept round with a whirring of wings, and settled, again darkening the spot they chose'. Such an encounter would be very rare in twenty-first-century Britain, but that of Jefferies' – common enough once – shows us how the very life of places centuries ago must have been utterly and unavoidably charged with the sounds, no less than the sights, of birds.

Guthlac would have known places alive like that. Happily enough, in yet another medieval telling of his story, it is cuckoos that bring in the spring to Guthlac. When Guthlac has done fighting the devils that beset him, the fenland bursts into vernal magnificence and *geacas gear budon* 'cuckoos proclaimed the year'. It is a lovely addition made by whomever wrote the Old English poetic version of the saint's life, poignantly bequeathing us with a single mention of cuckoos in the medieval fens. A single mention in a single copy of a single poem, in a certain single manuscript. The Exeter Book, of course.

Poetic flourish though they are, the Guthlac poet's words conveyed truth. The real saint on his island hermitage will have heard cuckoos each spring, just as the good people of Yaxley did, because everyone did. The poetic image declared a seasonal certainty; the reliable, unquestionable fact that this bird *will* return next spring, *will* sing here again. If it was a simple truth for them, it is an enviable one for us. Cuckoos had become a symbol for me of Yaxley and its fenlands (gone but not wholly gone, just traceable when you search or imagine hard enough), but this resonance was unhappily accompanied by an awareness that this was a stark contrast to the bird's former presence and power in these parts. Perhaps that was part of the disconcerting detachment I'd felt in Yaxley earlier that day – my struggle with a sense of place there, a past, was widening the distance I already felt from the bird. To hear a cuckoo in Yaxley, or Exbourne, today would thrill me for reasons that would make no sense to my ancestors, but would nonetheless be to hear the bird as they did. To utter either bird name or place name was, for them, to sing the cuckoo's notes one's self, to bring forth its being. It was to capture the *geac*, far more effectively than the efforts of Gotham's old fools.

3

Pathless Ways

Swallowcliffe, Wiltshire ~ Solway Firth, Cumbria

The cuckoo riddler very likely knew something else about cuckoos, something described in Pliny's *Natural History*. The cuckoo, it was thought, had the ability to transform itself into a hawk, which would have made a superb detail in the riddle, come to think of it – another changeling trick. There's a good reason why the poet didn't include it, however, and that's because this transformation had nothing to do with parasitism as far as he was concerned. Instead, the hawk metamorphosis explained the cuckoo's absence from its breeding territories for most of the year. 'The cuckoo', Pliny says, 'seems to be made by changing its shape out of a hawk at a certain season of the year, as the rest of the hawks do not appear then, except on a very few days, and the cuckoo itself also after being seen for a moderate period of the summer is not observed afterwards.' It is, in short, a migration myth. Or more correctly an absence of myth.

As it turns out, the hawk similarity among certain cuckoo species *is* about deceit (looking like a hawk is a useful scare tactic), and nothing to do with why cuckoos appear and disappear at certain times of the year. But those early observers were on to something, nonetheless. To those of us living in an age when the phenomenon of bird migration is simply common knowledge, the idea is preposterous, but if you live in a time or a culture when physical transfiguration is no barrier to truth, it's logical

enough. After all, the truth – that small birds, some
weighing merely grams, fly thousands of miles from one
continent to another, even from one end of the globe to
the other – is hardly less implausible.

We have been marvelling and pondering the mysteries
of birds' seasonal movements for millennia. These birds
mark our places through patterns of opposites –
permanence and transience, local and global – and our
sense of these places are in thrall to their comings and
goings.

There is a moment in early May when the fullness of
spring, though well begun, has not yet been confirmed.
You wake one morning, all still to happen, and in less
than a second, at any second, everything is underway,
surging headlong into unstoppered summer. My particular
second this morning catches me out as it always does,
even though I'm primed, expectant: with quick and
unmistakeable clarity a swift tears right past my window.
The sound comes first, then the thing itself, swifter than
my thoughts, hurtling with such defiant velocity it seems
to catch up, then outpace, its own shriek, and then the
shriek, dazed and piercing the tremulous air, chases to
overtake its owner again.

Swifts have obtained a certain rockstar status in recent
times, off the back of Ted Hughes' famous poem about
them. They are the current poster birds of summer, and as
such they have become a measure of the failing health
and rightness of our places, and of our own dubious place
in this world. It's certainly not difficult to see the attraction
to these swarthy dagger-birds: the air-slick, air-speed
hedonists of our summer skies. By all accounts though,

swift adoration is quite a modern thing. There is little evidence of it in pre-modern cultural appreciations. The word *swift* itself is Old English, but we don't know when people started using that adjective as a noun to describe the bird. And, moreover, there are no swift place names.[1] Whatever early people thought and felt about swifts, it was another species that made its name as the sharp-winged, sky-flinging bird of summer place in the Middle Ages.[2] The swallow, *Hirundo rustica*, had a considerable head start on the swift in this respect, being a species that had already been deeply and proverbially associated with summer in Europe for thousands of years, perhaps for even longer than the cuckoo.

Swallowcliffe is typical of many English villages: a small nucleated settlement built around a church, a pub (now smart and swanky under celebrity ownership), quaint architecture, and the sense that it passes much of its time in agreeable, peaceful anonymity (celebrity pub notwithstanding). Swallowcliffe was a rural backwater until the early twentieth century. Most of its 'old' buildings date from this period, in fact. Even the church, Victorian but built to look Norman, is deceptively modern. The village is old, there's no doubting that, named in documents that go back pre-Conquest to the year AD 940, but to really appreciate Swallowcliffe's significance you need to look to the surrounding landscape.

Geologically, it is located right on the edge of a tongue of chalk downland in the south-westerly limits of that great sweep of white Cretaceous bedrock that stretches north-east like a ceremonial sash across England's breast.

It is this proximity to chalk that is most important, because it locates the medieval village down in the valley between hills and plateaus that are full of far more ancient signs and remains of human habitation. To the north, most famously, there is Stonehenge on the Salisbury Plains, but the whole ridge of chalk down that extends south of Swallowcliffe is littered with round barrows and long barrows and cross dykes and field systems, all variously of Iron- and Bronze-Age or Neolithic antiquity.

I'd been hoping for some time to make a trip to Swallowcliffe. After more than one aborted effort at the time of the Covid pandemic, I palmed the kids off with my mother and persuaded my wife, Ginny, to join me for two days in Wiltshire with the promise of a night away at the fancy Royal Oak and more prehistoric monuments than she could wish for (she'll go a long way for a sarsen or a tumulus). The prize for me at the end of our march was a Bronze-Age round barrow with an Anglo-Saxon secret interred inside. It is a precious but little-known site – a chalk downs Sutton Hoo – long and mysteriously known as *posses hlawe*: the tumulus belonging to someone, probably, called Poss (whoever that was, and whatever they had to do with it in the Middle Ages). When the mound was excavated in 1966, archaeologists discovered that the original chamber had been reused in the seventh century, some 2,000 years after the original construction, to inter the body of a young, elite Anglo-Saxon woman – the Swallowcliffe Princess, as she has been termed. She was laid on an ash wood bed along with various status items, the best known of which is a roundel attached to a wood and leather satchel, made of bronze with gold and silver leaf shaped into tiny interlace decorations.

And so we arrived early one completely cloudless summer's day and set off, booted and backpacked, for a

morning in pursuit of ancient grass humps. We had a map,
but there was no way of missing the Down: its long,
sweeping escarpment dominates the whole south-facing
prospect, hard-shadowed in certain lights, but softly
curved too, like the brow of some ponderous chalk giant
sleeping out the epochs. This is *the* cliff. The swallows'
cliff. More than anything, of course, I was on the lookout
for them. I carried a slender-winged hope that they were
still here; that they'd been gracing the air above *posses
hlawe* thousands of years ago when someone first made
the chamber, blessed the seventh-century day when the
Swallowcliffe Princess was laid to rest, and had never
gone away.

We saw our first before we'd even left the village. A
single swallow led us out of town, swooping between
farm buildings and then away south towards the Down,
tilting and blinking into the sun. It was quickly lost to us,
but we followed it towards the cliff.

Medieval ideas about bird migration weren't all fantastical
myths. People living in the Middle Ages certainly knew
about bird migration in principle. Beliefs and anecdotes
about birds' seasonal disappearance are evident in ancient
texts and last right up to comparatively modern times.
While it was understood by classical and medieval writers
that some birds migrate seasonally in the way we
understand today, this knowledge didn't stop people
believing in other possibilities until long after the Middle
Ages. In the case of smaller birds, it was sometimes
assumed that they coped with the grand ordeal by hitching
a ride on the backs of larger birds. Isidore of Seville, the
indisputably mighty father of medieval encyclopaedic

writing, wrote in his seventh-century *Etymologies* of cuckoos that they are 'taken up on the shoulders of kites … fatigued by the long expanse of sky'. Both Aristotle and Pliny say some swallows migrate and some hibernate.

The swallow is an excellent bird for tracing old explanations for birds' seasonal disappearances because theories and experiments were repeatedly attached to this species, probably due to its long domestic familiarity to humans. Even in the eighteenth century, naturalist Gilbert White was still unable to dismiss the long-lived belief that swallows hibernate through the winter (he made considerable efforts to find hibernating hirundines in the ponds of Selborne, which is something I'd rather like to have witnessed). In the same century, others claimed that swallows spent winter on the moon, and the celebrated man of letters Samuel Johnson claimed confidently that the species 'certainly sleep all the winter. A number of them conglobulate together, by flying round and round, and then all in a heap throw themselves under water, and lie in the bed of a river.' And this was in the Age of Enlightenment. Fanciful notions about where birds spent the winter were not a peculiarly medieval habit.

What seems to have fascinated medieval thinkers most about migration, and bird flight in general, was not so much the facts that might be discovered and explained, but actually the opposite – its great unfathomability. The most repeated observation in natural philosophy texts was that birds have a characteristic ability to disappear and cover up all traces of their presence. An author of the twelfth century, known as Bartholomew the Englishman (who spent much of his life at universities abroad) says this best when he writes in *The Properties of Things* that 'after the [bird's] flight the air closes itself and leaves no signs or tokens of their passage'. I imagine these vanishing flight paths like the vapour trails of planes, slowly dissipating to nothing. For Bartholomew, birds required 'special mention' because they 'are between the two elements [earth and air] that are most heavy and most light' and compared to other creatures are 'more pure and light and noble of substance and swift of movement'. These characteristics feel most apparent in birds that migrate because flying becomes such an extreme feat in their case, and because for so long we could only guess as to where on earth they might have flown. In his *Etymologies*, Isidore of Seville states that it is impossible for humans to know birds entirely because we cannot hope to 'penetrate the wildernesses' where they go. They are, quite literally, *beyond* us. Indeed, Isidore tells us (incorrectly, but with an ingenuity you really want to believe) that birds are so called because they cannot be traced: 'They are called birds [*avis* in Latin] because they do not have set paths [*via*, as in Italian for 'way' or 'street'], but travel by means of pathless ways [*avia*]'. It is a wonderful thought: birds are birds because the purposes and destinations of their flights are secrets known only to them. I think Isidore would be interested to know that, more than 1,500 years after his death, we still do not know the migratory destinations of some birds' ways despite all our technological advances. That is a wonderful thought too.

At the top of Swallowcliffe Down, cresting the ridge of the ancient military road, you are at the highest point for some distance around. You can look north to the village in the vale, east and west along the backbone of the Down stretching between Salisbury and Shaftesbury, and south to where the hills slope away towards Dorset and

the Channel. No wonder prehistoric peoples liked this
place. It feels poised at the edge, open to the gods and the
wide world. Ginny and I rested here, on the north side,
lying down among buttercups in early summer warmth
to skylarks' inexhaustible sky-song. On a sharp, cloudless
morning like that, in a place like that, with your head at
skylark height, Bartholomew and Isidore's words might
easily come to mind; it is an in-between realm among
birds, pure and blue and unearthed. There were swifts, a
few, passing through fast, fired from their own cross-bow
bodies. But most of all it was swallows: scissor-sharp
swallows cutting the edges of our vision, opening and
closing the air instantaneously so as to leave no sign nor
token of their ways. I tried to follow the pathless paths of
individual birds, but they quickly outflew my sight and
patience. For Isidore, the swallow's very name revealed its
innate airy substance and habit: *hirundo*, he states
(inaccurately, but beautifully, again), derives from the Latin
word for 'air' (*aer*), and thus refers to the way birds of this
family feed on the wing.

They've probably always been here, returning year after
year since long before Swallowcliffe ever existed, swooping
and sheering over the escarpment that, like the village in
its lea and an Anglo-Saxon princess, came to bear their
name. But it wasn't the idea of swallows' ancient faithfulness
to this site or the promise of their annual returning that
struck me while we lay on the Down that morning, so
much as the impending and certain prospect of their
departure in a few months' time. Swallows always suggest
their own flickering transience to me. From the moment
they arrive on our shores, it is as though they are preparing
to leave; always urgent and fast, tireless, fidgeting and
fizzing like electric impulses down the wires on which
they perch briefly, gathering in twittering anticipation of

the southbound autumnal moment. How was a place like Swallowcliffe a place at all when the bird that gives the place its name is only present for half the year?

One possible answer lies in the fact that in the Middle Ages (and long before) societies could be transitory themselves. The common practice of transhumance – the movement of livestock from one grazing site to another in accordance with the seasons, as was practised in the Weald and on the edges of the Fens – meant that there were, quite literally, 'summer places' and 'winter places' binding season and site together. If you look due west from the hills of Wiltshire across into Dorset, just over the border into Somerset, about 30 miles west from Swallowcliffe, there is Somerton, 'the summer settlement', from which the county name itself is derived. Perhaps, then, it occurred to these people on the move that their arrival in the summer lands coincided with and might be measured by the advent of migrant birds.

Was this the case at Swallowcliffe, I wondered? Was the name the legacy of transhumance between low and high ground on these Downs, maybe even descending back to Iron- and Bronze-Age occupations? The idea appealed that day as we strode along the old drover's track in the swallow's burly season. I imagined yearly congregations in these summer places; happy folk relieved to see the back of another winter, hailing swallows in confirmation of season, sun and life, and when the time came, bidding farewell to the departing birds, hoping they might be granted luck enough to see this place again the following year: *Meet me here again, God willing, at the time of the swallow's return.*

There is no doubting that these chalk heights were busy places in the pre-modern world, as the wealth of archaeological sites indicates. We eventually found *posses hlawe* along a barbed-wire fence, at a sharp north-west bend in the line that marked the boundaries between the parishes of Swallowcliffe and Ansty on the highest point on the whole Down. Or rather, we think we found the spot where old Poss's tumulus *used* to be. Disappointingly, there is nothing there now. The same went for any remains of the nearby Iron Age village we'd hoped for. The clarity and confidence of the map's marks, which seemed to identify so precisely these sites in relation to the lines of paths and field margins, were not matched by anything that was visible on the ground. Geophysical surveys of the area have revealed evidence of pits and ditches and earthworks and roundhouses, but all of that is below the surface. Writing of rural Wiltshire in 1910, naturalist and author W. H. Hudson lamented 'the destruction of the ancient earthworks, especially of the barrows, which is going on all over the downs'. So it was here, the sites slowly lost to the plough over the decades of the twentieth century.

Even so, it was something, at least, to stand on that spot by the barbed wire on the chalk-scattered ground and think on all that had come to pass. Desecration notwithstanding, the Down certainly felt like a place where things endured. The ancient structures that strew the hilltops and plains of England's chalklands were built for lasting legacies, big and solid as the earth and our stoney will to remember.

Ginny and I stood talking about the might of these monuments and of the swallows right above us. There was contradiction in this, an incongruity of fleeting, restless birds against the height and broad, firm sweep of hill, but we felt acutely that this place – *all* place it felt, so open and wide and clear was the Down to everything – was alive with moment and motion. For us, it was alive *because* of the swallows, and a feeling for that place could not exist apart from them any more than the Cretaceous chalk beneath our feet. It felt like an axis, or the origin point of Swallowcliffe's coordinates: the Down and the birds, the bedrock and the swallows' flightlines plotting a course. Is this what the old Cornish felt too at Brown Willy on Bodmin Moor – the 'hill of swallows', famous as the highest point in Cornwall? This is what birds can bring to a place. Their movement and momentum are a dynamism in the force of a place. The dwelling mind and heart are oriented to the solid sureties of hill and rock, river and tree, yes; but so too the arc and swoop of a bird's flight that describes and shapes its own topography, casting out the dimensions and trajectories of place in all directions.

This paradox may ultimately be why species like the swallow are such good place-makers to us. The most ephemeral of all birds, the most fleeting and untraceable, but what they bring, what they give to place is the season itself. The very life of a place ignites in the wake of these birds' desert-dusted, sudden arrivals, and then bursts with full summer light and living. To see a place, your place, when swallows sheer down the hill's high steep is to know it truly and vitally alive. And to name it after that brief but precious time is a confirmation.

The same goes for our feelings at the other end of summer: grief at their departures, fear that they will not return the following year. The absence of these birds, withdrawing or withholding spring's arrival, has a similarly profound effect on our sense of place. Charles Foster, an avowed swift aficionado, has written of the funk he suffers when his favourite bird leaves for Africa in August. He makes every attempt to 'avoid that sudden sickening emptiness', to reduce the 'desolation and despair'. Without swifts, Foster's street in Oxford is devoid (they breed in the eaves of his house), and the 'sky has no form, no structure. Its beams have been removed'. For him, there is 'no use pretending' that the world is 'not worse' but 'just different'; the very fabric of place, of the air we breathe, is rent in pieces, disintegrates to nothing.

No wonder, then, that people might once have dreamed about preserving that essence of summer place, or may have been so stubbornly attached to die-hard myths about birds sleeping out winter at the bottom of ponds. If the birds never really leave, after all, then neither has summer. A small wick sputters through the dark cold months, a flame aglow in the benthic gloom. That's a myth to believe in, to keep alight, at a historical time when the success or failure of your harvest could literally mean the difference between life or death. It's a way to convince yourself that the summer state, as Foster says of swifts in our lives, is 'how everything, all the time, is meant to be'.

I'm thinking of cuckoos again, of the wise men of Gotham and their cuckoo bush. To prevent that bird leaving in midsummer, were it possible, would somehow be to capture and distil aestival substance, to be shelved alongside jars or flagons of summer's golden yield, as though the matter of the bird itself – fission of light, energy, song – is that of this long-day, revolving moment of our year. To call a place after a cuckoo, or a swallow, or any summer bird, seems to me a similar magic, another sort of capture. The name pinpoints the most life-affirming, life-full moment of a place, calls it out, and then keeps it tight, clutched in a fist close to the praying heart.

It is mid-April again, one year after my visit to Swallowcliffe. My brother, Richard, and I, up for a few days' hiking in the Lake District, arrived today on the English side of the huge Solway Firth, at Burgh by Sands, looking across to

Scotland. There are swallows here, freshly arrived, sleek and glossy. I am not here for them though. In fact, I'm not here with thoughts of summer at all. Quite the opposite.

There are people, me included, who long not for the swallows of spring, but for winter and its birds, for what they bring to our places. These hibernal spirits arrive as vanguards in autumn, escaping the severe temperatures that will grip their arctic homes. Today though, in the far north-west of England, rather than greeting winter, I want to catch it before it departs, bid it safe passage north on the wings of birds that have been gathering here in huge numbers for the off. One day soon they will go. Twenty thousand barnacle geese. For now, they are over there, feeding safely across the channel on the Rockcliffe peninsula between the Rivers Eden and Esk. A long way from me, on private land, miles and miles of private land. We need to get closer.

What did the early English make of winter birds? There are no unequivocal examples of winter species in our place names (which is perhaps unsurprising given how our ancestors must have felt about this cold and bleak season), but there can be little doubt that people noticed when these birds were in residence, arriving in autumn with the north winds and then leaving places suddenly empty of all that brumal hustle in the spring. The hold that they might have had on the medieval imagination can be glimpsed in the pages of one illuminated manuscript known as the Sherborne Missal. The book is famed for its exquisite marginal illustrations of nearly 50 native British birds (including a superb, displaying crane, as it happens), and among that collection there are remarkably accurate and intricate portraits of various winter visitors: a fieldfare, a great grey shrike, a 'wyld goos' that looks very like a white-fronted goose, and a barnacle goose in all its piebald beauty – a deep black neck and head, white face patch, and stippled grey, silver-laced back.

There was, in fact, a double intrigue concerning the pathless ways of winter migrants, because not only did they come and go each year from God knows where – they also reproduced out of all human sight as well. People in medieval Europe never encountered nesting barnacle geese or their chicks. No one did until the Svalbard population was discovered in the late sixteenth century (the Greenland population took another 300 years more to find). It is little wonder that, no less than was the case with summer migrants, far-fetched theories were proposed to explain the sometime presence and absence of winter-residing birds. And the wonderfully eccentric myth surrounding the barnacle goose, still relatively well known, has to be the most incredible of all.

Barnacle geese were thought to spontaneously generate from driftwood (or, in some depictions, grow directly from the trees that produced this driftwood, drooping like hanging fruit). Their embryonic forms, it was said, grew in dense clusters on sea-tossed timbers, attached 'by their beaks as if they were seaweed', as Gerald of Wales states in his twelfth-century *Topography of Ireland*, the source of our first written explanation for this bizarre theory. Gerald claimed to have seen, 'with my own eyes, more than a thousand of these small birds, hanging down on the seashore from one piece of timber, enclosed in their shells and already formed'. Those seaweed geese were actually goose-necked barnacles, as we now call them: a crustacean so peculiar-looking it seems right that some sort of myth should have involved them. The species that washes up on British shores has a long fleshy, black 'goose neck' (the peduncle, by which the creature anchors itself) attached to a brilliant white, goose-head-shaped shell, in which is housed the creature. You can see the logic, the thought process of some inquisitive individual long ago: it's an ingenious genesis for a bird that, as Gerald wrote, does 'not seem to build nests in any corner of the earth'.

Gerald of Wales is sometimes credited with inventing this story, but it goes back at least two centuries before he was writing. Once again, the Exeter Book – God bless that Leofric – provides us with our earliest-surviving written source. It's an exact depiction of the myth, even referring to the plumage of the bird, and its appearance in the riddle collection strongly implies that people were familiar enough with the story to be able to guess the answer, and that there were probably earlier sources for the myth, which are lost to us.

My nose was in a tight nick, and I beneath the water,
underflowed by the flood, sunk far
in the salt-streams and grew in the sea
buried by waves from above, my body
fastening on a floating wood-drifter.
I had a living spirit when I came out of the embrace
of brine and beam in a black garment;
some of my dressings were white.
Then the air lifted me, living, up,
wind from water, then carried me way
over the seal's bath. Say what I am called.

The Solway barnacle geese have been turning up from over the seal's bath 'since the memory of man', Hugh Gladstone grandly remarks in his voluminous *Birds of*

Dumfriesshire. Seeing their huge, swelling flocks today, I can believe it. It feels as though an annual gathering of this magnitude, such monumental arrival and leaving, has its origins in the formation of earth's raw elements. For Aldo Leopold, geese joined cranes as the great avian progenitors: 'In the beginning was the unity of the Ice Sheet. Then followed the unity of the March thaw, and the northward hegira of the international geese'. It's possible that these Solway birds have been doing just that – making their tremendous journeys between here and Spitsbergen every year since some time after the last Ice Age when the Firth and its estuarine flats first formed. It is, and likely has long been, *the* place for barnacle geese in England.

Today, confronted by the vastness of the Firth's tide and sky and sand, I'm overwhelmed by that possibility. It is one of the most remarkable and affecting of all ways to connect yourself to a place: to know and to see before you the great turning and passing of the world made constant and solid each year in a single location. All of Svalbard's barnacle geese, the entire population, here on one estuary in Britain. Perhaps this, too, is why seasonal birds matter so much to our interactions with place. It is true with swallows and all their summer kin – this feeling that they've always been doing it, that they return to the same spot, even the same nest, each year – but for me it's heightened when you witness the magnitude of winter bird flocks. It makes me vividly aware that the outlandish barnacle goose myth is really all about place, in the end; about how and why the birds are here and then not here, about conceiving where this bird is in the corners of the earth when it is not visible to us.

When the place where this yearly magic happens is your home, the sense of wonder and connection is all the more. That was what I wanted to get closer to today. There was no goose place name to find, but by meeting those who live alongside the geese's migrations year in, year out, I hoped to connect with the old legacy of Solway geese, people and landscape.[3] That local link was also, I knew, my only sure chance of getting closer to the birds themselves. I had a two-week window in mid-April, which I desperately hoped would coincide with the traditional assembly of barnacle geese on the Rockcliffe Marshes in the restless weeks before leaving town. When I contacted the Cumbria Bird Club, my enquiries were eagerly answered, and then a period of quiet followed while I was shuffled between various authorities on the subject. Finally, I received a short message that simply read, 'Brian Hodgson. He'll get you among the geese.'

There can be few people living today who know the Rockcliffe birds and their landscape better than Brian. He grew up here, running free across the estuarine plains, fishing for flounder and paddling in summer, collecting mushrooms in autumn, and watching birds. Straight from school, Brian started as gamekeeper for the Castletown Estate, which owns the marshes and surrounding farmland (some 4,000 acres), a job he held for decades. Although he now works on the railways, Brian has been involved with Castletown in one way or another for 42 years. He still spends every spare moment he can on the estate participating in conservation projects, often with his young grandson Archie, as is the case today when we meet him outside the mansion house.

'Either of you driven one of these before?' Brian says, pointing to a pair of quad bikes. My brother recalls doing so once on a stag do, so he saddles up and reacquaints himself while Brian points out to me a feral colony of greylag geese on a nearby pond that he hatched and raised himself. He's convinced they still recognise him as 'mam' because they'll tolerate no one else getting anywhere near them. It turns out Brian has a knack for rearing: I'm astonished to hear he breeds willow tits (with a dream of supplying reintroduction schemes in extirpated locations in this region).

'And the barnacles?' I ask casually, trying to hide my anxiety that they might have gone.

'They're out there.' He smiles, sensing my keenness. 'Won't be long though. It could be days or weeks, but they'll go soon. Most go together. For several afternoons or evenings before they'll do test flights, going higher and higher, spiralling round and round, and then one day that's it. Until October.' It was strange to think of that; they'd not even gone yet, but they would be back on site in six months. 'Autumn's begun when you hear the geese on a full moon in October. Always a full moon. If it's full they land at this end, if it's not they'll go to the Scottish side. No one knows why, but that seems to be the way it is. It's the same when they leave; all the birds gather here at our end before leaving. If the moon is right, all the geese from Spitsbergen start as well as end here.'

Brian climbs onto his quad, Archie nestled in front between his legs. 'Shall we go then?'

I quickly discover that travelling on the back end of a quad bike, perched on a shelf above the driver's seat and grasping a makeshift fender, is a deeply uncomfortable experience. The machine's lurching, exaggerated by every gear shift and throttle turn, jolts and throws you, so that just about everything is sore and you've no hands free to do anything but cling on. To relieve our backsides and give each other a chance to see what Brian points out in every direction as we speed across the marsh, Richard and I take driving in turns. There's no doubt though, this is the way to travel out here; there's so much land you'll barely cover anything on foot.

Brian's aim is to get me closer, something he said isn't too difficult on the bikes. As we leave the sea wall he points out the cottage where he lived with his family for many years as gamekeeper. His children were 'fetched up' on the marsh. We drive out west, Brian speeding off and slowing at precisely the right moments over creeks and undulations, us keeping up as best we can. The topography and routes are long-learned for Brian and so ingrained in memory I wouldn't be at all surprised if he could navigate his way to the sands on a moonless night, or blindfolded.

To us, the marsh is route-less and timeless. There is such a feeling of space out here. Although the main waters of the Firth are further round the Cumbrian coast, out beyond the mouth of the River Esk, it looks to us that we can see it all from here; the marsh so seamlessly becomes mud and sand and water in the big mouth of the estuary that nothing is distinct and all are one. Suddenly, when Richard and I are beginning to feel that we can't endure too many more butt-aching turns on the bike's backend, Brian pulls up short, turns off his engine and points again, standing up on his seat. We draw up level and turn off too. Now there is only the sound of wind and birds. Curlews, lapwings, gulls, and the puppy yap of barnacle geese. We look out to the sea-sky and there they are, a few hundred maybe, flying low along the shore. There is more than one group, and through our binoculars we soon pick out the many gaggles and skeins. We are much closer than we were at Burgh first thing this morning, but the effect is the same – the tremulous, shimmering creature, glinting like mica or quartz. It's not the same as a wader flock, which twists and turns so that the whole body shifts colour as one; the effect of these geese on mass is caused by every individual registering itself discrete in the many.

'Just look from one side to the other, lads. It's like the Serengeti. My Serengeti anyway.' He's right. As far around as we can scan with binoculars, twisting our bodies left to right, there is a bright seam of geese-light between the land and sky, lifting and rising like a tide.

'Not as many as there should be though. Looks a lot – it is if you've not seen them before, but I've been with them all my life. We've lost nearly forty per cent of the usual population this winter. We get over 40,000 birds on the Solway, but our counts reckon on 25,000 now. Not far off half the Svalbard birds dead. I've not seen anything like that sort of loss in my time.' Brian had mentioned the impact of avian flu on the geese in our email exchanges, but I wasn't aware just how severely impacted the geese were. 'It's easing now we're into spring, but last November and December the poor things were dropping everywhere on the marsh, like their shit. You could walk right up to them and they'd do nothing; just sat there, dying. Twenty-four hours, that's all it takes, from catching the virus to dead. And it wasn't just the barnacles either: we get thousands of pink-footed geese on the Solway too, and they were copping it, though nowhere near as badly for some reason – seem to be more resistant. I found dead raptors out here too, dead from feeding on the geese: peregrine, buzzards, white-tailed eagles. And waders, from probing infected mud I guess.'

A curlew interrupts our conversation from very close by. Brian's ring tone it turns out, so while he takes the call I walk over to inspect a dead barnacle goose a short distance away. As I get closer I can see that its body is

gone, gnawed and drenched to bone. Even in this state
though, it is beautiful. The upward-facing wings, the back,
neck and head are so pristine, covering the shock of
plundered corpse under their feathers, it seems as though
the bird might have died just hours ago. It's likely the
closest I'll ever get to a wild barnacle goose, and I can see
how its plumage is the perfection of monochrome. Every
shade between purest white and purest black is in there
somewhere, the extremes of the spectrum boldly contrasted
in piebald parts, and intricate gradations of the subtlest
silvers and greys striped and suffused.

I daren't touch the thing, but find a lone primary
feather from another bird on my way to rejoin the
others and can't resist stowing it in my bag. It is at once
thrilling and disheartening to hold. Dull and inert,
detached from its purpose as from the bird, useless and
earthbound as me, but to have the feather in hand is also
to connect myself with some residual flight magic, the
miracle it should have performed, only weeks, even days
from now.

Brian says we're likely to see moribund geese as we
head west to the point, but there are none, just more
deceased birds in various stages of decomposition. I think
of a medieval battlefield after the bloody event is done,
strewn with wretched bodies that lie right where they
were struck down. The plaguey ravishes of avian flu make
this a surreal place to be this year. Beyond are thousands
of geese, as there always are, readying to return north as
they always do, but close to, at our feet, is a distressing
reality that contaminates the illusion of normality up
ahead. It's a sign for our times.

We've driven as far as we can go, and most of the geese
have now settled across a channel on an island off the
peninsula. We watch the birds from here, and Brian points

out landmarks on the Scottish coast across the Esk: Gretna
Green to the east, and Caerlaverock Castle to the west, the
most famous site for wintering barnacle geese on the Firth.
I ask him how this season of flu has affected him.

'It's heartbreaking. Out there is a place of geese, always
has been. They're here for more than half a year, so
although they're truly birds of Svalbard, you feel like this
is their home, and when they come back in October the
place is right again. We've lots of other birds on the
marsh: nesting golden plover, more lapwing here than
anywhere else in the country, but it's the geese that make
it. They're everything that is adventurous about a wild
place. It's them that make it wild. These birds will recover
from this year's losses I'm sure, but they've got lots else to
face. Traditionally the birds don't leave till early May, but
we've noticed it getting earlier in recent years. It's because
the ice up north is thawing earlier. They seem to be
responding to that. Polar bears in Spitsbergen have
apparently changed their habits now because there's so
little ice. They've taken to predating barnacle geese eggs
and chicks much more.'

'What do other people think of the geese?' I ask. 'Do
the locals pay much attention to them?'

'Ay, the older ones do. It's part of their heritage. They
know like I do what the sound of geese in autumn means.
In the past the geese would have been a food source as
well, so there's that. There's one old boy who still takes his
gun out once a year at Christmas to bag a bird. Am I going
to stop him? He's been doing it all his life. When I was a
kid I used to beg my dad to take me along wildfowling
with him; I was fascinated to see the birds he shot, to hold
them in my hand. That was a connection. It's what got me
started on birds in the first place. My bairns were weaned
on the birds. They ate all sorts. I still control vermin on the

Estate, but I wouldn't shoot anything else now. Those were different days. You can only kill something once, but you can have the pleasure of watching it forever.

'The younger ones couldn't give a toss though. I do what I can with local schools to encourage an interest in the kids – making nestboxes, giving talks and the like. Hopefully something will stick. I donated a taxidermy collection to the local primary for display, but the headteacher took the lot when he left!'

The tide is on the turn now. At the right time, Brian says, it is possible to cross to the island where the geese are, but we must leave them, and we turn back east. Tides can come in frighteningly fast here: the second fastest ever recorded in the UK was on the Solway Firth. At high tide, these geese-lands are totally covered, and spring tides have breached the original sea wall before now, rising to above 10 metres.

I watch the gathering geese on the island one last time, thinking again of the old riddle, the transformations of a bird that transforms this ebb-and-flow landscape with every coming and going. They are coming now. The strange creature grows, restless and ceaseless, swells like the incoming tide. Soon they will vanish, gone again over the seal's bath. I cannot know exactly what long past generations of Solway folk thought of these birds, but it seems inconceivable to me that anyone could not sense the daily and seasonal movements of the geese as part of the ever-changing soul of this wild place and the wide world.

4

Charterlands

Frilsham and Bucklebury, Berkshire ~
Bishop's Cleeve, Gloucestershire ~
East Brabourne and Sellindge, Kent

In a lifetime that spanned all ten decades of the twentieth century, the historian W. G. Hoskins pioneered a new way of seeking the past: not in written sources or artefacts, but in the folds and fields of the English countryside. His expeditions and studies were the foundation of his profound and original belief that the English landscape itself is the most precious and informative historical record we possess. Hoskins' work in landscape history is known best in his classic book, *The Making of the English Landscape*. Published in 1955 and never out of print, its deep love of England's long rural past is suffused with a post-war grief and indignation at modernity's monstrous destructions. *The Making of the English Landscape* is a plea to recognise and defend the hidden, often overlooked heritage right under our noses.

One of the most poetic and affecting moments in the book concerns a little-known early English landscape feature that clearly fascinated Hoskins. He describes how, 'armed with a copy of a Saxon charter and the 2½ inch maps', he scrambled and traipsed across the countryside in pursuit of the boundaries of former Anglo–Saxon estates. For him, he writes, there is no exercise that leads to a 'truer and more detailed knowledge' of 'some few miles', or by which these local terrains are more 'indelibly printed on the mind and heart'. I imagine him with gaitered trousers muddied in boggy streams, tie, tweed jacket, and hair all brambled from hedgerow escapades along narrow and deep lanes.

A summer ago, I took up Hoskins' hobby for myself, headed to Gloucestershire for my own adventures in the charterlands, as I've come to call them. I went, like him, armed with documents and maps, and a hope to trace medieval secrets in the land. It was a task, I discovered very early on, that involved me losing my way more often than I found it, arriving upon certainties no more than they escaped me.

I stood on the highest land in the county, looking due west. This was the hill. I was sure of that. There was nothing to see at first. I'd arrived in a squall that had me hastily pull on waterproofs and hole up in a disused quarry, but the rain blew east and the sopping skies were suddenly blue and cloudless, and sunlight filled the Severn valley below. It was one reason I'd chosen Gloucestershire – that famous view over the wide vale to the Malverns and on to the black tops of Wales.

This was the hill alright, and I was on it, and down there was Bishop's Cleeve. Or plain Cleeve, as it was once known, and before that, Clif. Good Old English: say what you see. Like the medieval people of Swallowcliffe beneath their chalk down, the Clif dwellers looked up and named the view: high ground to the east: a steep escarpment of limestone with outcropped ledges dropping to the river plain.

But there were other landmarks that caught my eye when I first read the directions in the charter, and that enticed me to make the journey no less than had the view from Cleeve Hill. The landmarks that sounded as

though they belonged to some immaterial world beyond
our dimension, only visible on certain nights of the year
when the moon was right: the apple tree and the maple
tree that grow together, the black shining pool, the wolf's
glade, the lonely thorn, the hanging wood of stories.
These places sounded too fantastical to be real.

The day before I was chasing mysterious landmarks in
Berkshire. I'd read about some at a wood called Hawkridge,
and the place being situated not even a mile off the
motorway on my way west to Gloucestershire, and close
to a friend who knew the lie of the county's land, I
arranged to meet for a morning's wander and an excuse
for lunch at a nearby pub.

I arrived early and sent instructions. 'Meet by the well.
Straight up the hill opposite the church,' I said. 'Straight
up the hill and past the red phone box. Turn right into the
woods. You'll find it there, just a little further up, among
the holly.'

A good place to start. A well, a spring, a beginning, and
one with illustrious medieval origins to boot. It has long
been said in these parts to be Saint Frideswide's, struck by
prayer from the ground in the woods where she performed
miracles during her years on the run from marriage in
Oxford in the seventh century. It's a typical narrative of
wells and springs – the subterranean gift of precious water
sanctified in a time of saints, miracles and relics. Whether
Saint Frideswide's or not, the well on the hill at Frilsham
is a traditional landmark, and however truly ancient or
holy, it occurred to me that perhaps generations of locals
have been meeting here, and known it always to be
familiar to everyone they knew. People were collecting

water from it up until the 1950s. Its importance might be
as deep as its own echoing darkness. That local
understanding is at the heart of this book and the very
idea of place, but its power had a new force for me now as
I approached the charterlands.

Activist and nature writer Nicola Chester knows a
thing or two about local knowledge. Little knowledge,
we might say, where little does not mean ignorance or
lack, but the opposite: precise, focused, careful,
intimately attentive. Nicola has spent a lifetime
consciously and intensively gathering these little
knowledges of place. She grew up and has very nearly
always lived inside, along, or just over Berkshire's
borders. Those boundaries have surrounded and
marked her life, and more than once she has been faced
with a need to defend or confirm that irreplaceable
sense of belonging – at Twyford Down, at Newbury, at
Greenham Common. She moved around often, as a
child and as an adult, but learned to put down roots
defiantly wherever she went.

Nicola arrived to find me sat on the well, pondering
directions. As at Cleeve, I knew I'd found the hill alright
– the hawk's ridge. For a while we looked over the OS
map together at intriguing local names: Burntbush Lane,
Oxley's Shaw, Boar's Hole Farm. There were birds too,
lots of them: Rook's Copse, Cuckoo Pitts, Pheasant Hill
Wood, Magpie Farm.

'Why Hawkridge then?' Nicola said.

'Hawkridge is ancient. Old English. The others aren't.
It's first mentioned here.' I handed her the piece of paper
on which I'd copied out my directions. 'But it's more
about this,' I pointed, 'the bit that comes after the name.'
She examined my writing for a few seconds and then
looked at me.

'Is this here?'

'Yes and no. It is, but not as we see it now. Those are local landmarks in this parish over a thousand years ago. It's from an Anglo-Saxon charter, giving land at Hawkridge to the Church. It's a deed describing the boundaries of that land, all the way around the edge.'

Nicola read aloud. 'First to Pang's stream … to the ditch … to the hedge.' She laughed. 'Well, the Pang I can do, but the hedge – which hedge?'

'Some sort of raised earth-bank probably, maybe with a hedge on top.[1] It would have been a very particular bank. The Hawkridge people would have known exactly what was meant by that. And the ditch.'

Nicola read more, calling out landmarks. '"Cuthwulf's cottages … the crucifix tree?" What's that?'

'Probably a tree with a cross marked on it, a signpost.'

'"The titmouse's pond!" Oh, I love that! A long-tailed tit?'

'Could be.'

'Finding your way by titmouse pond. Wonderful.'

The charters are full of these treasures. They are maps of lost places, some long gone, others half-hidden or darkly submerged, like the refracted, shadowy world beneath the surface of a river. Many of these locations and landmarks are possible to find, if you know where and how to look. In their descriptions of linked landmarks making up medieval boundaries, the charters go beyond place names alone; they expand the dimensions of place, show us the wider countryside beyond and between. We 'catch sight of an earlier world', Hoskins wrote. In this 'rich tapestry preserved', as another scholar, Della Hooke, has described the charters' jigsaw vision of the English landscape, we glimpse how 'local people actually saw their countryside'. As the late archaeologist Christopher Taylor remarked in his beautiful edition of Hoskins' classic, the early estates 'are the real framework of England'.

⋆ ⋆ ⋆⋆⋆ ⋆

Anglo-Saxon charters do not make for bedtime reading. They are some of the most unlikely sources in which you'd expect to discover a feeling for place, or detailed knowledge about the natural world. There are nearly 2,000 of them, the earliest dating from AD 679 – a huge corpus of legal documents that are typically to do with granting land. The script in each charter is packed tightly, with little space between words in continuous lines of Latin prose (the language of everything important for centuries). They tell us about the administrative business of royals and nobles, the Church estates, noble privileges, land tenures, and so on. Reading charters, once you've made the transcription and translation, is like settling down with all that small print that comes with an insurance policy, or the will of someone you've never heard of.

And yet, if you take the time to examine a charter or two, amid the royal personages, entitlements, oaths and decrees, you'll notice something in all that dense Latin; something noticeably different, maybe even recognisable. That's because many of the charters include words or passages in Old English, the common language hidden in the elite, inscrutable script, detectable if you look closely enough. Sometimes it's like listening to a foreigner speaking their native language, then suddenly, comically, inserting an English word or two for which there is no translation. Hawkridge first appears in

writing in this way, an English word springing out from
the Latin.

Cui uidelicet nemori ipsius diocesis solicole notum imposuerunt
uocabulum Heafochrycg, quod his undique notis circumgiratur
limitibus.

There it is, halfway through – *Heafochrycg*. There is a mud-
spattered immediacy to the English name in among the
Latin, like a thin English winter interrupting the flourish
of Mediterranean heat. Here, we are told, are the
boundaries surrounding the place that the locals
specifically call Hawkridge, a part of which was now
granted as a small woodland estate in this charter by King
Eadwig in February 956 to a certain Abbot Æthelwold
and his monks.

   Immediately beneath this, in English, with an ornate
green initial, is the description of the estate's boundaries,
the description I had shared with Nicola. They are written
as though spoken, a vivid and detailed set of instructions
guiding readers or listeners around the estate border from
one landmark to the next, such that anyone with good
local knowledge could pace out a circular, clockwise
route. Sometimes that perimeter is intact, where parish
boundaries have maintained parts of the ancient estate
borders (which, we now know, might themselves have
inherited even older demarcations from Roman, or
possibly Iron-Age, patterns). Those dotted lines marking
boundaries you find on OS maps can be far older than
you imagine in certain cases: Old English memory alive
in 2½ inch-to-the-mile print.

   The early English *landscip* was to be walked, traversed,
known and sensed through contact and repeated
encounter, and to read the charters now is to be, quite

literally, guided through a medieval world.[2] *Þis synd þa landmearca*, the charters often state; 'these are the landmarks'. Out of context, it is as though we approach a conversation part way through, overhearing the response to some foot-weary traveller asking their way of a local. 'First to Pang's stream', the Hawkridge description begins.

> *Thence to the ditch. Then, always by the ditch, go to the hedgebank, and from there to the crucifix tree; thence along the hedgebank to the thorny patch of wood, and on to the ford at the bridge, continuing always by the hedgebank to stone way. From stone way, proceed always by the woodbank to the acres of flax, and thence always by the woodbank to the titmouse's pond, and from there to Cuthwulf's hamlet, and from the hamlet to Pang's stream, heading up midstream back to the ditch.*

This is how charter boundaries work: start here, go from here to there, and so on until you are back where you began. The descriptions, again, do something that place names cannot: they give us a speaker, and the speaker breathes life. The extraordinary sense of an Old English voice is so distinct it feels as though the gap of 1,000 years has been closed in an instant. Not simply because it has the force and clarity of direct speech, but because the words spoken reveal an insider's knowledge, memory maps, held in a head stuffed full of remembered places: meeting places, passing places, know-your-way-by-this-place places, all passed on by word of mouth, teaching others to know the ditch and the hedge and the birds at the pond.

Many charters do not have boundary clauses. Some may have included them originally but lost them when the texts were copied out into later manuscripts. In others, blank spaces patiently wait for the scribe's return and the stain of ink, now permanently suspended in time. And in others still, insider knowledge is so readily assumed and trusted that the charters simply refer to the 'well-known boundaries' and nothing more. What memory maps there must have been!

Here is another, from Chertsey in Surrey:

> *... up between east wood and otter shaw to the hoary thorn ... to the three trees along the deep brook ... to the black willow, then straight on to the Britons' hythe along the Thames on the other side of the hemmed in land where the dung heap is ... along the water straight to nettle island ...*

And in Wiltshire:

> *... from the elder stump, and from there to town way, and thus to the dove thorn ...*

or Staffordshire:

> *... from the marten's strip of wood and so forth, over the bare wood ... to goats' bridge ... to the sour apple at the narrow dwelling and from there to the hollow brook at Wulfgar's marsh ...*

The charters, like our place names, are ancient glossaries of flora and fauna.[3] That they are, however, is entirely incidental. They do so unintentionally. Accidental natural histories, as it were. They do not care for a sense of place, but rather the limits of place, because their bureaucratic purpose was to provide a written record of a land transfer that would stand in perpetuity, 'firm and unshaken', as one example states. Charters deal in boundaries for a reason, and with that emphasis comes the realisation that what all this amounted to, for the ordinary person living

on and working the land, was a potential loss of rights,
restricted access, and the threat of penalty. That many of
the charters included detailed boundary descriptions in
English, and those responsible for writing them gleaned
that oral wisdom directly from the locals themselves, was
partly a measure to ensure that the locals knew exactly
what land belonged to whom. The charters, in effect,
turned local knowledge and the vernacular language
against themselves: there can be no excuse for not being
clear about the bounds of the new estate, and anyone
who interferes or transgresses will be, the charters state,
excommunicated and condemned by God to the avenging
fires of hell. A frightening prospect indeed to any good
Christian soul.

But nonetheless, there they are – the wild lives and
landscapes in parishes all over medieval England: the
woodcock's valley, raven's ridge, finches' den, kingfisher's
clearing, wrens' spring, yellowhammer land, alder shaw,
great willow, nettle island, wild garlic lea, ragwort well,
rosehip bridge, wolf's gully, beetle's marsh, beaver stream,
fox cottages, the old badger hole … the list goes on.

These appellations are, in one sense, place names in
waiting; the stage before habitation occurs and a name
from the nearby environment is transferred to a new place.
The names of some of our towns and villages must certainly
have come about in this way. In another sense, they appear
like the contents of a field guide. To view the boundary
descriptions like this, though, is to miss the bigger picture
and point. It is to overlook the experiences alive in these
memories of creature and place that over generations have
shaped the cultural geographies of communities. The birds,
mammals, amphibians, insects, plants, trees, stones, waters,
lands and weathers that fill the charters and intersect with
human spaces are not isolated or independent of one

another. They form whole ecologies, each living thing observed, understood and located in its habitat, which has its place in turn alongside the next, and the next.

In their charter contexts these animal-habitat pairs appear to me like tiny poems, distinctive in workaday rhythmic patterns. They are found 'in the field', to use John Clare's famous phrase of his own work, who, he humbly claimed, 'only wrote them down'. The charter voices carry through the centuries like folk songs passed from ear to ear, committed to heart. Down-to-earth, worked-in-earth voices of ordinary people shaped necessarily and assuredly by the 'imaginative sufficiencies of the parish', as American poet, Wendell Berry, has said on the subject of small-town living and farming. Agricultural labourers in the nineteenth century would still have understood the tune, the deep connection with home turf that knew reed and oak and the bare hollow on the east side of a hill as naturally as the thoughts in their own heads. The same song would be recognisable to many, even at the turn of the twentieth century, but there can be relatively few now who know the land in this way, who could rely on such precise, shared communal knowledge that they might guide another by the thorny acre and map one's place in the world by elder, rook, beetle, wind and ditch.

⋆ ⋆ ⋆ ⋆ ⋆

Nicola and I walked that morning in the spirit of the charters' wild inhabitants, not with any great success in tracking them or their locations, but happy enough in stepping out our own clockwise route according to Nicola's memories and whichever landmarks we happened to pass by: from the eastern edge of Frilsham Common by the road to the Pot Kiln pub (just a 'glow in the woods', as Nicola remembers it decades ago – 'no electricity, and rough, bare floors'); from there to the top of the horse paddock by the footpath, then always by the butterfly brambles to the road where nipplewort grows on the banks …

We made for Bucklebury, where the road runs parallel to the chalk-fed Pang on the south side of the ridge, and the river itself becomes the parish boundary for a stretch. Here, at least, we had met in some way with the charter's closing words, following the Pang's route 'up midstream'. We took a dogleg through the village and turned west, the river to our right, and on our left, Nicola pointed out, the northern limit of Bucklebury estate, the oldest landed estate in Berkshire – 900 years and only ever in the hands of two owners. It's nothing new, we said, all that land belonging to the few. (Berkshire, in fact, is especially crowded with aristocratic demesnes.) We spoke as we walked of rural poverty and inequality; of public anger in a post-Covid world towards trespass laws, the intractability of landed wealth; of Dartmoor and the rights-to-roam furore. Too often it feels as if nature is granted incidental existence and space, forced to find accidental footholds, to survive in the gaps between. And we must discover it that way too, with incidental access, snatching our moments to be close to nature and love it, whenever and wherever, defending it as best we can against powerful oppositions.

We watched the river where we could, at bridges, on the bank, at the notorious Bucklebury ford. It is an old source for Nicola, the little Pang, a first place. Moving from the early childhood home at Pangbourne, she writes in her memoir, *On Gallows Down*, 'felt like a coming away of skin'. I thought of Nick Acheson and his Wensum, the river of his life. Clear waters both delivered clean and pure from chalk-bedrock. I envied them that connection, that closeness, their personal wellsprings.

With increased rainfall compared to previous summers, the water levels were not so low and the ford was not dry. At other times in the year though, especially in winter, the ford is unfordable by car; too wide and too deep. Not infrequently, non-locals get caught out. We stood on one side to watch waving tendrils of crowfoot in the glassy flow, hoping for the lane-changing dash of a small trout on the feed.

'I've a story about this ford,' Nicola said. 'It happened with an old boyfriend, Rob; he and I met in a record shop in Newbury and protested at the Bypass together. In the early nineties we often drove to the Pot Kiln for live music (Rob was a drummer; I sang). One winter's night – I remember cold, and starlight on the water – we came to the ford on our way to the Kiln. Rob had a red and white Citroën 2CV. After trying to judge the depth, we thought, heck, let's risk it! Of course, the water came in, under the doors, into the footwells, and then the car stalled. We got out into freezing water, right over our knees – I had to tuck my dress into my coat belt – and waded round to the back of the car to push her out. When we got to the pub, there was another couple there ahead of us drying out, and a row of steaming boots and socks by the fire. Everyone cheered!

'On the same night,' she continued, 'on the way to the Pot Kiln I think – actually maybe not, but I remember cold and clear and dark, so definitely another winter's night – there was a huge black dog walking towards us and its eyes reflected red in the headlamps. I turned around as we passed by it, and it turned as well to look back at the car, and its eyes were still red. The brake lights perhaps, but I'm quite sure those eyes were red when the dog was in front of us too. It was all a bit spooky!'

Nicola's stories stayed with me. I thought about how moments such as that bring places to life for each of us, turning them suddenly into places that matter, our personal crucifix trees, though we could not have known this beforehand, or in the moment itself. Places are transformed in this way, settling into memory, claimed by memory, made into precious possessions, although, truly, it is the places that possess us. Bucklebury Ford, and Frideswide's Well no doubt, must be thick with dank, mossy stories imprinted 'indelibly on the mind and heart', as Hoskins wrote.

The charters have their place stories too, somewhere deep, irretrievably deep perhaps, in those descriptions of local landscapes, as accidental as the trees and creatures to which they are attached, but there nonetheless. What passings or meetings occurred at the stone way? What words were exchanged? And when did those tiny tit-birds at the pond a stretch from Cuthwulf's cottages settle in someone's consciousness? A sense of place as tree-scurry and titter of titmice.

There is another place like that in the Gloucestershire charter. The following morning, having more successfully tracked the Cleeve boundary by car from Stoke Orchard in the west to the cockerels' fort in the north, and then on foot up the old green way,[4] from where I diverted up to the Common to admire the big view, I set out to find the woodpecker's meadow.

I left the sunlit ledge of Cleeve and marched fast along the northern edge of the Common, hard east along hedgerowed tracks gloriously pink and purple with thistle, vetch, scabious and harebell, and then sharp south where the path turned and declined. From here, the modern parish boundary appears to follow closely, maybe even exactly, the original estate line as marked out in the AD 777 charter, descending and zigzagging into shallow valleys where spring-fed streams cut through the Common's lower steeps. I walked alongside paddocks and pastures by Postlip Hall, thinking of all the curious landmarks I'd wondered at earlier in the charter description: the hanging wood of speech or tales, the shining black pool, the lonely thorn. If my reading of the boundaries was right, the 'apple and maple trees grown together' might have been somewhere round here all that time ago, close to the wolves that once roamed the wooded combes. An orchard, perhaps, but I fancifully imagined two trees entwined around one another as if in some Jacobean ornamental garden.

When the footpath stopped at Isbourne spring, I left it and followed the boundary line on my map further south to where I hazarded a guess the south-east corner of the estate circuit might have been before it turned west over the hill to meet up with the Tirle (the brook is still there and still a boundary). The valley slopes were humming loudly, and grasshoppers, dry-brown as the grass itself, popped in front of me like a scatter of seed heads with every foot I put forwards. The insects' fizzing energy besides, there was a drowsy, simmering motility to everything, and I dropped my pack, wet with sweat, to lie in the grass.

This was it. Or as close as I was going to get, anyway. Thirteen hundred years ago, when the lands around here were united under the rule of Mercia and home to the Hwicce people, before the Vikings had set foot in England, a whole century before Alfred became king and some notion of a united England started to become a political vision, this place, or somewhere near this place, between the 'calf's hill' and 'wheel corner' as the charter describes, was the woodpecker's meadow.

Beneath the skittering grass and a sky now white-hot with midday sun, I tried to imagine a place defined by these birds. A great spotted? Smartly pied, red-banded, sharp pips from nearby woodland fringes that reverberate with springtime drumming, like a bright coin on a tabletop. Or a green woodpecker? King of the ant barrows, stitching up the meadow's corners in pleated flight and laughing at its own parting jokes.

I thought again of the tits by the Berkshire pond. Old English for the family is *mase*, which means 'little or tiny thing'. The crane's opposite. Everything about these birds is smallness – the upside-down deftness, butterfly buoyancy, finicky feeding, peep and scold. I think of long-tailed tits most of all; dainty and downy and whiskered. They seem light as one of their own feathers, and their tinkling calls are so delicate it is as though their tiny frames are transfigured into their own tiny fairy notes.

Woodpeckers and titmice are surely some of the less likely birds in the names of places. They are not alone. There are tiny wrens, cock-tailed defenders at the village of Warmfield; buntings at Amberley (yellowhammers perhaps, little luminous hedgerow gods); mouse-grey mistle thrushes at Shrigley; sandpipers at Stinsford; finches at Finchhampstead and Finchley, or the nook in a river bend where finches are to be found that gave its name to Finchale in Durham; sparrows, or some other small bird, feeding on the flooded land that gave (Stretton) Sugwas its name. And then there are the dunnocks of Dunnockshaw. Imagine that: the antics of little brown jobs in a copse in Lancashire as place-defining elements.

All these birds come as an equal delight and surprise. Their appearances in place names, unexpected as they may seem, should remind us of how locally people once lived in and viewed their surroundings, and the minute particulars of the charters' boundaries made that realisation feel even more apparent to me. Those qualities of birds we might think of as unpredictable, unreliable or unsuitable in matters of place-marking presented no such contradictions or limitations to our ancestors. Both the birds and the charterlands are a 'finely particular phenomenon', to borrow a phrase from Robert Macfarlane's discussion of traditional ecological vocabularies in his book *Landmarks*.

It is a phenomenon shared by delineations of place in cultures all over the globe. For the Inuit peoples living in Alaska, Canada and Greenland, for instance, a place name such as Arvinnguaq, meaning 'the hill that looks like a bowhead whale', finds its Old English equivalent in Purbeck and Swineshead. Itirviluk, the 'bay that looks like a butt crack', recalls the crude humour in Calders, the 'cold arse' hillside in Cheshire; and Qaumajualuk, the 'lake with a light-coloured bottom that seems to shine', matches the 'black shining pool' that turns up as a marker in the Bishop's Cleeve boundaries. There are plenty of birds in Inuit toponyms too, as you might imagine: gulls, eiders, guillemots, Canada geese, ravens, all of which are valuable food and resources in the Inuit hunter-gatherer culture. Then again, there is the island remembered because it is so encrusted with Arctic tern excrement, or the one that legend claims is slanted because of the weight of all the terns that breed there.

England's place names are a direct link to a time when our language reflected the same attentiveness and vital connection to the land. The many Inuit words for the subtle degrees and forms of snow and ice recall, for instance, the precisely differentiating medieval English terms for hill. To any modern English speaker, by and large, a hill is a hill is a hill, but our medieval ancestors had a whole orographic spectrum available to them: *beorg* for a rounded hill, *pic* for a pointed hill, *copp* for a narrow, cresting summit, *hoh* for a projecting ridge with a slight rise to the peak and a concave slope, or, conversely, *ofer* for a flat-topped ridge with a convex slope.

Our place names are the vestige of our own traditional ways of living that are largely lost to us, a fate that is also now threatening Inuit communities, where knowledge is no longer being passed down to younger generations. This has prompted urgent projects to collect and record Inuit place names by talking to elders, who are still keepers of the old knowledge. Records of early English toponyms have been compiled the hard way, in reverse: the painstaking, century-and-more-long efforts of scholars working backwards to retrace and recover by meticulous linguistic study the origins of meanings lost or diminished over time, and conducting vital fieldwork to see things as far as possible through the eyes of those who created and spoke the names.[5]

The charters take us a step closer. Their networks of boundary points, which describe a continuous, joined-up landscape are miniature, localised equivalents of the interconnecting memory maps that stretch vast distances in the Inuit Arctic terrains, or, closer to home, those still recorded in Gaelic in Scotland and Ireland. And the charters' voices, too, evocatively alive when we read or speak out the boundary directions, are the closest we'll get to indigenous elders letting us in on place secrets for posterity. It's quite a thought that once, any space you cared to pinpoint blindly on a map of Britain would have been littered with names describing every topographical feature, understood intimately and necessarily in relation to one another to map out the intersecting places of individual and collective lives. As Michael Bond has written in his discussion of traditional methods of wayfinding, a 'community's place names reflected what was important to them'. Somewhere in that scale of what was important to our ancestors, there was room for something as subtle as a dunnock's dun hedgerow business, as slight as the filigree flight or pearl-string notes of a goldfinch charm, as sudden as a woodpecker's yellow-bright yaffle, or small as a tit flock's weightless, treetop roving.

To enter the charterlands is, as we have seen, to encounter loss in various forms. Hidden or irretrievable landmarks; the remains of old knowledges, locked in language that is strange, half-recognisable, not entirely recoverable. The charters deal in the transience of living landscapes caught in a vivid instant in medieval time, the features of which we would not expect to be with us now. It is the half-lost or just-remaining aspect of these sites and landmarks that can be most eerily appealing, as is often the case with ruined human settlements. Even fully surviving habitations flourishing in modern times can sometimes *feel* lost, as I'd found at Yaxley, with its submerged cuckoo past. What, though, about human dwellings that are truly lost; not in the brooding imaginative sense, but which have quite literally disappeared?

Late on that summer, weeks after I had returned from Gloucestershire, I found a charter place of this kind, just a half-hour or so from home in Kent. Somewhere between the North Downs and the low country at Romney that leads to the silting sea, somewhere just north of the juggernaut M20 bound for Folkestone, not far from the eastern end of the great Wealden forest where Vikings ventured up the old Rother in AD 892 with 250 ships, where I was married in 2016 in the castle at Lympne on the prehistoric seacliffs, is the lost village of Ulaham. The owl's home.

It is not actually hard to find lost medieval villages. They are a sort of speciality, a phenomenon of the age. More commonly known as 'deserted medieval villages', these are the settlements, among a total of 3,000 or so deserted at various times in England's history, that were largely, and now famously, abandoned in the fourteenth and fifteenth centuries in both direct and indirect consequence of the Black Death. In other circumstances many of these settlements might have survived into modern times, but the Plague devastated populations so severely that some sites were emptied suddenly and never resettled, while others were gradually vacated as residents living in marginal lands retreated to homes in more accessible, fertile, and recently depopulated country. The remains of deserted villages, such as those at Wharram Percy in north Yorkshire or Gainsthorpe in Lincolnshire, can often be observed in the grassy rises and ridges on present-day farmland, which reveal the outlines of ground plans, like giant mole tunnels just beneath the surface. Or there remains a ruined church or manor house all alone in a bare field, as though it has just emerged from the earth.

Ulaham is a deserted medieval village with a difference. Unlike most, which are visitable locations, still with more or less identifiable remains, still justifiably places in their own right, there is nothing whatsoever left of Ulaham. It is, literally, a vanished village. There is no evidence on the ground, no names passed down to us today. Nothing. As the novelist Henry James said of Dunwich – the medieval port city in Suffolk that fell into the sea – 'almost all you can say of it is that it consists of the mere letters of its old name'. And were it not for the charters, we would not even have the letters of an old name.

Once, probably between the remains of twelfth-century Horton Priory to the north, and modern Sellindge to the south, the Ulaham community lived somewhere near the site of the modern-day hamlet of Moorstock, working the surrounding fields and wet pastures more than 1,000 years ago.[6] However old the village was upon the arrival of the Normans, it may have already disappeared by 1086, or perhaps, like Cranbrook, it was subsumed under the records of another settlement, because there is no mention of it in Domesday. Nearby Sibourne ('Sibba's burn') is recorded in Domesday, though that too vanishes sometime after. The only trace of Ulaham's existence is the soot or oak-gall ink inscribing the name in three charters. The earliest of these dates from AD 853, in which Æthelwulf, king of Kent and Wessex, grants to his minister, Ealdhere, one 'sulung' (roughly equal to 240 acres). As with Hawkridge, we find the English name in the midst of Latin:

hæc terra suprascripta æt ulaham his notissimis terminibus undique circumcincta est ab occidente hodoworða ab aquilone winterburna ab oriente prata illa to liminge a meritie bromteag

Here are the boundaries of Ulaham, we are told. On the west side is Hodoworth; on the north side the winter burn; on the east the meadows belonging to Lyminge; on the south, the broom enclosure (where broom shrub can be got). From this description you can get a fair sense of where Ulaham once was: while the meadows and the broom scrub have mostly long since been swallowed up by development, Hodoworth is remembered in Hodiford Farm, and the winter burn still flows, just north of Moorstock.

How had Ulaham come to be? The village is mentioned only in passing, as a boundary point for the granted lands of Brabourne (now East Brabourne, a village north of Sellindge at the foot of the North Downs). Such a slight survival, right on the margins of both land and record. In whatever way and in whatever century the place was deserted or dissolved, it was known well enough in its time that a local in the late tenth century, advising or reciting land boundaries for another charter, this time for King Æthelred in AD 993, refers in shorthand to 'the people of the homestead of the owls'. *Ulhæma.* The Old English is elegantly concise – a neat suffix specifically denoting inhabitants belonging to a *ham* place name. *Hæma*, in its loosest sense, simply means 'people', a community. These were the owl-people.

I spent hours that day walking the boundaries. It was fiercely hot again, and my efforts felt like sweltering ritual – circumambulations to an owl-god. By afternoon I couldn't stand it and went to rest in the shade of St Mary's church in Sellindge. I sat on the cool floor with my back against thick church stone for an hour, guzzling tepid water and half-remembering that I have some roots in this place. I phoned my mother that evening. Yes, my maternal ancestors, clergy for generations in Kent, ended up here in the mid-twentieth century. My great grandfather, John William Horsley, formerly vicar of the church at Challock, retired to Sellindge and lived in tied accommodation by the church until he died in 1966. His passing so affected my great grandmother that she was found more than once wandering the graveyard at night in deranged bereavement. My mother spent childhood holidays here, exploring brooks and rooky fields in the surrounding countryside. Strange to think of all that family business and wandering half a century ago, not half a mile from ghostly Ulaham.

The mystery of the vanished village was more than enough to hold my interest, but there were, of course, the owls too. What of them? They had nothing to do with Ulaham's end, but belonged somewhere in the irrecoverable story of the place's beginnings. Barn owls, most likely, in this farmland habitat, which a thousand years ago was scrub, grazing land and marshy meadows. There are still parts of this brook-crossed, dyke-cut landscape that feel as though they could hold owls in a nook or two, where rough pasture runs by the burns, where once local farmers at task on summer evenings might have known the bird's silent sunset progress alongside their labours. Generations of people and generations of owls.

I have never seen an owl of any kind at Ulaham, not in all the times I've returned to where nothing marks the spot, when the burns are dry in drought and raging in winter deluge. But I did know something of what it meant to have a place graced by these birds. If Ulaham left me wanting, the opposite was true back home in the parts of Kent I knew best. We hear and see owls often. They are hallowed and hailed dwellers to us, and as we'll see in the next chapter, the many surviving owl places of England make it clear that we are not alone in our experiences.

5
An Owl's Cry

The Kentish Weald ~ Devon's owl-combes ~ Ulley, Yorkshire

My memories of my daughter's first moments cannot be separated from owl encounters. An owl shook its song from the forest fringes of the hospital car park the night she was born. A votive. She arrived in the winter I began writing this book, and in the first months of her tiny life she was companion to my work. That owl transfers one time and place upon another from that January, so that I can no longer separate sensation and occasion: frost-cold and owl-shriek, slumber-warmth at the lamp-lit desk. Islay slept like a dormouse at my chest, attended my thoughts, absorbed my mutterings, snuffled to the rhythms of my typing. Mostly, our time was the night. She kept irregular hours, as babies do, adjusting from her own turning in the womb to the big earth's revolutions. When she roused and cried in the very late or very early hours, when feeding or shushing would not soothe her down, we went out.

Those nights were a time of knowing newly, of re-knowing places I knew well by daylight. It began as nothing more than practical resort. A new father learning the trade. I drove circuits round the town, taking care to keep gear shifts smooth and the engine purring low, glancing at Islay in my rear-view mirror, checking, checking. Often it did the trick; the steady motion and hum sent her to sleep like rocking. Sometimes it didn't. Sometimes it was all distraction: brand new astonishment.

Before long I was venturing further afield, out to the Wealden country lanes. Many are narrow, deep and wooded. Some are true holloways; others are bordered by steep banks that give the same subterranean impression. The trees on either side meet above the road, forming vaulting arches in places where grand oaks or beeches stand tall and thick as the columns in St Dunstan's Church at Cranbrook. In summer the colour and light are magnificent in these grand green aisles. At night, the glaring beams of car lamps collapse this perspective to a low, cavernous highway, distorting the curvature of branches and their multiplying shadows to a mine shaft or a burrow in which the trees become their own fibrous, tangled roots.

Those drives became something ritual to me, the first lucid intimacies in a father and daughter's lives together, slipping into the accomplice dark. Mother and the town abed, and we alone shared the owlish night.

There is no doubt that medieval people would have encountered tawny owls in this *miclan wudu* – 'great wood', as the *Anglo-Saxon Chronicles* describe the Weald. But if they had a particular name for the bird, or indeed different names for different owl species, these names have not survived. The great number of folk terms for owls in more modern times suggests the situation was probably no different in earlier centuries. Take the barn owl. It is known by various, fabulous dialect terms across the British Isles, all suggesting different ways of encountering the bird: church owl, white owl, yellow owl, screech owl, screaming owl, Billy Whit, Pudge, Moggy, Woolert, Gillihowlet. None of these names, as far as I know, is directly medieval in origin, but it's likely that some have roots that go back to much earlier days of our language. People must surely have recognised and categorised owl differences somehow. But the fact remains that our word for this order of birds descends from an Old English word that described all owls. *Ule* ('*Oooo-luh*').

Ule, like crane and cuckoo, is another very ancient, Indo-European word. It is imitative and vocative, owl essence in a shamanic utterance. With its sustained, lamenting vowel, *ule* is the quintessential owl cry. It goes deeper than this. It is the primal utterance associated with other creatures inhabiting the nocturnal void ('owl' and 'howl' are of a kind) – night's intimate familiars, thriving close to us in shared darkness, but also strange as fearsome forms in bathybic depths. *Ule*, too, is the ululating wolf and the shrieking fox; the mysterious 'night-raven' (*nycticorax*)[1] or archetypal 'night-bird' (*niht-fuhel*) found in classical and medieval lores, all wailing otherworldly sounds that seem designed precisely to amplify everything we think is most exquisitely terrifying about night. In the Middle Ages, owls' suspicious connection to darkness was firmly and routinely cemented in religious texts: creatures that love darkness cannot be good. They are a model of the sinful person who seeks shadows and flees the light of virtue.[2]

If *ule* is the definitive owl sound, the ur-cry in the real and mythic darkness, then its most characteristic owner, the ur-owl, must be the tawny owl. This is probably the bird meant by *ulula* in Latin too (we retain *ulula* in the species' scientific name, *Strix aluco*). Whatever species were identified by Old English *ule*, the tawny owl's unmistakeable hoot echoes most clearly in that name. In its vast range across the Western Palearctic you're likely to find it anywhere with even a little woodland. For our early ancestors – for people in most centuries – nearly all living rurally and probably close to at least some woodland, tawny owls must have been well-known neighbours. Today, the species' willingness to seek territory in every type of urban space makes it no less familiar. These birds are opportunists, like much wildlife that has adapted to our built environments, but they prefer big, broadleaved trees with suitable, age-worn cavities for nesting. The Weald, with its surviving ancient and semi-ancient woodland, is perfect habitat.

I wasn't looking for owls on those night drives with Islay, not to start with anyway. The first one was so suddenly there and gone I doubted I'd seen it at all. My headlights projected a sliding dome of light across the road ahead, the edges dissolving quickly again to untainted black the second we passed by. Momentarily, where the lights cleaved darkness, there was the phantom of an owl.

It was a thing so briefly present it seemed to know its own uncanny timing for suspense. I braked, already some way past before I could fully register what I thought I'd seen. Islay slept on. I put the car in reverse and crept back 20 yards or so, to a point I guessed was previous to the manifestation. I drove forwards again, this time at walking pace, eyes on the ceiling of branches. I could see well directly above me, straining through the windscreen, though only for the bright second at which I passed any particular point. It was raining, soft, fine rain that steamed on the hot bonnet – and there, still there, brightly white in the beam, was an unquestionable tawny owl, so deadly still I thought of the stuffed old thing in a glass dome that watches down on drinkers in a nearby pub. I dipped the lights and turned off the engine, surprised at its apparent indifference to what had just happened; all that roaring bright commotion hadn't startled it to flight. In all the hours of darkness, night after night, perhaps the birds grow accustomed to cars passing through their territories and the strange moments of artificial daylight.

Nearly all owls are nocturnal to some degree, or at least crepuscular. Hunters specialising in the margins of light: 'owl light', as twilight was sometimes called in medieval parlance. Time and light perceived as winged movement. Tawny owls though, more than any other British, and most European, owl species, are true night creatures. They inhabit the dark – and all its associated bugaboos – like no other. For a tawny owl, day is just something to get through. Tawny owls intimately match their woodland environment, their intricate plumage patterns and gradations the stuff of tree itself: the full arboreal spectrum. I think of autumnal bracken; its fronds great folded wings, pinnae delicate and slender as feathers. There are the colours and forms of tree barks: the imbrications of reptilian pine, creviced oak, the pocks and nicks of birch. The exact browns of tawnies also depend on geography. In temperate zones, they appear rich chestnut – the most familiar colouration to us in Britain. But in colder climes where it is more likely to snow, they are a softer, hoary brown; the colour of beech or ash bark.[3]

It's the eyes that strike you most. Tawny owls' eyes don't have the aquiline force of many other owls' – sharp black pupils on fierce orange or yellow. If you could look a tawny owl right in the eye (not advisable; they can take yours right out), you'd see the same subtle browns of their plumage. From any distance though, those eyes are all black. Docile and ponderous as cows' eyes. Fearsome and unpredictable as a white shark's. In the monochromatic shades of night, sharpened to high contrasts by the glare of intrusive light, a tawny owl's huge eyes are sunless planets. Or nothing at all – just vacant sockets, two gaping bores, as though someone blew the night clean through the back of its skull. Darkness pours.

I looked over my shoulder to Islay. She was awake and looked at me. She couldn't see what I saw, but she was there at least. The owl continued its vigilant stare for prey, shifting its position on the branch, focusing intensely on disturbances in the verge that we could never hear, adjusting its head by minute degrees to shift the acoustic balance. I drove on and left it to the night.

We got lucky that winter. You don't so much plan to *see* tawny owls, but we did. For a time, we found them repeatedly on those night drives. I drove further out in the lanes each time, investigating new spots I thought might be good, trialling new routes and new sites. I was learning a mental map, reconfiguring my hinterlands according to the places I saw tawnies. There were owls in all weathers; more than once, quite unexpectedly, we saw them in banging rain and tilting wind, presumably forced out in such appalling weather by the need to hunt.

Seeing tawny owls was exciting and addictive in stark winter when Islay came into the world. I felt, though, for all the marvel of seeing this bird of night, that this wasn't the truest way of knowing tawny owls. It is the song, after all, that most defines the species. For most people, in fact, it defines all owls. The *tu-wit tu-woo* refrain – that call and response between two communicating birds, often partners, that many mistakenly think is the complete song of one individual – is the generic owl sound children learn alongside dogs barking and sheep bleating, as definitively owlish as ear tufts and wisdom. But this apparent familiarity with tawny owls masks a contradiction: this is a bird whose haunting song is deeply embedded in our cultural psyche, a bird we all 'know', and yet which most have never actually seen. More than any other common British bird, the tawny owl probably best exemplifies this strange, sightless intimacy in our encounters with some species, largely because we tend to think we know it so well. This owl is not for seeing; superbly camouflaged and strictly nocturnal, twice invisible. The bird's casual presence near or right by human habitation intensifies this paradox for us: so proximate and conspicuously vocal, and yet so elusive. This might seem debilitating. Robbed of our sight, our experiences feel partial or incomplete, as if to know the world at all is to know it – to verify it – with our eyes. But listening to owls connects us to them, however feebly by comparison, through the sense that characteristically and most keenly shapes their perceptions. It is a reminder that other creatures exist primarily, some entirely, through senses other than sight. Listening to owls seems the right way to become part of their night world.

It is also the best way to get closer to medieval experiences of owls. 'Night has its own songs', wrote Saint Ambrose in a lyrical passage from his fourth-century *Hexameron*, a popular text with medieval theologians. The 'melodies' of the owl and other night birds, he writes, are a 'solace' to the 'vigils of mankind'. In listening to the owl's melodies we are reminded of the great capacity of that little word, 'owl', when we speak it. Despite a simplicity that has inured us to its power, its onomatopoeic potency nullified by repetition, that same simplicity still reverberates with summoning force. It is present in the word's long evolution to modern 'owl' (*ule, ul, oule, olle, ouel, wol, houl, hule, hole, howle, owl*), suggesting that for our earliest ancestors, on some elemental level, owls existed and materialised as sound. Not sound as poor substitution for sight, a second-rate removed encounter, but as a first and true singularity. If there is a contradiction for us in this – the invisible bird we think we know so well – it cannot have been so apparent to them.

In one of the most remarkable poems of the whole English Middle Ages this attention to sound is striking. *The Owl and the Nightingale* is a debate poem, probably written in the thirteenth century, in which the title birds insult each other all night long. The nightingale (we'll meet her in chapter 8) offers a good description of a tawny owl, intended as insult: squat, no-necked, big-headed, with huge 'col-blake' eyes. It's the owl's vocal presence that holds most attention though. The narrator happens upon the pair right at the beginning of the poem because he *hears* them, and he informs us that in their anger they are exercised especially by each 'oþeres (other's) song'. The owl's range includes yelling and hollering, hooting, shrieking, and even bill-snapping. The owl herself describes her song as *ilich one grete horne* 'like a great horn'. The poet is knowledgeable about real owl repertoires: it is part of the marvellous comedy of the poem that the nightingale is so aggravated by the owl's sheer variety of calls. The poet knows his owl sounds, but he would also have been familiar with the various Latin names for owls, which are no less onomatopoeic than Old English *ule*. Latin *strix*, *bubo* and *ulula* are wailers and screechers and howlers. In life and art, owl is sound.

We're only beginning to really understand what tawnies' complex and varied vocalisations mean to the birds themselves. To most of us, a hoot is a hoot. But to tawny owls each note and strophe contains highly nuanced, unique information that not only distinguishes between individuals, but also conveys specific details – sex, health, aggression – about them. The length of a male's hoot, for instance, its frequency, its pitch, its harshness, all contribute to how it is received by another owl. There is also a sophisticated relationship between sound and place for tawny owls. The spatial characteristics of an owl's habitat, even the locality of its exact territory, can affect its vocal communications with other owls. Woodland, for instance, the classic tawny owl habitat, requires lower-pitched utterances because they travel better through the obstructed space, but higher pitches suit more open locations, such as farmland. If you're an owl used to dealing with strong winds on your home turf, or your neighbours live some distance off, the calibrations of your particular song dynamics will also reflect those demands.

That astonishing relationship between tawny owls' songs and their environments occurs to me each July when we holiday in Devon on a small manor farm on the eastern edge of Dartmoor. We happened upon it in a rush one year, a last-minute booking, but we were so immediately attached to the place that we returned several times in the years following. Our accommodation, a converted barn, sits on the edge of a grassy hill, sloping away to a brook at the valley bottom and rising again to hill-top woods across the way. It's what's known as a combe in those parts – a valley.

There are always buzzards. We arrive in late July when fledglings are on the wing, mewing and wheeling with their parents all the light, warm hours. There are swallows too, swooping in and out of the stables the whole summer long. It is tawny owls, though, that charge the life of that place for us most dramatically. The occasion of our first night in that place had the force of a portent, and we have never forgotten it. In the hours after midnight, an owl started up in the big sycamore tree right outside our bedroom window overlooking the valley. Its first, startling note pierced that stuffy night in the hottest week of the year like long-awaited thunder or downpour releasing heat from agitated air. The sound, talon-sharp, ripped through silence and pulled us out of sleep. It had an independent, physical form of its own.

The sycamore owl woke us again on following nights, though with less alarm and fury. It was not alone. Often, its calls were met by another's across the hill; softer, more distant. There was a pleasing symmetry in the way the two birds and their duet echoed across the combe, making a chamber for the antiphony of owls. Listening to the birds' music each night, I thought of a favourite Edward Thomas poem. Our combe, too, resounded to 'An owl's cry, a most melancholy cry / Shaken out long and clear upon the hill'. In his poem the 'night was quite barred out' from the hill-sheltered inn where a weary traveller stops to rest. Barred out, that is, except the 'melancholy cry'. The speaker is 'Salted and sobered' by the infiltrating sound, and the moment of the poem's sombre scene is distilled to an owl's voice 'Speaking for all who lay under the stars'.

I didn't know it at the time of our first visit, but that part of Devon is surrounded by owl-combes, each one actually named 'owl combe'. One, in a secluded, wooded vale just north of Buckfast, is now remembered only in a cluster of habitation names: Owlacombe Cottage, Owlacombe Bridge, Owlacombe Farm. Another, Ullacombe Farm, is just four miles north, near Yarner.

The following summer I went to find each one, tracking their former existences in old records, then finding more and more across Devon, listing the medieval names like an incantation: *Ulacomba* 1086, *Wollecumbe* 1242, *Hulecombe* 1244, *Oulecomb* 1330, *Ullecumbe* 1290, *Owlecombe* 1531 ...

Almost every ruck and fold in Devon and the wider south-west is called a combe. The word, Old English, but thought to derive from a primitive Welsh word for 'valley',[4] is a reminder of those Iron-Age peoples living in and farming these lands long before the Middle Ages, and whose languages, customs and lives coexisted or hung on alongside those of the Germanic newcomers even while they were suppressed or replaced. In the south-west of England, there was a strong and sustained presence of Brittonic people for centuries into the early medieval period: the *Dumnonii* tribe, from whom the county gets its name, and may derive from an even more ancient Celtic word meaning both 'deep' and 'world'. In this world of deep and wooded valleys, I wonder when owls first entered the hearts and minds of people, passing through into their mythologies of place. Probably long before the word *ule* even existed in these lands. I think of owls pealing in the land and in our imaginations, further and further, out across the old parishes and hundreds and shires.

The combes of Devon are more associated with owls than is any other landscape in England's place names, but, like the birds themselves, you'll find owl places right across the country. There is Ulgham ('owl nook', still known by Northumbrian locals today as the 'village of the owls')

and, in the same county, Outchester ('owl's Roman fort');
in Warwickshire, Oldberrow ('owl hill') and Ullenhall
('owl's nook'); Ullenwood in Gloucestershire ('owls'
wood'); Ousden in Suffolk ('owl's valley') and, meaning
the same thing, Ulcombe in Kent. The habitats in these
names don't give hard evidence for any one species. It's
not clear, either, how literally we should take the
association between bird and location, but that uncertainty
leaves plenty of room for fanciful imaginings: maybe barn
owls nested in the ruins of a Roman fort, or the 'nook' in
Ulgham (*hwamm* means 'corner') belonged to wintering
long-eared owls huddled in a stand of trees or a wedge of
scrubby thorn.

A number of these names, though, must surely invoke
the hooting tawny, particularly those that mention
woodland or that once had woodland close by, such as
Oldberrow and Ullenhall in Warwickshire, two owl
villages just a mile apart. They are now largely
surrounded by pasture fields, but in centuries past
places such as these were well within or adjacent to
woodland – the once extensive Arden Forest. Ullenhall
was probably in or near a dell or sunken clearing in
surrounding woodland.[5] It's likely that for the namers
of these places, the names they chose were not so much
visual markers (owl sightings, as it were), but indicators
of sound. These are places where tawny owls were
surely *heard*; perhaps, even more excitingly, could still
be heard.

Since encountering the owl combes of Devon I had
begun to imagine places in these new terms, as though
through a strange synaesthesia, perceiving the forms of
woods and vales and hills in aural degrees, trying hard to
lose the insistency on sight. I thought of Saint Ambrose's
night-songs. I would make my own vigils, go somewhere

where I could imagine the geographies of night raised up by owls' lugubrious song.

If you're driving up the centre of England on the M1, not long after you enter Yorkshire, as you pass by Sheffield some eight miles away to your left, where the wind turbines are, look west; if you can steal a glance between the roadside trees you might just catch sight of a cluster of buildings seven fields away on a knoll rising above the surrounding farmland. This is Ulley. The 'owl wood', or 'owl wooded clearing'.

Late afternoon in late summer, with two precious days to myself and a makeshift bed in the back of the car, I drove north to find this village on the hill. My first view from the inter-urban highway felt strange – that sensation again that old and new collided, that somehow my experience of the past was both distanced and made more striking by contrast with hard modernity. I was glad to leave the motorway after hours in its surge, and follow the rural lanes and signposts up to Ulley. Sunset was hours off yet. Time enough then to get a proper feel for the place and, God willing, a much-deserved pint at the local pub.

The Royal Oak was closed. By the looks of it, it had been for years. There were huge boulders positioned across the car park entrance, presumably to deter noisy groups of young drivers or bikers making the space their own. I was too tired to bother looking elsewhere so I left the car opposite the pub and wandered across to the church. It was open, and I briefly contemplated making my bed up in one of the aisles for the night before remembering that a parishioner was bound to lock up at some point. The building, like some of the older terraced houses on the street, was Victorian, constructed of hefty, dark masonry that evinced to me a steely, coalface grit suited to the region's industrial heritage.

There is little obvious evidence of a more ancient past. Pottery and coins have been excavated (just behind the Royal Oak, in fact) that revealed a one-time Roman presence, and a few fragments remain of a medieval chapel that was demolished in 1850 to make way for what is now Holy Trinity. If there was a church here at the time when the village received its Old English name (it's likely there was), it too suffered demolition. Ulley was established enough to make it into Domesday Book, but *Ollei* has very little to report in 1086: the names of the Norman landowners, a paltry two ploughlands and valuation of two pounds a year. There is no record of any population. Instead, like many places in Yorkshire, it is described as 'waste'. Very probably, Ulley was one of the sites destroyed in the infamous 'harrying of the North' that occurred in 1069 following rebellion in this region. Yorkshire was badly hit. Orderic Vitalis, an English chronicler who was a child at the time of the Domesday survey, wrote later of the event that William the Conqueror 'burnt homes to ashes' and commanded that 'all crops and herds, chattels and food of every kind should be brought together and burned to ashes with consuming fire'. The resulting famine was devastating.

This village of razed fortunes between Sheffield and the M1 was where I would spend the night, hoping for owls in a place where the most distinctive sound now is the distant but constant drone of traffic.

I returned to my car and prepared for the night, plumping the pillows and blankets I'd brought with me to make them as comfortable as possible over the reclined back seats, pinning up the black-out curtain I'd stolen from my daughters' bedroom, pulling a rain coat over the front seats to conceal me further, getting in place everything I thought I might need to lay a hand on in the night. Then, with light enough yet, I took the footpath south of the village this time. The signpost pointed the way down a farm track by cattle sheds, accessible to the side of a padlocked metal gate, upon which was another sign in bold red letters: 'GUARD DOGS. ENTER AT YOUR OWN RISK.' As if to confirm the threat, there was a German shepherd dog sprawled territorially across the path. I thought better of my plan and kept to the road.

Even the little elevation of this hill gives good views from all sides. The early English might have called it a *dun*: a low hill with a level, extended summit upon which a settlement might be built. From the farmyard wall I could see the M1 and beyond, so it felt, across the counties. I knew somewhere in that direction, nine miles east of Ulley, was Oldcotes (I might have seen it if the hill was higher, peeping over into Nottinghamshire). The name means 'owl cottages', although the most prominent building you'll find there now is a carvery restaurant. The *dun*, in one sense, is the greatest link of all to Ulley's past. It has been there longer than any human – since the last glaciation – and is probably the reason why people chose to settle or station here in the first place. What, I thought, did people one or two thousand years ago see from where I stood? Not wind turbines or motorways, that's for sure. Farmland and, as the name tells us, woodland. Woodland and owls, somewhere in all that human history of oppression, atrocity and ruin.

There are few trees in Ulley now. I stood under sycamores lining the roadside by the farm for the extra

darkness their canopy created. It was difficult to tell
how dark it had really become. Streetlights were on
now in Main Street, and they intensified the blackness
beyond their own brightness. Despite its rural location,
Ulley's night sky is affected by Sheffield's illuminations
in the west, and if you had nothing else to guide you
the motorway glare would quickly help point you east.

Finding absolute dark is a modern problem. It's a point
easily overlooked, but our experiences of night are not
the same as our ancestors'. The changes to our modern
night sky are so recent and rapid that it's no exaggeration
to say that up until the nineteenth century, the twentieth
century even, it was a simple condition of people's lives
that night was dark; that it was distinctly divided from
the day; that this cycle, by and large, determined
rhythms; and that darkness could only be relieved by
the moon or the shadowy flicker of firelight. The
differences with modern experiences are probably more
apparent now in the twenty-first century (which has
never known a time without intensive, global
industrialisation) than has ever been the case in human
history. In our own times, light pollution violates the
solar pattern so aggressively that only the most rural or
unpeopled parts of our country are spared the star-
blinding sky glow. Urban lights right across the West
can be seen from space. If you take a look on Google
Earth at our planet it's not so much night's space-
blackness you see across half the globe but the
astonishing light show illuminating that blackness. It's a
startling realisation. When we speak of 'dark' now, it is
infected by these dazzling intrusions.

The word itself is rooted in a purer, different understanding that traces back through Middle English *derk* to Old English *deorc* and back further to a much earlier **derkaz* past. There were other words, too, that have gone from our vocabulary, leaving us with a single word. In *The Owl and the Nightingale*, there is no *derk*. It is all *þeostre* ('*THAY-os-tre*') and *þustre* when the birds talk about night-time owlish haunts and habits. Sadly, *þeostreness* and its many derivatives never made it into modern English alongside its familiar synonym. As a term in our once richer nocturnal lexis, it could not have envisaged or encompassed the industrial twilight that now passes for night in our metropolises and conurbations.

Devoid of the distractions of anthropogenic light noise, *þeostreness* sharpens sounds' presence and clarity, as well as our senses to hear them. To people living in past ages, accustomed to *þeostreness*, owls must have seemed, *were*, intensely the 'first true sound of night', as J. A. Baker puts it in *The Hill of Summer*. For him, in response to the tawny's 'dark release of song', the 'dusk bristled ... like the fur of a cat'. Conveyed through blurred senses in Baker's description, an owl's sound is an animate, shaping force on the landscape. I thought of Oldcotes away to the east, imagining superstitious inhabitants waking in the candleless dark in cold bedrooms to the devilish, goblin screeches and hoots of one or another owl species. Or perhaps these routine night-songs accompanied people's activities as they roused after midnight from their first sleep – owlish nocturns to accompany Matin prayers.[6]

If you want to hear tawny owls, get out in autumn and winter, when pairs are at their most vocal establishing or consolidating their bonds and territory. It's also when you're most likely to encounter the remarkable range of sounds tawny owls can make: excitable duets, caterwauling, strangling screams, horrendous shrieks, alien pulsing hoots (as though someone is shaking the bird mid-'tu-woo'). I, though, was in Ulley in August, not getting lucky.

I turned in when rain began. It was certainly dark enough in the car with my makeshift curtains. Getting undressed and into my sleeping bag with barely room to sit up was some operation, and anything forgotten (socks, locking the car) required a tight reversal of the procedure. When I was as comfortable as I was going to be, I lay on my side, jackknifed into position with my feet rammed down to the boot, but after an hour of caterpillar wriggling and failing to will myself to sleep, I decided perhaps I could be bothered to brush my teeth after all.

I heard it mid-task, mouth full of toothpaste. I straightened up. Cat? Rabbit? Someone drunk? The noise came from the grand house next to the church. I walked down with toothbrush and tube in hand and stood on the street looking up into the trees above the property's wall. Whatever it was, it was silent now. I made to go back to the car. Then it sounded again, high-pitched and ridiculous, like a dog's chew-toy or a giant mouse. Repeated now, close, somewhere directly above me. It was only when a far more familiar sound joined in that I realised what I was hearing: these were the begging calls of a young tawny owl, and its mother was right there, kekking encouragement, or reproach. The youngster seemed to gain in confidence, louder, insistent, then stuttering into a 't-t-t-t-t-tu-witt!' When both birds got going the voices merged as one – squawks and seeps spluttering intermittently into eerie ululations – as though the little one was trying on adult song for size. And then they flew. Silent but for the slightest whisper in their wings, right over me so that I might have reached up and touched them, both birds glided from darkness, passed momentarily through a streetlamp's orb, and then dissolved into sound again on the other side. They were in the churchyard now. I listened from the shadows of a tree. I didn't see either bird again, but it seemed to me that they moved with spectral swiftness from one tree to another, disembodied cries that came from all places. At moments, I couldn't help feeling that they gamely spooked me when one or the other called sharply and suddenly as though right at my shoulder.

Just as suddenly, they went quiet. It was no less unnerving, for now I had the distinct sense that they were invisibly watching me from somewhere in this graveyard haunt. I left promptly, closing the gate quietly in obeisance, and went back to the car, feeling simultaneously foolish and thrilled at what had happened.

I consider myself lucky that there isn't a place where I've lived for most of my adult life where tawny owls haven't been audible from the night-time household fringes. In fact, it's probably the case that every house I've ever lived in has received the benediction of owls at one time – whether that's in sodium-orange suburban streets, city centres, or moonless-black country hamlets. They call, invisibly and darkly, from the penumbra of our introverted, domestic lives.

We moved house not long after my encounters with the Ulley owls. Our landlord was selling up, so, most unexpectedly, Plot 14, a new build in the village of Headcorn, became our first owned house, because the price was right, it was available quickly, and it made good sense with two young children. We felt the loss of Crown Cottage's history all the more because we had moved somewhere without any history at all – we were the settlers, the first scuffs on the walls.

But from the start there were owls. When we'd first viewed the place we'd noticed that it was built just off Ulcombe Road, which leads to Ulcombe, the 'owls' valley', three miles to the north – a Domesday village with a twelfth-century church on the western lip of the hill where the original settlement likely was. It's the only one of the owl-combes in England you'll find on a standard road map, and here we were considering a house literally just down the road. Ginny and I joked: we couldn't pass up on such an omen!

We discovered with delight that the Headcorn locality is still very owly. There are little owls in mature oaks all up Ulcombe Road, easy to spot on long light evenings. In our first summer we found a family of them frequenting Ulcombe's playpark, perched proprietorially on the swings and climbing frames whenever we turned up. Of all the British owls, little owls feel to me the most suitable *genii loci*. It's their squat rotundity, like souvenir Buddha idols, and their fierce, yellow-eyed intensity. Their brows suggest an elder wisdom: old-man grey and furrowed as oak bark (mimicked on the rear of their heads, Janus-like, as though they're always watching you). They are crabby old-timers, always where you expect them, as though hunched over an ale at the local pub, cantankerously guarding their plots. They carry out their duties to place with an irascible but unerring loyalty.

The first Ulcombers wouldn't have known little owls; this species didn't appear in the British countryside until the nineteenth century, when they were introduced by Victorian collectors. But they certainly would have known the barn owl family I discovered in a tiny brick, ramshackle barn just five minutes from home and have

watched with Islay ever since, and they would have known
the tawny owls that hooted close by our house on the
first night we spent in the place. They have continued
hooting close by. Some nights, even when it's raining or
cold, we open the windows to let the sound in. We love
the sense that wildness has got to us, passing doubly
through the window and the threshold of sleep. The owl's
song enters our dreams.

Marsh Dwellers

The Essex Marshes

When winter and geese had returned, and temperatures fell near freezing, and lead-heavy clouds sunk so low to the land it seemed nothing was left between, I drove out to the earth's end on an island's end. I left the car where the road stopped, and walked to meet the day where the land became sea.

The island was mine all morning. Who else would come to such a place, especially now when the lights and music of Christmas offered their glittering attractions? A low mist steamed, as though the land dreamed of warmth. The island's far eastern tip is named, with an eerie sense of mystery, School House viewpoint. It is a reminder that there was a community here once, remarkable as this seems in such a place. It was easy to imagine the ghostly shouts and forms of those island-dwelling children, like so many Pip Pirrips running across the lonely marshes, each a 'small bundle of shivers' running in fear from the sea's 'savage lair', as Dickens describes in *Great Expectations*.

In truth, Wallasea Island in Essex is not so very remote in the twenty-first century. It is a little more than eight miles from Southend-on-Sea, under 30 miles from the M25, and just around the corner from the Thames Gateway. All of this, though, the near presence of so much dense habitation and heavy industry, only made bleak and unpeopled Wallasea feel that much more distant and wild to me. I am glad for these places; so close to our metropolises but feeling like other dimensions entirely, accessed through some invisible threshold that transports you suddenly and you can't quite say how – especially if you make the journey out as I did on a black winter's morning before the sun is up.

Wallasea is a paradox in other ways. It is a bewildering combination of past and present; unquestionably ancient, wildly natural, and yet deceptively new, artificial as a drainpipe. Owned and managed by the RSPB since the beginning of the twenty-first century, it is the site of a tremendous project to recreate lost coastal marshland. Over the last two decades, millions of tonnes of excavated soil from the London Underground have been relocated here to raise the height of the island. The sea walls were breached so that the tides could flood farmland, transforming parts of it into saltmarsh. The whole island is now a carefully managed landscape of mud, sea and marsh, as well as inland dykes and lagoons. The wildness encountered on Wallasea today provides a thrilling sense of the past, but it is a very new past, in which the recreated old is the product of just one more humanmade change altering the shape and function of the island. The RSPB's work at Wallasea has recreated territory not seen there for hundreds of years, but it also, ironically, reverses the very act recalled in the place's medieval name: people have been building walls to keep the sea out for a very long time.

Our efforts to control the sea notwithstanding, Wallasea is, and has been for nearly all its history, a place of marsh and marsh birds. That was certainly the case on the morning I visited. I was accompanied only by the sharp wind in my ears and the birds, birds in their hundreds and thousands: curlews, redshanks, dunlins, oystercatchers, grey plovers, golden plovers, godwits, shelducks, brent geese, wigeons, teals, all whistling and piping and moaning. There are few places that genuinely feel so entirely given over to birds, but here is such a place, and it is the huge number of waders and wildfowl at this time of year that makes the intertidal marshes along and close to the Thames Gateway internationally important, protected (in name at least) by just about every status designation possible.

Whatever changes to the land have occurred, the former residents of places like Wallasea knew the estuarine birds as close neighbours. The name given by the RSPB to one of the lagoons on the reserve today, Pool Marsh, remembers a medieval forbear, *Polemersh*, a site that at one time was known as *Bridepol*, 'bird pool'. Even more compelling is the name of the tantalisingly close, off-limits island just across the tiny River Roach channel. I could see it from School House viewpoint, could have alighted its shore in no time if I'd fancied a courageous and very cold swim. Much bigger than Wallasea, Foulness is owned by the Ministry of Defence (MOD) and usually inaccessible to visitors. Foulness is nearly all agricultural fields, as Wallasea was for much of the twentieth century, but the military presence is still imposing. From where I stood at the viewpoint, I could make out the barbed-wire peripheries of MOD buildings. They had a sinister secrecy beneath the day's low skies that put me in mind of those mysterious American operations in deserts that monitor paranormal activity.

Beyond where I could see, though, at the far northern tip of Foulness, there is small patch of saltmarsh wildness. When the tide is right out, there are exposed sands beyond it that stretch along a low bar of sand, extending the island's pointing finger far out into the North Sea. This nib of the island, its furthest, remotest spot (and surely one of the most difficult-to-reach and dangerous marshes in Britain), gives the island its name, and is our link back to a time when all the little, interlocking islands

on this part of the Essex coast, intersected and separated
by creeks and fleets, would have been given over to birds.
This is *fugla næss*, 'the birds' headland'. Once, all of
Foulness must have been saltmarsh, as was Wallasea, and
the entire place, its shores and creeks and flats, must have
thronged with birds. Not given over to the birds, then,
for it was *theirs* to begin with.

Foulness was not alone in this respect, as suggested by
other place names elsewhere in England, such as Fulstow,
Fowlmere or Fowley.[1] In centuries past, many more of us
would have been far better acquainted with marshland
and its birds because, quite simply, there was a lot more of
it and a lot more of them. In Oliver Rackham's estimation,
a quarter of the British Isles 'is or was some kind of
wetland'. Like our ancient woodlands, the history of our
wetlands is characterised by its steady loss, but despite our
attempts to block, contain and drain water over millennia,
wet places were much more prevalent even into relatively
recent times (unlike our old woodlands), and even more so
in pre-modern Britain before the big enterprises to drain
our greatest former marshes. Famous survivors, such as the
Fens, Somerset Levels, the Derwent Ings, or the blanket
peat bogs of Ireland and Scotland, were not exceptional in
this sense. The ubiquity and marvellous variety of these
terraqueous landscapes in England alone is revealed by the
number of place names referring to soggy locations (just
the word *mersc* 'marsh' alone appears many times all over
the country) and the great range of early words that specify
the different types of wetland. From *hamm* or *eg*, meaning
'marsh-bounded dry land', to *slæp*, 'a slippery place', from
Norse terms for swamp such as *kjarr* and *myrr* (from which

we get carr and mire), to *soc* (literally 'suck') and – alas that
this did not survive – *cwabba,* meaning 'a boggy place', the
vocabulary of marsh seeps deep into our language and
land. Ours, indeed, was the marsh country.

My home county of Kent, bordered by the sea on
nearly all sides, is a good example of this former marshiness
in Britain. In the Middle Ages the central landmass of
Kent was squeezed in between saltmarsh islands in the
north and a repeatedly advancing and retreating shoreline
on the Romney Marshes that once, and not that long ago
at all, came much further inland – the result of a centuries-
old struggle for dominance between man and tide. But
even in the most seemingly unexpected of places today
you can find evidence for the old marsh.

I grew up in Worthing in West Sussex, a typical south-
coast, pier-and-arcade seaside town to which, I admit, I
never formed any serious childhood attachment. Only
much later in life did I learn that celebrated Victorian
nature writers Richard Jeffries and W. H. Hudson are both
buried in a cemetery right by where I cycled across town
to school. And only later did I discover Worthing's marshy
foundations. Near the town centre, where a deserted multi-
storey car park once stood, and a shopping centre before
that, there once ran a stream, the Teville Stream (hence
Teville Road in this location now), which became a
substantial, three-tined, tidal channel further to the south-
east, forming an inlet that flowed inland as far Broadwater,
in the north of the town. The stream still flows behind the
industrial estate and municipal tip, close to where I lived
between the ages of 5 and 14 – but it has been concreted
and culverted into invisibility for much of its course. Such
were the damp mists rising from the stream at certain times
of year that one road was once named Vapours Lane. Best
of all to me, one of the outlying villages that was engulfed

in the nineteenth-century urban expansion of Worthing, and which is now split across the very busy A27, was named Sompting, meaning 'dwellers in the marsh'.[2]

I am a marsh-dweller at heart. A *sumptingas* tribe member. One of the *merscware* 'marsh-folk'. I cannot fully say why I love it so, only that I feel an instinctive pull towards any sodden, wind-whipped, wind-flattened place. It is where, as on that dark and cold day at Wallasea, I feel most in place and at peace. In part, this chapter is an attempt to better understand that call to the marsh.

I didn't need to travel to Essex. After all, the Kent marshes are on my doorstep. But it is their kindred lands across the Thames in the old kingdom of the East Saxons that have most affectingly made a miry place in my heart. I first visited them as a child and have been going back ever since.

Essex excels in one particular type of marsh. Saltmarshes, or saltings as they are also known, are an Essex speciality. Not the sort I had visited earlier in the year, at Rockcliffe in Cumbria – all short turf and wind-blown sand that has the appearance of a football pitch – but the stuff with deep, squelching, glossy, silted muds interlaced with serpentine creeks. Above, inhabiting the surfaces at their own precise and different tolerance levels, are the plants: eel-grass and glasswort, the tender purples of aster and lavender, marsh-mallow and golden samphire. Beneath, making their own little creeks, are the marine creatures: mud snails and shrimps, lug-, rag- and catworms.

You'll find lots of saltmarsh all along Essex's coastline, but, as so often with any of our remaining habitats, there was once much more, as Wallasea and Foulness remind us. The effects of coastal squeeze (sea walls one side, rising sea levels on the other) have reduced the county's share of this precious habitat by over 90 per cent in the last 400 years. Some of the biggest losses are along the Thames estuary where Essex merges into London. This intensive site of heavy industry and cargo was once marsh. Lots of marsh. Daniel Defoe, in his grand tour around Britain, remarked of the south Essex coast that 'there is nothing for many miles ... but a continued level of unhealthy marshes'. In this 'damp part of the world', it was apparently common for men to have one wife after another because 'young lasses' from the uplands – all wives came from elsewhere it seems – died swiftly from the ague among the fogs. No less ubiquitous than fever were the birds: 'an infinite number' and 'vast flights' of wildfowl.

Look at an eighteenth-century map of the region and you can see the terrain Defoe describes – coastal marshes all the way along the Thames as far west as Stratford. There are surviving pockets still there, such as Rainham Marshes (thanks to the RSPB), but if you want proper saltmarsh, the sort that goes on for miles, you need to journey east along the Thames as Defoe did in 1722, detouring north up and around the River Crouch – he 'being not able to travel [there] without many windings ... by reason of the creeks, and waters' – until you arrive on the Dengie peninsula, where, in Defoe's century, there was a kilometre-wide tract of saltmarsh right up its eastern length. It's still there today.

The same is true further north, across the Blackwater River that divides the Dengie from the northern half of Essex. Where slender fingers of marshland reach into sea and clasp Mersea Island like a pendant jewel, where black stumps of Saxon fish traps can still be seen in the sands like rotten teeth, where Vikings landed just upriver to defeat Ealdorman Byrhtnoth and his army in a famous battle at Maldon, there is a twining channel in the Blackwater's

yawning brown mouth that leads to a wide, enclosed bay,
all sea twice a day, but when the tide is out this inlet where
the land doubles back is a wilderness of saltmarsh. It is,
quite possibly, my favourite place in the world.

My wife and I have holidayed on the Blackwater estuary
between Maldon and Mersea every year for as long as we've
been married. My children know it well now. I was here
when I heard that my father had died. For even longer, I've
been visiting with a dear friend whose own emotional ties
to these marshlands go back long before I was born. Jeremy
Mynott grew up near Colchester, and the marshes down
this way were his boyhood birdwatching haunts in the post-
war decades when it was possible to roam wherever he liked
across the pathless, unfenced acres inside the sea wall. He has
seen the marsh harrier become a common bird here, and
others, such as the red-backed shrike, go extinct.

As usual, I met Jeremy on a short winter's day just after
New Year on the marshes north of Tollesbury, at the end
of another lane that leads nowhere else. When I arrived
he was up on the wall by the old wharf. I climbed the
steps to greet him and he pointed out a little egret
immediately below us, stalking prey in the creek bottom.
It was immaculately white in all that mud, far too bright
for the austere spectrum of saltmarsh chroma. It's one bird
that was certainly not here when Jeremy was a boy, having
rapidly and prolifically colonised Britain only since the
late twentieth century. It stepped round a corner, like the
sun suddenly behind clouds.

This view across the marsh from this far inland corner
of the estuary is one of the most impressive standpoints.
With your back to ploughed fields, looking down the

full length of the bay, out along the fleet, and beyond
that, further than you can clearly make out, into the
mouth of the Blackwater, the old *sealtmersc* looks like
miles of solid, uninterrupted terrain, as though you could
walk out to greet your future where sea meets horizon.
It's a view that feels outrightly medieval to me, not just
because of that sense of sweeping time, but also because
ancient saltmarsh, where you find it, is one of very few
landscapes in this country that can appear to us as it did
centuries ago, with no trees to fell and no solid ground
on which to build. On the far side of the Blackwater, just
visible with the naked eye, is the tiny medieval chapel of
St Peter-on-the-Wall, squat and solitary on the Dengie
north coast, like a miniature sibling to the great hulk of
nearby Bradwell power station. It is one of the oldest
churches in Britain, standing alone on the marshland
edge, looking out to sea for more than 1,300 years.

The view is medieval in another sense, seen from
above. On a map or an aerial photograph, you grasp the
true beauty and geography of saltmarsh, all the creeks
that interlace the mudflats, and do so here in more
complexity and profusion than anywhere else I'm aware
of in Britain. The labyrinthine patterns formed by the
creeks are as beautifully intricate and fractal as the brain's
lobal crevices or a nutmeg's fissures when you slice it
open. Some place names suggest that the bird's-eye view,
so easily achieved by any of us in the satellite age, was
actually an instinctive mode to the early mind. Not far
from where Jeremy and I stood, up the Colne River
beyond Mersea Island and inland towards Colchester,
there is another place surrounded by marsh known as
Fingringhoe (a name that never fails to elicit smutty
comments). It means 'the hill-spur belonging to the
people who live on the finger of land'. Immediately

south of Foulness, there is Shoebury, which might mean the 'shoe-shaped heel of land', and Swineshead in Bedfordshire or Wroot in Humberside refer to protruding land resembling a snout. Similarly, Purbeck in Dorset is thought to be so named because the hill ridge in that location recalled the shape of a bird's beak. Ancient dwellers visualised earthly forms from above in such powerfully whole terms that they were able to transform them, as though cloud watching, into landmarking metaphors.

I've tried more than once to 'island hop' the saltmarsh on this edge of Essex, just to see. I've never got far. Not only are there so many riddling, intertwining creeks as to make it impossible to pick an easy path across the tops, but some are so wide and deep that there's no chance of leaping across from one island to the next. Viewed from creek level, taking a horizontal cross section, the terrain is a mountain range, beset with ravines, canyons, treacherous passes and dead-end tracks. Down in the valleys below the sea-level plateaus, it is not height that's perilous, it's the thick, oozing muds that blacken beneath the surface and suck your boots straight in. They offer no passage, not on foot anyway. It's a place for no one, and I am no exception. Marsh prohibition makes it all the more a place of others, the waterways of seals and the birds.

A mile or so along the coast, heading east, the saltmarsh peters out and the sloping wall drops down straight into deep, glassy mud. Behind you, on the other side of the bank, are high grasslands, as wide open and vast as the estuarine flats. It's a familiar situation of coastal marsh habitat: the sea walls – many of which were first built or improved in the Middle Ages – straddling saltmarsh or estuary on one side and reclaimed land for farming on the other. At one time, but probably not since early medieval or even Roman times, what exists on the landward side of the wall would have been saltmarsh too; it was the construction of the seabanks that transformed one into the other – engineered, piecemeal enclosures of the saltmarsh (known as 'innings' or 'polders') created bit by bit over centuries for the traditional purpose of grazing cattle and sheep on rough pasture. The innings along this stretch of coast are still grazing marsh, unlike those on the Dengie peninsula, which, typically, were converted to crop fields that come right up to the sea wall.

Grazing marshes, although human–made and managed, are still wetlands, and they can be just as rich in life as their tidal counterparts on the other side of the wall. The marsh is closely intersected with straight dykes and fleets, as well as winding channels like the branches of winter trees. In their own ways, these freshwater marshes are no less impenetrable or thrillingly treacherous than the clutching mud creeks over the wall. You still feel that you could march out, put a foot wrong, and disappear into watery blackness. They recall, especially in half-light mists, the fearsome *morhopu* 'marsh lairs' of the famous old English epic poem *Beowulf*, from which the monstrous Grendel stalks at night to seek his hapless victims. Not that any of this inhibited Jeremy's adventures in these boyhood hinterlands.

In the early nineteenth century, more than a thousand years after the *Beowulf* composer sang about the *morhopu* of medieval Scandinavia, the Romantic poet John Clare wrote no less evocatively about the wetlands of his native fenland regions. For him, these were places where 'fear encamps' and the 'trembling grass' will not admit the 'weight of man to let him pass'. The memory of Grendel haunts those lines too. Clare's poem, however, is not actually about the marshes. It is about a bird, but a bird that is so curiously marshy in its substance and essence that the poem *is*, in the end, inescapably an ode written as much to marshy places as it is 'To the Snipe'.

Jeremy and I stopped along the sea wall at one pool enclosed by dense, shifting reeds that we knew was usually good for something. I scanned the sodden margins, hoping for Clare's 'Lover of swamps' and 'rancid streams'. The snipe is a defining creature and emblem of all-round marshiness. It is the embodiment of its bog-dull world. In appearance, snipe are the very stuff of their habitat (or, which is the same thing, their habitat is the stuff of snipe), so often the trick to finding one is to carefully examine the wet edges of promising territory and hope that some tiny part of it materialises as snipe; or, conversely, start from the premise that everything you're scrutinising is snipe until it gives itself up as mud and grass. Even so, such is the soil-and-sedge bird's skill at hiding in plain sight, that looking for one can be like a game of hide-and-seek with a child who stubbornly insists upon invisibility even once they've been found and called out. The snipe's beady black eyes appear intently to watch you watching them, as if they know you know, or they know that you *think* you know, but hope to confuse you into admitting, after all, that you're actually just staring at a clod of mud.

Before long I found one in this way, carefully teasing bird from vegetation. It was sat on a tussock, openly enough, but roosting with its head tucked back along its wings, its long bill hidden in feathers among the beak-straight barley stripes on its back (it's thought that this diagnostic length of bill is probably responsible for its name, originating from an ancient word meaning 'long, protruding instrument'). Through the telescope I had an eyeful. What you lose up that close is the sense of how snipe merge, chameleon-like, into their backgrounds. But what you gain is an inspection of snipe crypsis: how brilliantly and perfectly the bird's plumage mimics fenny colour and substance; the full spectrum of bog browns in the sedgy stub and loamy sod of each feather, which in the aggregate gives the impression that the bird constructs a piece of marsh right there in front of you. It is a simultaneous coding and decoding of the marsh genome.

Even the noises snipe make give away as little as possible. If you disturb snipe from the ground, they burst up at the last second from your feet, uttering an almost inaudible 'snick' or 'sneck', which is very difficult to describe or translate. Even scientific literature reaches for inventive similes: one field guide entry to snipe describes their flight-call as 'like a rubber boot being pulled out of soft mud' or 'a muffled sneeze'. To me, the utterance is somewhere between a kiss and a sharp tear of cloth, as though the bird has just ripped up from the grubby fabric of soil.

For all these reasons, I count snipe as a favourite marsh bird, just as Clare did. What's more, according to our place names, so did some of our early English ancestors. You'd think that maybe the species' inclination to understatement, like the dunnock, might rule them out of any criteria for useful place-marking. But no, there they are, in names such as Snitterfield, Snitemore, Snydale and Snite. Perhaps some of these refer to locations where snipe could be hunted, as other wetland species certainly were by a *fugel-bana* 'fowler' with a *fugel-net* somewhere *fugel-wylle* 'full of birds', but there is keen observation, local knowledge and a nuanced alertness in these names too. In the last, Snite (a field name), apparently the name of the bird alone was enough to evoke a whole environment. For those place-namers too, I like to think, snipe were embodiments of the marsh, 'governed', as C. A. Johns describes in my grandfather's schoolboy copy of *British Birds and Their Haunts*, 'by laws of which we know little or nothing'. The marsh-mysterious, marsh-keepers divining earth's secrets with their long, twitching bills, like solemn priests at their esoteric rites.

If there's one *morhop* bird that makes an even more extraordinary skill of obscurity, it has to be the bittern. Having perfected specialist reedbed living with such effective imitation, it is a wonder that no origin myths have passed down to tell of how this bird sheared from reed in Ovidian metamorphosis, ripped up from the very same material in which it skulks. Its colours and striations mimic the close, vertical world of reedbed marsh exactly, especially so when the bird transforms its heron plumpness by lifting its beak skywards, narrowing itself to reed-thinness and swaying gently with the wind-rustling stems. Like snipe, these are very particular birds of place in this way – integral elements of marsh substance because of the ways in which they literally embody their environments.

At home in reedbeds impenetrable as fog, and with such shapeshifting expertise, bitterns are rarely seen, and only heard at the right time of year. When you do hear one booming, though, it is unmistakeable – a breathy bassoon note, basso profundo, not so very loud in reality but far-carrying, with an undeniable and reverberating sonic presence that feels like great volume nonetheless. It's hard to believe it is really a bird producing the sound, and this oddity inspired marsh folk in centuries past to devise fantastical explanations as to how the bittern fashioned such strange properties of sound: was it the result of blowing through a reed, in the way that small children do with a blade of grass? Or, as Chaucer famously describes in his 'Wife of Bath's Tale', maybe the bird thrust its beak under water to produce a subaquatic blast, and thus the 'bitore bombleth in the myre'.

The playful alliteration in many dialect terms that have come down to us – butter bump, bog bumper, bog blutter – reveals just how elemental the bird's distinctive boom has long been for those living in bittern-haunted places. The same is true of onomatopoeia in Middle English *miredromble*, or Old English *raredumle* ('reed-boomer') and *pur* (pronounce it foghorn-low with a long vowel with your head underwater in the bath and you'll see what I mean).[3] The last of these names appears, happily enough, in a bittern place overlooking the Blackwater, a little way south of Maldon and the lands where my paternal ancestors once lived (solid labouring stock who no doubt knew a bittern from a handsaw). I've only ever seen one bittern on the Essex marshes – a hapless bird skidding gracelessly across an icy fleet one frozen winter's day – but Purleigh hints at a time when the bird must have been more common in these parts, bluttering and bumping in reedy clearings. Round medieval Purleigh in spring the uncanny noises of territorial, courting male birds inflated like tuning bagpipes must have sounded as Daniel Defoe heard them in the Holland district of Lincolnshire. Even in the eighteenth century, when the draining of much of the old Fens surrounding the Ouse Washes was already well underway, Defoe was drawn to 'the uncouth Music of the Bittern ... so loud that it is heard two or three Miles Distance' as the main point of note on his travels through this region.

Even the diminutive snipe delivers a mesmerising courtship song. While you'll get nothing more out of a snipe than piglet disgruntlements for most of the year, in spring the male bird performs a display flight at a great, difficult-to-pinpoint height, the purpose of which is to emit an eerie, wavering song that sounds like some far-off lamentation carried on the wind. This aeolian refrain, however, has nothing to do with the snipe's voice. Instead, confounding your perceptions again, it is produced by the splayed outer tail feathers as air rushes through them on the bird's swooping descents. This strange display, although not frequently heard, clearly struck the ears of some early peoples in Britain and elsewhere as the defining snipe aspect, because many regional names for the bird, both ancient and more modern, refer to the peculiar winnowing sound in which they heard caprine equivalents, as in the alternative Old English name *hæferblæte* ('goat-bleat') or the Scots Gaelic *Gabhar-athair*, 'goat of the air'. In Ireland, unsuprisingly, given the extent of that country's former boglands, the snipe turns up in place names no less than in England, as does the bittern. Tullineaskey in County Cork (Cork itself derives from Gaelic for marsh), is 'the snipes' little hill', and Curraghbonaun, a townland in County Sligo, is 'the bitterns' marsh'.[4]

As snipe and bitterns demonstrate especially well, the sounds of marsh birds are deeply integral to our perceptions of these quaggy, drowned places. I would go as far to say that it would be difficult to imagine such places *without* the sounds of birds. Partly, it is the unearthly quality of the birds' songs and calls. They invoke will-o'-the-wisp otherness, reminding us humans that these are not our places; we are unsuited, blundering things out of our depths (quite literally at times). Partly, it is how this otherworldliness is intensified by invisibility, as in the case of the snipe and bittern. The disguised birds of marsh seem to transfer or lend their weird voices directly to place, as though the washy tussocks or reed forests or the skies' extremities issue sound themselves. The marsh raises its own voices: small protests at human intrusions – sneck! snick! – straight from the sucking soil; reedy booms from gas-burping swamp depths; marshes' watery skies quivering with their own snipe-sad sorrows.

It is also the great multitude and variety of these marsh songs. If Vaughan Williams or Holst or Sibelius had ever composed a marsh symphony, I imagine it would have sounded like these birds, all voices entwining together in the cold wind. Williams' tone poem 'In the Fen Country' captures something birdy perhaps in its plaintive evocations, but for me Finnish composer Einojuhani Rautavaara's 'Concerto for Birds and Orchestra', *Cantus Arcticus*, comes closest, invoking the mysterious operations of marsh magic through its inventive interlacing of orchestral parts and recorded bird calls. The phenomenon of marsh song is at its best in winter, when the biggest number of species and individuals have gathered on the UK's estuaries and coastal marshes. Not all voices are there in the symphony at once, and while some play lead parts others are momentary or barely audible, but each announces and excuses itself at its right time, overlapping, combining, interweaving a thread of notes into the whole. It rivals any spring woodland chorus in my view. Arrive on site before dawn, as I did at Wallasea, and let the birds alone, instantly, tell you where you are.

You are struck, too, at such moments, alone in the dark on the frontiers of these big spaces, of that other deeply transcendent and transformative property of marsh birds in their evocations of place. To our ears, nearly all the species register somewhere along an intricate spectrum of lonesome despair that ranges from gentle solemnity to full, wailing dolour: the piteous wee sobs of teal and wigeon; the alarm of redshanks; sombre defiance in a greenshank's three-note plaint; plover sighs and descents. If we think of marshes as bleak, unforgiving and wretched, this notion has much to do with the sound of birds – they sing that sadness into our perceptions so firmly that it is difficult not to imagine that they suffer a tearful, marsh-sodden melancholia.

Back on the other side of the sea wall and much further east along the peninsula towards Mersea, Jeremy and I stopped to scan through wading birds out on the flats. We tucked in tight against the seaward side of the sea wall to escape the wind and keep off the skyline, kept warm with tea and chocolate, and made our way carefully and slowly through the birds with binoculars and telescopes. At high tide, especially a spring tide, the waves come right up to the wall here, covering everything so that the bay looks like a vast lake, but for now the muds are bare and we can see them stretch far along Tollesbury Fleet into the mouth of the Blackwater. For just a few hours, the exposed flats are so covered with feeding and resting waders and wildfowl that the mud writhes with life.

Of all these birds, the curlew, the largest European wader, is instantly recognisable, not only from its size but also by its famously long, curved bill that has the flourish of a scribe's immaculate curlicue, extending and reflecting the slender arcs of the bird's body. Because of this distinctively shaped bill (recalled in the Latin scientific name, *Numenius*, 'new moon'), the curlew is one of those birds that is easily learned and familiarised, and to many people there is none to rival its close associations with wet and wild open spaces, or its placemaking abilities to cast a spell on the land and us.

As with other species of marsh bird, it's the curlew's song that really does the trick. It is everything that goes to make a marsh. In *Cantus Arcticus*'s first movement, 'The bog', the curlew takes centre stage, beautifully suggested and echoed by a flute's swirling melodies, mimicking the bird's giddy tremulations. As elegant and attenuated as its bill, exquisitely afflicted, so uplifting and disquieting all at once, curlew song perfects the note of elegy pronounced by other avian voices in the mire and mud, contributing its call to the scale of marsh desolation while simultaneously articulating that very scale within in its own song. The curlew's song *is* a scale: if you listen to the refrains slowed right down, it's possible to detect how it slides chromatically up a small interval somewhere between a tone and a minor third, creating curls of sound like fine scrolls of planed wood, and then, when the bird is ready, these intervals crescendo high and fast up the octave and hold a bright, shivering semitone, which peaks sharply and repeatedly on minor thirds again, before the whole performance descends the octave in platforms, returning steadily to silence.

Curlew song is one of the first we hear in English literature. It appears in a poem, once again, from the Exeter Book – *The Seafarer* is an elegy in which a forlorn sailor battles against stormy winter seas and his troubled, world-weary soul. The narrator describes a journey along a rocky shoreline, emphasises again and again his location and discomfort, and mentions how he takes solace in the calls of birds, including that of *huilpan sweg* 'the curlew's cry'. This is the earliest-surviving curlew in English literature, in the earliest-surviving written description we have of birds being evocatively associated with place (we'll return to this description in the next chapter, such is its importance).

Frustratingly, it seems there are no old curlew place names. In the north of England and in Scotland you will find some names with *whaup* (a dialect term for the curlew), and across the North Sea in the Netherlands there is Wulpenbek, meaning either 'triangular wedge of land where curlews or some such wader are seen', or 'wedge of land shaped like a curlew's beak' but none of these is likely to be ancient. The *huilpe* in *The Seafarer*, then, is not only the first curlew, it's the only curlew in all Old English. It's what's known as a *hapax legomenon*: a single recorded instance, and the only clue in this case we have to the old name for this bird before similarly onomatopoeic *curleu* replaced it later in the Middle Ages.[5]

Precious though it is, *The Seafarer* is not the only surviving artefact from early England that tells us how birds such as the curlew resonated in people's imaginations. In the eighth century, a series of coins known as *sceattas* (pennies), probably associated with King Offa (he of the Dyke), was distributed in coastal regions depicting long-legged, long-beaked waders, powerfully suggesting a mental attachment of these recognisable birds to their habitats, or even that the birds functioned as a civic symbol in particular parts of the country. In archaeological finds from medieval coastal sites, too, a wide range of estuarine birds turn up, revealing that they formed part of the medieval diet, but also that people clearly encountered these species at close hand. Excavations at Anglo–Saxon Bishopstone in East Sussex, located right by what would have once been saltmarsh where the River Ouse flows into the sea at Newhaven, turned up the bones of numerous species such as golden plover, oystercatcher, dunlin and curlew. Whoever the poet of *The Seafarer* was, they seemed to be drawing upon a real connection between these birds and their landscape that could be relied upon to evoke a powerful sense of place.

It was easy to visualise *The Seafarer's* maritime scene with Jeremy that day, hunkered in grey grass on the sea wall looking out on the glistening flats, and the fleet unravelling itself out into grey sea and low grey clouds, and the chiming clinks of moored boats across the way at Tollesbury. Curlews fed determinedly and silently among knot and redshank and grey plover and dunlin – the last, to the naked eye, like hundreds of scuttling crabs that had generated from the oozing clay. There were lots of curlews. There always are when we visit in winter. But this abundance is misleading.

The great winter curlew flocks on coastal marshes all around Britain (of which some were in front of me probing good Essex mud) might give the impression that all is well with curlews, but they belie a desperate situation for our breeding populations – the birds that are actually here, ours, all year round. It's a situation I'd not realised until I read Mary Colwell's *Curlew Moon* – the story of her 500-mile journey across the species' breeding range in Britain and Ireland to raise awareness of their desperate plight. As she explains, estimates place overall wintering curlew numbers at about 150,000 individuals, but only about a third of that number accounts for resident birds, breeding on inland moors, pastures and bogs; the rest are winter migrants who arrive from northern European countries such as Finland and Norway in autumn and who return to breed in the subarctic tundra each spring. The fact is – and it's a distressingly familiar story regarding so many other species – Britain's homegrown curlews, which are thought to support 25 per cent of the global European curlew population, declined by some 60 per cent between 1994 and 2015 (98 per cent in Ireland), and the future trend looks to be decidedly and steeply downhill.

Watching winter curlews in Essex, I wondered if some of our resident curlews were on the Blackwater in front of me, feeding indistinguishably among their Nordic relatives, but with considerably more desperate outlooks. I'd met with Mary a month before, on the same day I visited Wallasea, for a spot of curlew-watching and conservation talk. We'd agreed to meet at Rainham Marshes for a few hours (a sliver of surviving marshland, I thought, for a slender-fortuned bird). A single curlew, wind-flapped and roosting with eyes tight shut on the Thames estuary, was all we found. A coincidence – elsewhere along the Essex coast, there can be many more – but we couldn't help commenting. A solitary curlew seemed about right. *Hapax legomenon*. A single survivor.

I asked Mary what she thought the future really looked like for these birds that she's spent years working to save.

'I think we'll lose them. From most of the UK anyway. It's not that you won't see curlews; there will still be wintering birds – although they're on the down too – but it's not the same. It doesn't sound like much, but when we're talking about a creature that has defined particular types of places for us for so long – places we're losing too – then it *is* a big deal. It alters the way those places matter to us, and the emotions we feel about those places. You lose some of the magic.'

I thought about Mary's words again on the Essex sea wall, trying to imagine what the place would be without the birds. What would it be without their presence, their hemisphere of sound? More than any others, I think, birds of the marsh make me realise the very sombre truth and threat of a birdless place. The landscape would look the same; it would still convey some sense of wildness no doubt, or elicit feelings of bleakness for us, but that same vastness and wetness would echo emptiness and desertion, not mystery and uncanny thrill, bereft of those energies and properties that exhilarate our sensations and deepen our bonds to place.

Jeremy and I arrived back at the main saltings just before dark. Redshanks were all alarm, piping urgently and flashing white wing edges. Curlews, undisturbed, called from the creek tunnels. Under-gods of the salt labyrinths. When my family visit these marshes each autumn we hear them across the way from our cottage at night, like wind down chimneys or an old kettle on the hob. Their bubbling trills come down the invisible watery channels, an estuarine substance rising free of its own matter.

I hope I will end my days somewhere like this. When my time comes, take me to the marsh. Let the wind carry me down heron-necked creeks that wash me wild and clean and dissolve me below the curve-billed horizons. Listen for me there in the curlew's liquid song.

7
The Gull's Home

Islay, Inner Hebrides ~ The Farne Islands, Northumberland ~ Earnley, West Sussex

In one interminable winter – the season by which lives and events are measured and recorded in Anglo-Saxon writing – another sea-bound traveller, bereft of his long-dead lord and kin, the world wasting and falling, rows alone, far from land on the ice-cold seas. Rain, hail, snow have him all at once. He is hall-sad, yearns for the mirth and comfort of his lord in the bright mead-house of feasting and fellows. Driven on by anxious thought for his heavenly redemption, the speaker suffers this grim but resolute dedication to the wave-tossed paths of self-exile. This is the dark abyss to take him, God willing, to the heavenly promised land. Homeless, he is now at home abroad, bound on the journey of all journeys for faithful souls.

He drifts into frozen sleep in the hull of his boat, dreams that he is reunited with friends in the great hall of warriors and warmth. *Đonne onwæcneð eft winleas guma* 'Then the friendless man wakes again':

sees before him dark waves,
seabirds bathing, spreading feathers,
rime and snow falling, mingled with hail.
Then are the heart's hurts the heavier,
sore with thinking on the loved lord. Sorrow is renewed
when the memory of kinsmen passes through the mind.

He greets them joyfully, keenly looks upon
the companions of men. They so often swim away.
The souls of floating ones do not bring there many
familiar voices.

This haunting and fleeting encounter from the Old
English elegy known as *The Wanderer* is an example of
how seabirds and their realm resonate in our imaginations.
The Wanderer's birds are very real to him, so real that he
reaches out to them in hope. But the poet also implies
with graceful ambiguity that the birds might just be
imagined – a ghostly vision of sea-drifting souls
hallucinated by a half-conscious, delirious sailor. The birds
are momentarily companions to the friendless man, and
yet also utterly remote from him, indifferently preening
and bathing, swimming away beyond reach, as
contradictory as his relationship with their habitat: the
'gannet's bath', the 'swan-road', the 'gull's home', as the
sea is variously and inventively known in Old English.
This is what seabirds do; they put us out of place where
they are supremely in place.

Seabirds, or *brimfuglas* to give them their Old English
name, the word that is used in *The Wanderer*, are a large
and characterful group of birds dependent to one degree
or another on the depths and bounties of the saltwater
spaces that cover over 70 per cent of the earth's surface.
Some go no further than the intertidal and neritic
(shallow) zones, making a living in coastal waters; others,
entirely pathetic landlubbers, only touch down on *terra
firma* for as brief a time as possible in the summer to
breed. The multiple islands, bays, skerries and inlets of
Britain and Ireland's anfractuous coastlines are
internationally important for their millions of *brimfuglas*,
and these defining inhabitants have long contributed to

the allure of maritime places in our cultures. In the early
Middle Ages seabirds featured in one very specific
connection to Britain's seascapes – a relationship to place
that is utterly alluring, dumbfounding, and, at times, quite
literally incredible. In search of the unbelievable then, I
went north; north and far out of England.

From here there's nothing before me but ocean, with
nothing but more of the same big ocean beyond that.
Infinity, viewed from a precipice of bare black, salt-
spumed rock at the edge of myself and an island's finitude.

This is westernmost Islay, one of the largest and best
known of Scotland's Inner Hebrides. A western edge of a
western isle on Britain's far Atlantic-facing west. It's not
my first time on the island (my elder daughter is so
named for my love of this place). I'm here, as before now,
with old friends for good whisky, and plenty of it, but
this time with an added quest. I've left carousing for the
day and made the slow and winding drive out west in
search of this very particular spot that I can see on my
map is only accessible by a trek across difficult terrain
with no footpaths. Even on making it this far, there was
still the business of finding somewhere to park on these
narrow roads across blanket bogs, walking back on myself
to a track showing on the map as a route past a sheepfold,
then getting across very uneven ground without twisting
an ankle or getting wet, all the while warily keeping to
the edge of the field because more than one furtive
source I consulted about how to get here warned me of
a bull. The final phase had me clambering and sliding
down steep dunes to what is advertised as one of the
most unspoilt, secluded beaches on all of Islay.

With a journey like that to reach it, I'm not surprised it is unspoilt. And it is, just as I was told, pristine and utterly deserted, as though I were the first person ever to discover it. I followed the brook across the immaculate sands, harassed by circles of irate common gulls vexed by an unwanted visitor to their bay. It was well-earned, as perfect a destination as you could wish for. But Lossit Bay wasn't what I'd come for. I was headed a climb and a scramble away over the hill from the beach, and the sight of the mewing, ganging gulls lifted my heart in hope. I was after a specific outcrop of rock, just one of many promontories along this part of the island's coast that I never would have noticed had it not been for the Gaelic word written alongside it on the map. *Faoileag*. Gull. *Rubha na faoileige*. The gull's headland.

The gulls led me here, to the summit overlooking their rock, on which, like some tribal overlord, there is a territorial great black-backed gull, and overhead, overlooking me, are the cat-calling common gulls that will not quit. A short distance away to the north there is a smaller *rubha*, this one the property of shags. *Rubha nan sgarbh*. They, too, are out to prove their place today. There are several at home, sea-ravens, pegging out their wings, black and motionless and prehistoric-looking as the gneiss slabs on which they sit, as if they've been carved from the stuff itself. They make me sharply aware, in a way that can only occur when you are surrounded or immersed in the ambience of a place, that this spot has me at the centre of several transecting routes to a deep past. I am atop Dun Bhoraraig, a Bronze- or Iron-Age hill fort – one of several along this coast – built on bedrock that is nearly two billion years old. All of that is easily felt here, in the roaring wind on this Atlantic edge, in the sun-bright, sea-white gulls, and the shags' metamorphic stance.

Gulls and shags (though *sgarbh* can include cormorants too) are common in place names all around the Scottish coasts and islands. So too in Ireland. The names of these birds embody the two major linguistic, cultural and seagoing influences in this part of medieval Britain. Looking out from Dun Bhoraraig, *faoileag*, the gull, flies south to Ireland. The word is from the more ancient of the two languages, deriving from Old Irish, the Celtic tongue that came to Scotland from Irish settlers in the early Middle Ages, or possibly even before that. The shag, *sgarbh*, takes us in the opposite direction, north and then east, right around the head of Scotland and on to Scandinavia. The word is Gaelic still, but derived from Old Norse for shag (*skarfr*) as are many Scots Gaelic terms relating to the natural world, such was the Viking influence over many centuries all around Scotland, as in parts of Ireland and England too at this time. From Norse we have Foula, one of the Shetlands, Fugloy in the Faroes, both meaning 'bird island', and Sula Sgeir, 'gannet skerry', the island 40 miles north of Lewis where the centuries-old harvesting of young gannets, or 'guga' as they are known, still occurs once a year (a controversial practice now, officially restricted by NatureScot to 2,000 birds killed annually). What can we say about the days when these names came into existence, when the gulls or shags on their Islay rocks first became emblems of this place?

Unfortunately, not as much as we'd like to. When it comes to Gaelic place names in Scotland, although the original language may be very old, older than English by far, there is not the same body of evidence that exists for English place names confirming early provenance. Outside of settlement names, many Gaelic place names were unrecorded before the nineteenth century, when the first Ordnance Survey maps were being produced. It may be that a good number of the highly localised topographical names that litter the Scottish highlands and islands are only a few hundred years old, bestowed by crofters and shepherds in a time before the clearances emptied the land of human communities.

This doesn't mean, though, that some of the names couldn't be, or aren't, much older. There is certainly no doubting that the lives of seabirds and people on this western fringe of Britain have long been intertwined. Along this sweep of north-west Europe, perhaps especially in the west of Scotland with its intricate coastline and archipelagos, the sea dominates geographies and perceptions. It is always close and present, land is surrounded, or thin and all edges, smoothed and cut and invaded by a sea that is always reaching in, and whose weathers are big and wild and quick and won't let you forget it. No wonder the birds of such sea-shaped places made their mark in the names and minds of cultures immersed and skilled in maritime existence, who dwelt in and between lands of coastal cliffs and crags – those land-leaving habitats where so many seabirds choose to breed. Little wonder, too, when we remember that for nearly all of human history in these remote fringes and islands of Britain, these places were not so remote as they seem to us now. From the Mesolithic onwards, a network of well-known, well-sailed sea-roads enabled trade, travel and communications right across the Scottish seaboards and far beyond.

One group of unlikely seafarers in the Middle Ages using these Atlantic highways were early men of the Church, voyaging in search and in the name of heavenly eternity. They brought with them the Word of God, and the Word travelled on the seabird's way, bound for the places where the seabirds are.

I might have seen them from here a millennium and a half ago, those nautical churchmen. I'm looking out on what was an important meeting of sea-paths across the early medieval, Hiberno-Scottish kingdom of Dál Riata. Islay is a gateway and stopping-off point to the Hebrides, the most southerly isle before you reach the northern coast of Ireland. Those holy men, cross-channel voyagers, came up from Ireland in the sixth to eighth centuries along the flightlines of *faoileagan*, just as that word itself journeyed here to find its way into the memory and vocabulary of place. They sailed in currachs – the traditional, seagoing, Irish vessel made from wicker frame and calf hides caulked with tar (a *naomhóg* in the southern Irish vernacular, meaning 'little holy one'). To any northbound crew passing Islay's coast, the secluded sandy bays interrupting the dark igneous rock and fierce surf must have looked good for respite. Did holy men in their holy boats ever come ashore here? Perhaps. Legend has it that Columba himself stopped at Kilchiaran Bay, a little way north of where I am.

Suddenly you see one there, a *naomhóg* cresting the waves into Lossit's safe harbour, men leaping the stern into knee-deep water, then hauling their craft up the beach in a white flurry of gulls. They wear simple habits and their heads are tonsured, not as a crown of thorns in the Roman style, but at the front from ear to ear.

Who were these eremites and missionaries bent on masochistic living? Their ideal has settled deep in the cultural psyche. It is a medieval phenomenon. In the Age of Saints, wandering monks across the Celtic-speaking regions were seeking new lives closer to God in the remotest locations the British Isles have to offer. That ambition involved a radical way of thinking about and being in place. Emulating the Desert Fathers, the Irish monk hermits saw in the Atlantic their own 'desert in the ocean'. In pursuing isolation, they were enacting the very root of that modern word: to be isolated is to be an island (*insula* in Latin), and there were plenty of those off the west coast of Britain. Islands were necessary for the practicalities of living, but what these *peregrini* really wanted was ocean: waves lapping or crashing at their senses, sea brimming to the edges of sight. The *peregrini* (from the Latin *peregrinus*, 'far wanderer', from which our word 'pilgrim' derives, as well, of course, as 'peregrine falcon') drew upon and literalised a Christian tradition in which all human life was metaphorically perceived as a sea-bound exile, a lifelong pilgrimage destined for the Kingdom of Heaven *pro amore Dei* 'for the love of God'.

The *peregrini* got everywhere. You will be hard pushed to find an island off Ireland or Scotland's west coast (or indeed the Welsh or Cornish coast) that doesn't have some saintly connection.[1] Most impressive of the remoter locations is the monastic community that Saint Finan (or Finian) supposedly founded when he sailed to Skellig Michael, 12 miles out from Ireland's County Kerry – a place and a feat to defy belief and imagination, with its sharp, precipitous peaks rising like monstrous teeth from black sea, upon which terrifying heights are poised a monastery with its bee-hive cells and a teetering hermitage on the very south-western, uppermost jagged point. It is a place belonging to an otherworldly realm, the stuff of legend, but it is utterly real. Others went further out still, to the Flannans, the Kildas, the Shetlands, possibly even the Faroes and Iceland.[2] The most extreme *peregrini* set off in their curraghs with no specific destination at all, such as the three monks who fetched up in Cornwall, having sailed from Ireland in an oarless boat in AD 891 because 'they wanted for the love of God to be abroad – they did not care where'. Such were the places of the *peregrini*, who renounced the body to pursue a wind-sharpened purity of the soul and a clear line to God through a relationship with rock and sea and the wild birds.

You might reasonably assume that the Farne Islands, a tiny archipelago of island-specks off the Northumbrian coast, only a mile and a half from the mainland, were a world apart from the *peregrini* islands clear and far out the other side of Britain. Not so. Seventh-century Northumbria was profoundly linked to these Atlantic extremities, and itself became a mighty centre of ecclesiastic influence and production to rival Iona. The Farnes, satellite hermitages to England's Holy Isle, the tidal island of Lindisfarne, were connected and opened to the world by the seaways. From Iona, the great and famous Hebridean centre of Columba himself, Saint Aidan set sail in AD 635 around the north of Scotland and down to Northumbria, establishing the first monastery on Lindisfarne in deliberate imitation of the insular tradition he had brought with him. And it was from Lindisfarne that Saint Cuthbert, decades later, made Inner Farne his own salt-desert – an association of saint and island that has been intensely venerated and memorialised ever since. And from Lindisfarne too, a bright young monk with ambitions by the name of

Cedd set out in AD 653 to evangelise Essex, and when he arrived off the Dengie Peninsula he built himself a chapel. St Peter-on-the-Wall. All things are connected by the seabird's way.

The Farnes lack extremes and immensities: oceanic distance and dark hostility, summit-breaking waves, dizzying stack heights. But their modest achievements make the Farnes much more accessible and the birds unbeatably close. They are one of Britain's very best locations to get up close with seabirds, to experience for oneself, with remarkable intimacy, the rawness of a place alive to seabird existence. In the summer of 2019, with tremendously fortunate timing before the chaos of Covid and the devastations of avian flu closed operations down, I made my own, long-awaited, pilgrimage to England's foremost place of rock and sea and wild birds.

The day was desperately hot, one of those scorchers we've come to expect in British summers. From the harbour at Seahouses, just south of Bamburgh, I could already see the birds, a shimmer and glint of activity made doubly hazy through the magnification of binoculars. The heat intensified everything. My senses and thoughts were seared, sun-baked as the guano that was easily visible on approach to the Islands, bright and abundant as the birds themselves: a sense of belonging shit-stained on the place itself. Ashore Staple Island – one of the larger of the Outer Farnes – the stuff burned bright. Black dolerite was luminous as chalk. Whiteness was all: sea, rock, sun, sky and birds, whose staring alertness and hard glares were fierce.

I sat by a shag for a time with its woolly chick. Each as stultified by the conditions as the other, I drank water greedily, and it panted on what breeze there was, its beak agape and gular flaring. The shag, of all birds on Staple, felt most distant in slow, simmering time to me. Its viridian eyes did not communicate sympathy or understanding, but there we were, only feet apart, both enduring under the high sun.

I thought of *Rubha nan sgarbh*, and of another shag, this one from saintly literature associated with Brenhilda, sister to Saint Ronan, a very rare example of a named female *peregrinus*. The siblings lived together as hermits on North Rona, but, so legend tells, when her brother was tempted by bodily desire (her body to be precise), Brenhilda set sail 11 miles west, trying and failing to eke a living alone among the gannets of Sula Sgeir. In macabre mockery of Brenhilda's doomed time among the birds, similarities are made disturbingly real when a shag makes its nest in the hollow of her ribcage, as though enacting some grotesque resurrection. Cohabitation *in extremis*.

Close interaction with non-human creatures was a saintly convention. It demonstrated their miraculous, intercessory powers. Cuthbert did it repeatedly: otters dried his freezing, wet feet; an eagle delivered him a salmon to feed the poor; apologetic ravens provided lard to grease boots; and famously, so legend has it but with no real evidence, Inner Farne's eider ducks enjoyed his personal custody. Cross-species intimacy is there too in Brenhilda's case, though its outcomes and implications could not be more harrowing, with nothing of Cuthbert's cosy relations, and appearing to us like a severe cautionary tale.

The extremes of Cuthbert and Brenhilda beg the question: what did those early eremites actually make of the birds with which they shared their ocean deserts? Those who took themselves off to seabird-inhabited spots must have found it impossible to avoid or ignore the screeching colonies in the chaotic midst of sheer-cliff breeding. The author Adam Nicolson has said that an absence of seabirds on the Hebridean Shiant Isles that his family owns (and that may have had a medieval hermit of two) is like 'a book with only half the alphabet'. Medieval inhabitants of islands such as the Shiants, the Farnes or Sula Sgeir could not have shared a modern quixotic or conservationist love. On the other hand, we can't dismiss the idea either that they marvelled at God's creation in the life around them, felt awe at the elements' might and scale, even if in dismal terror. In the lines of early Irish poetry, nearly all of which was written down after the Age of Saints, but much of which is indeed focused on the life 'Solitary in a small cell', we can easily and equally read perverse as well as straightforward pleasure in a voice that exclaims, 'Delightful I think it is to be in the bosom of an isle / On the crest of a rock'. Did Nicolson's Shiant predecessors curse the birds' raucous interference in matters of prayer, and bless the birds' departure in late summer for the peace it brought? Did they welcome the racket as simply part of the privation and penitence they chose to face in their unswerving devotion to God? Quite probably.

Like everything else about the *peregrini* and their disciples, it is next to impossible to know anything for certain. But we may be able to get a little closer yet. Not to the wayfaring monks themselves, but there survives a dramatic medieval imagining of their saintly travails that may carry in it a scintilla of those early voices. The most vivid and detailed articulation of an ocean exile was written down, not in Latin or Irish from the Atlantic edges of Britain, but in the south of England, in Old English, in a poem we already know, *The Seafarer*. And it may be that Lindisfarne, or another Northumbrian monastery such as Bede's at Jarrow, was the sphere of influence from which the fascination for Irish wanderings passed south through England and eventually found its way into this poem.

The single-surviving, Old English curlew who made an appearance in the previous chapter is not, in fact, so very alone. It is accompanied by five other birds in *The Seafarer*. Five other seabirds. The mariner–narrator knows all their names and speaks of them as ocean companions on his journey in the earliest written description of birds evoking place in the English language.

> *Sometimes the swan's song*
> *I took for my game, the gannet's sound*
> *and curlew's cry for men's laughter,*
> *the gull's singing for mead-drink.*
> *There, storms beat stone cliffs, there the tern answered them*
> *icy-feathered; very often the eagle yelled,*
> *dewy-feathered. No protecting kinsman*
> *can comfort the desolate soul.*

This well-known passage is the most precise and developed aspect of place in the poem. The weather and its effects are emphatically present too, throughout: appalling winter weather, as befitting the speaker's desolation. But the birds are most memorable and unique: they are the most exact, vivifying elements of the seascape, two of them inhabiting the shoreline – the curlew and the surf-sprayed eagle – and the others all at home on the waves, all long-distance, wave-crossing migrants and wanderers (particularly in winter, which perhaps helps to explain the otherwise confusing presence of a tern in this scene).

The Seafarer is a poem of two halves. The birds appear in the first, that part of the poem in which the narrator relates his time living 'in the paths of exile' on the 'ice-cold sea' for a whole winter. The second half becomes explicitly Christian and implores us all to strive towards 'the eternal blessedness' over the 'seaways'. All the references to exile, to the *merewerges mod* (a lovely Old English phrase meaning 'sea-weary spirit'), to the narrator's desire to endure this suffering 'time and again', encourage us to see this as a *peregrinatio pro amore Dei* ('Pilgrimage for the love of God') even while the poem is also heroic Anglo-Saxon, with its mead-hall, treasure-giving lord and warrior kin. And right there, named, alive and vocal in the materiality of ocean existence, as palpable and distinctive as the tossing of waves and the rocky cliffs, are the birds. The narrator, in the fashion of the saints, has intentionally and willingly exiled himself from the intoxicating pleasures of society, and now takes the birds in place of these temptations. In the symmetry of the lines and the narrator's contrast between what once was and what now is we sense a keen attention on the birds as adopted company, as new place-kin. It is a vividly realised scene and moment ('there', the narrator says, 'there') in which the birds' screech and yell the place into salt-flayed, storm-drenched existence.

As in *The Wanderer*, that other sea elegy from the Exeter Book, the narrator sails the exile-paths and encounters seabirds, wishing to interact with them. Both poets imagine and dramatise a relationship between the maritime exile and bird that might genuinely have occurred to the pilgrim mind. *Peregrini* and seabirds are, in several senses, joined in a common aim and live similar lives. Their shared habitat is the sea. For both, island dwelling is a necessary but tedious concession to the laws of physics that make certain things, such as laying and incubating eggs in the case of the birds, impossible to do at sea; islands, at least, create the illusion of being so close to sea that you are practically at sea. It's why many seabirds, including auks, shearwaters, fulmars and gulls, choose these locations; they are sea-empty and sea-isolated. One can't help feeling that those lunatic monks who scaled the outright dangerous heights of the tottering penthouse hermitage on Skellig cannot have missed the obvious similarity between themselves and the cliff-nesting seabirds around them, who also sought the most vertical, unreachable stack-ledges to spend a few months: if you can't be actually at sea, you may as well choose somewhere that gives you the best possible sea view and the exhilarating threat of a martyr's plunge to the gannet's deep.

Of all the Farnes' birds, of all the birds in *The Seafarer* too, the one for me that most epitomises the solitary's relationship with the gull's home is the Arctic tern. Farne tourism trades on puffins, but it was the Arctic terns I really wanted to get close to. Short of travelling to the Orkneys or Shetlands, you'll find nowhere better to do so than Saint Cuthbert's isle itself, Inner Farne.[3] You can't miss them. This is very true of all the species on the islands, concentrated as they are into such a small space, but it's even more true in the case of the thousands of terns, because they, repeatedly and violently, won't miss you. My first, on the quay, perched with arch nonchalance on a sign that read, 'The Arctic tern breeding season is in full swing', while we filed past only feet away.

The polite notice serves as a euphemistic warning to the unsuspecting, such as, I guessed, the bald gentleman in front of me in flip-flops. The typical tern encounter on Inner Farne is outright attack. The quayside bird was calmly, deceptively tolerant, but the others were ready with dagger-sharp, blood-red bills. You cannot hope to avoid them – the nests and chicks are everywhere, including the paths – and once you reach the island's plateau at the head of the steps the assault is immediate. Even with a hat (vital in tern territory), you feel the sharp strike at your skull and the shriek in your ear, like 'a thing being torn in two', as author Stephen Rutt puts it. Every so often they draw blood and you hear a yelp or see flailing arms as though their owner is suddenly caught in a midge cloud. This divebombing is a highly effective tactic that can drive even a lumbering, hungry polar bear to distraction. If you come to the Farnes in summer, you submit to this, forewarned or otherwise. This is their place, after all. You are the intruder.

Watching terns around the medieval chapel at the north end of the island, I wondered if these birds were here in Cuthbert's day (the chapel is purportedly built on the site of his original hermitage cell). There's no way of knowing; seabird populations at particular places come and go, and not all are ancient. Still, I like to think of him not commanding jackdaws or cuddling up with cuddy ducks, but in the maelstrom of terns, swatting away attacks as he makes a dash for it from his cell to the spring for water, or perhaps miraculously silencing their squawks while he kneels in concentrated prayer.

Saintly interventions aside, you can't tame the terns, or any seabird. The Wanderer and the Seafarer knew that well. However close you are, those birds remain apart. You reach out. They always swim away. I was closer on the Farnes than I ever thought it possible to be to seabirds, petting distance, close enough to smell fishy breath and pity their panting discomfort. It was exhilarating, but also disturbing. It felt unnatural to be so close. Islands, the Farnes especially so in their smallness, crystallise that perpetually transforming and colliding sense of near and far. They, and their birds, could not feel more precisely, more intimately local in one way, but they are also inconceivably vast and distant.

The Arctic tern, a seabird *par exemplar*, reinforces this notion more than any other. Its statistics are well known, for they rank among the most staggering feats in all the natural world and are never anything short of mind-blowing. The Farne birds, breeding at the southern global limit of the species' breeding territories, will end up, like most of their kind, on the Antarctic pack-ice over winter, before returning nearly to the opposite pole again in the following year, a journey a single tern could potentially do for two decades or more, notching up distances over a lifetime that equate to more than one trip to the moon and back. There is no creature on the planet that can match the Arctic tern for these migration distances. In 2016, in fact, it was a Farne bird that broke the longest migration record of its time, flying a total 59,650 miles in one year, departing from and returning to Northumberland. To touch an icy-feathered Arctic tern, or rather to have one touch you, is to be transported to the frozen top and bottom of the world, to make contact with the illimitable realms that are, paradoxically, beyond your reach.

Some facts pertaining to these realms and journeys are now within our knowledge, thanks to modern satellite technologies. We know the round-trip itineraries

of Arctic terns; we know that non-breeding kittiwakes
on the Isle of May off the east of Scotland head to the
waters south of Greenland for winter, and that a fulmar
on an Orkney isle is capable of leaving its mate and
travelling almost to Canada in search of feeding grounds.
To us, these revelations are no less miraculous because
we know them to be facts – we marvel at the magnitudes
– but they miss the point when it comes to understanding
what the magic of seabirds meant to earlier cultures. *Not
knowing* was the thing. It is Isidore of Seville's pathless
ways again.

The mysteries of oceanic mastery make the tern and
its far-wandering companions special in *The Seafarer*.
They are not just place-evokers, integrated elements in
the seascape. They are powerfully attached to the
narrator's inner geography too, recalling his own
tremendous spiritual undertaking and his terrifying
place upon the high seas, which, gannet-like, he makes
alone in winter. They are all pelagic brethren, solitary
wayfarers desiring open ocean and distant, wide horizons
where there is no such thing as the local. It is not far-
fetched to say that medieval seafarers would have
encountered pelagic birds, particularly when we
remember that Viking travellers, and even some monks,
made it to the Arctic regions. Those extremists who set
sail in oarless or rudderless currachs bound for God
knows where didn't just share the seabirds' environment;
in a way, they became seabirds. They did this physically,
taking to the sea in their fragile crafts, but figuratively
too, imagining their souls aloft, free of the bone-house
and land-woes, discovering a direction towards the
homeland where truth lies.

This is what appears in *The Seafarer*. A soul on
migration. The idea no doubt occurred to more than

one religious mind contemplating the soul's progress, thinking of the familiar conceit of pilgrims at sea who must, as Saint Augustine wrote, 'soar to the unchangeable substance of God'. The colour of seabirds must have appealed: 'white-winged flight' as one early Irish poet describes; the 'white thing' by which one might see 'secrets that took hold of God' as Herman Melville put it upon seeing an albatross centuries later: pristine, graceful, diaphanous, angelically attenuated. In evolutionary terms, that characteristic of plumage has a hard-edged function (it is predatorial camouflage, as seen looking up from underwater to the light sky), but to us it is ethereal and white as the purified soul. It is the colour of the *peregrini* themselves, who suffered what they called the 'white martyrdom'– privation and abstinence for the love of God.

The moment of transcendence in *The Seafarer* comes about halfway through the poem, just before the renunciation of land-life for the glory of heavenly eternity. Growing urgently restless, the narrator's spirit sets out on a soaring, out-of-body experience:

> *Now my desire roams beyond the breast-locker,*
> *my spirit with the sea-flood,*
> *travels widely over the whale's home [and]*
> *earth's corners, comes again to me*
> *eager and greedy. The lone-flier yells,*
> *urges the heart to the whale-path without hesitation*
> *over the oceans' expanses.*

The loner-flier. In Old English, *anfloga*. Soul. Bird. Bird-soul. Like the curlew, the *anfloga* is a *hapax legomenon*, another once-only recorded name. The soul, like a bird, and the bird, like a soul, calls out, back to the body it has transcended and urges it to follow, for the *anfloga* knows already that the journey is worthwhile and true.

There are very few seabirds in English names, even in regions such as Northumbria. This was one reason why I'd begun my journey in Scotland, on the Gaelic and Norse coasts. That north–south division points out one likely answer to the name absence in England – it is a consequence of geography. The most suitable and extensive habitat for the widest range of seabird species is to be found along our west and north coasts, particularly so in Scotland, which alone possesses 65 per cent of Britain's coastline. These are the true seabird places. Another possibility, however, lies in the way that Old English thought, as suggested in surviving writings, directly and closely associated seabirds with their immediate and proper place: Anglo-Saxon people named the sea, not land, after these birds: the gannet's bath, the swan's road, over which one travelled by boat 'most birdlike'. Not for them the modern associations of boisterous, chip-thieving gulls, cool cruisers of the promenade, urbane anthropocenists making their way inland to feed on human garbage. The gull's home was out there. Seabird place names do not belong on land.

There is one striking and important exception to this general absence. The last, and one of the two largest species on *The Seafarer's* (and Britain's) list has a suitably large presence in our place names as well. In the Middle Ages, the white-tailed eagle, as it's officially known now, the *earn* to Old English speakers (erne, still, in modern English), *ǫrn* to the Vikings, had a range across the British Isles to suit its magnificent wingspan. It rivals the crane in size, cultural stature and in the widespread presence of its name all over England. Like many of our raptor species that were shot to extinction, the white-tailed eagle hung on, mostly on remote, monkish islands, until the early twentieth century (the last, a portentously all-white bird, was shot in Shetland in the year the First World War ended), but the hundreds of hunting and museum records from the nineteenth and early twentieth centuries for the species also give a detailed picture of encounters until modern times in just about every single county. This was the seabird of English place names.

In one respect the erne feels like cheating. It's no seabird in the proper sense. All across their Palearctic range white-tailed eagles exist wherever there are suitably large bodies of water. But on the Atlantic fringes of Europe, white-tails are often coastal birds, nesting on sea cliffs or in wooded valleys not far from the sea where fish, snatched straight from the waves, form a characteristic and key part of their diet. In the *peregrini* haunts of Scotland and Ireland these eagles would have been intimately associated with sea stacks and crags, and in lowland England they will have been familiar cohabitants of coastal wetlands. In Scots Gaelic, the bird is *Iolaire chladaich*, 'eagle of the shore'. In modern English, it is often called the sea eagle. In *The Seafarer*, it is the surf-sprayed, screaming eagle of the stony cliffs and the terrible waves, in company with the gannet and the tern and gull. The Seafarer's word is good enough for me.

The sea-streams crossed again, connecting near and far, returning endings to beginnings. I'd left off for my seabird peregrinations from the tidal edges of Essex. Now, a different summer in a different place, I waded back in, so to speak, to the sea-fretting margins.

Shortly after dawn one Sunday, long before any tourists were about, I stood at the water's edge on Bosham quay in West Sussex. The tide was out, but on the turn. Cnut's tide, the site of that famous story. In the shallows below the harbour wall, fat grey mullet lounged like cud-chewing cows, almost as motionless as the water and the warm, windless air. A good meal for a sea eagle. Common terns patrolled, plunging for small fry. A curlew lamented on the far side. Black-headed gulls squawked and scrapped, some still in dapper summer getup, others already fading into white winter wear.

Bosham, in the Chichester Harbour waterways, is a long way from Lindisfarne, and even further from the Hebrides. But even here those surprising serendipities linking the histories and ideas of far places eddied and pooled in the intertwining currents. Bounded on three sides by estuary, the sea is no less present and shaping in Bosham than anywhere on the Scottish coast. It cuts off the coast road fringing the village twice a day, leaves its bladderwracked identity right up the tarmac at every high tide. The local pub and flinted-flecked houses, just metres away, have flood barriers. So does the tenth-century church, not many more metres away – flood angels, door dams, as they are variously referred to in the trade. To live here, I guess, is to live happily enough with the idea of flood, to be wide open to its threat.

So it really should have been no surprise to discover that at Bosham, three centuries before the village and Harold Godwinson are immortalised together in the Bayeux Tapestry, an Irish monk by the name of Dícuill had a small monastery built in this tide-worried place. The *peregrini* spirit was here too, daring the bare face of gale and flood, just like Saint Cedd of Lindisfarne in the same century on the Essex sea-brink. And no surprise either that in the eleventh century Bosham's church was in the possession of Osbern FitzOsbern, who became Bishop of Exeter in 1072, following the death of old Leofric, owner and bequeather of the Exeter Book, home of *The Seafarer*.

I had, it should be said, a significantly better chance of actually seeing ernes right where I'd started, in the Hebrides. Indeed, I did see them there. Following the reintroduction of white-tails on the Isle of Rum in 1975, hundreds of descendants have now bred and dispersed across the Scottish Isles and coastal Highlands, making this region the sea eagle centre of Britain. The names of their long empty haunts are all over the land. *Stac na h-Iolaire. Creag na h-Iolaire. Cnoc na h-Iolaire.*

But the names are here too, in England. What's more, at last, so are the birds.

Just a few miles east of Bosham as the eagle flies is the village of Earnley. It has always been very small – the historic part is now only a church at what probably marks the site of early settlement. It is surrounded now by grand modern residentials with swimming pools, a housing estate, and a caravan park to the west. But Earnley's origins are unquestionably old. It first appears in writing as *Earnaleach* in AD 780. The ernes' woodland clearing. It is one of many – some 70 or so – ancient eagle names that help map the past of this species all across England, from Cornwall to Staffordshire, Berkshire to Nottinghamshire, Shropshire to Yorkshire, Wiltshire to Cumbria. In all these counties, sea eagles might have made their homes. At least some of these names, those appearing in northern mountain and moor country, may well refer to that other, iconic British *earn*, the golden eagle. But not most. And there's certainly no doubt that Earnley, located where it is, was home to the *earn æftan hwit* 'eagle white from behind', as the bird is described in another Old English poem, *The Battle of Brunanburh*.

For any Earnley dweller of old there was no missing a
bird like the sea eagle. A pair in residence, each a metre tall
from beak to feet, is a landmark of magnitude, solid as a
rune stone, venerable as a grand oak. An established eyrie
in itself is an ancestral throne, a lofty monument with all
the broad, mighty heft of the bird's beating, totem wings.
Its place can endure in local knowledge, even when the
nest has long been empty. And eagles, like cranes, had been
regally cloaked in cultural reverence for millennia; on the
North Sea Frisian flatlands, on the Norwegian coastal
fjords, on the northern Scottish Isles where, as at Isbister
on the Orkney island of South Ronaldsay, ernes were
interred alongside human occupants in a tomb over 2,000
years ago. Old English *earn* is, in a sense, the bird of all
birds, the name descended from Indo-European, parallel
to ancient Greek for simple 'bird', *ornis*. All of that
proprietary splendour and talismanic authority is
transferred upon an eagle place. Seeing an eagle is always a
stop-and-stare moment for anyone – head up, hand
shading eyes, squinting at *Iolaire sùil na grèine*, 'the eagle
with the sunlit eye'. There is nothing else to be done.

Bosham, its medieval past so damply close, easily
summons visions of the *earn*, this most Anglo-Saxon of
birds: the famous, white-tailed battle-bird of legend and
poetry; horny-beaked and hoary-headed, stripping
corpses with the raven and the wolf. While Earnley now
has nothing beyond its name to suggest its old aquiline
majesties, the landscape in which it is located still recalls
Bede's Bosham country 'surrounded by woods and sea'.
Even in the nineteenth century Earnley retained some of
its woodland, right on the edge of now-drained saltmarsh
that then surrounded Selsea (the seal's island) to the east.
To the west were, and still are, the extensive estuaries
between Portsmouth and Chichester, and beyond that the

Isle of Wight dividing the Solent strait a few miles from the mainland. The Earnley eagles would have occupied a huge nest, perhaps generations old, high on the edge of the woods, surveying all of this, as would those across the Solent in Hampshire at Arnewood (now New Milton), those on the Isle of Wight, which bred until 1780, and those west of that in Devon, at Yarner and Yarnscombe.

It is precisely this extent of good remaining habitat that made the Isle of Wight and its seas the ideal location for a long-awaited English reintroduction of the species in 2019. Six juveniles from Scotland were released at a secret spot on the island – poignantly, the last recorded English breeding site for the birds – and more every year since, with the intention of translocating 60 birds in total. The young eagles have found their place, eventually establishing territories in the vicinity, although in their first year or so they made exploratory journeys all over Britain and beyond. One, a female, has been all along the south coast (from satellite images taken from her tracking device, it looks as though she must have passed close by Earnley) and summered twice in the far north of Scotland. Another, a male, wandered as far as Cornwall and Norfolk; then, touring the lands of our Germanic ancestors, he journeyed all along the north-western continental coast as far as Denmark and Sweden, before heading back to Hampshire.

The erne is no longer a figment. More and more people are looking up all along the south coast to see white-tailed eagles. It is still early days, but the hope is that slowly these birds will repopulate the south of England, and then spread beyond to other counties. I've yet to encounter one. I know what it is to see ernes on their island strongholds – the same type of remote, offshore locations where the last surviving individuals struggled on into the twentieth century: Hirta, one of the Kilda Isles 40 miles out to sea from the Scottish mainland; the Isle of Man, Fair Isle, the Shetlands, Lundy (this last, Norse for 'puffin island', is, coincidentally, the only other old seabird place name in England). These are outposts though, not a true picture of sea eagles as they ought to exist in these lands.

One day, there it will be, like an island in the estuary sands, attended by squiring gulls and crows. It heaves into air, heroic and steep, beats down the channel for open water on church-door wings. A Flood Angel. Perhaps this is what the Seafarer had in mind. I can imagine that: the lone-flier as sea eagle, spectral as the last earn of Shetland, bearer of souls over far horizons.

8

Everywhere and Nowhere

Heol-y-Cyw, Wales ~ Dering Wood, Kent ~ Whisby, Lincolnshire ~ Castor Hanglands, Cambridgeshire

There are no nightingales in Wales. Indeed, although no one can tell for sure, in most of its 21,000 km, there may never have been nightingales.[2] The same goes for Scotland and Ireland, but as far back as the Middle Ages, it seems to have been generally, even proverbially, acknowledged that 'the nightingale followed wise counsel, and never came into Wales', as Gerald of Wales wrote in the twelfth century. The western end of the species' range in Britain, at the point where it meets the River Severn, broadly locates the species along the Marches – the English–Welsh borderlands that formed contested and bloody ground in the Middle Ages. Crossing over the country border, then, once signalled a stepping in and out of nightingale lands, though now, with the species' range shrinking fast in western England too, it's only just about possible to still make that claim.

The possibility of nightingales in Wales is even less likely now. The last survey conducted by the British Trust for Ornithology (2008-2011) produced no breeding records of nightingales in Wales whatsoever. Online, there is a proud report from the *Powys County Times* of an individual heard singing in Machynlleth in 2020, the first record in Montgomeryshire since 1983,

and a few forum discussions in which people have
enquired about the chances of the bird they'd heard
singing being a nightingale, to which the answers were
invariably and emphatically – very little to no chance
whatsoever.

What then was I thinking, searching for my first
nightingale of the year one May day in a Welsh field?

In some back-to-front way it made sense to start a
journey for nightingales where there are no nightingales,
but it was more particularly a nightingale conundrum
that had brought me here. As it turns out, there are
nightingales in Wales, lots of them, if you know where to
look. Not the bird itself, but its name. Once I started
looking, I discovered it all over, as far north as Flint and
Denbigh, and as far west as Cardigan and Fishguard.
Welsh *eos*, bewitching as a Greek goddess, is everywhere.
But here's the intriguing irony. Wales, a country with a
long-standing reputation as a place with no nightingales,
has more nightingale place names than, probably,
anywhere else on earth, whereas England, the one place
in Britain where they have always been since sometime
after the end of the last Ice Age, the one place where
they reliably and numerously bred across most of the
country until the second half of the twentieth century,
has no nightingale place names at all. Not one.
Everywhere and nowhere. That's the nightingale. That's
the paradox that shadowed me wherever I went in search
of these birds.

And so there I was, briefly de-roading the family
holiday in search of an *eos* just off the M4 near Bridgend,
north of the village of Heol-y-Cyw. This one, Brin
Eos, was situated on the most southerly edge of the
South Wales Valleys, from which the field surely
received its name – 'nightingale hill'. It is, still, exactly

as shown on the early map I'd found; a pasture sloping down to shaw-shaded brooks with a public footpath alongside.

Ginny left me on the road leading out of Heol-y-Cyw ('the road of the chicken') I smiled to three cross-armed locals who seemed, reasonably enough, quite baffled by this English out-of-towner in shorts and sandals hurriedly thrown out of a car that had driven off at some speed. I enquired about the footpath for politeness' sake, to which they seemed even more suspicious, so, making my excuses, I walked on, back the way I'd come, which no doubt confused them further.

Brin Eos was a bucolic, sunlit vision – lush long grass with buttercups, cuckoo flowers, vetch. There were swallows overhead and a blackcap singing. I knew, of course, that there would be no nightingales, but there at the bottom of the field was the feature I'd spotted on Google's satellite images. The ruin of Ty Bach. In 1888, rented by one John Isiah, it was a farmhouse with several outbuildings and 56 acres of pasture and woodland attached, including Brin Eos. Now, it is rubble-and-nettle foundations and ivy-clad, tumbling walls. I stood where the farmhouse once was, listening to the shouts of boys playing in a stream beyond, which came to me like voices from the place's former life.

Exactly when and how Brin Eos got its name is impossible to say. Like the Gaelic toponyms I'd encountered on Islay, it might be no older than the century in which the tithe document records it; or, possibly, its origins could be much older, inspired at some unwritten moment by a real nightingale singing from copsy scrub. Whichever is true, it occurred to someone at some point. What was going on here? Were these really places where nightingales once were in

Wales and have since disappeared? Many of the place names do pair the bird with very believable nightingale habitats: *Cileos* 'nightingale nook', *Pant-y-eos* 'the nightingale hollow', *Llwyn eos* 'nightingale copse'.[1] And some of these are in the parts of Wales where nightingales were once reported to breed. Even in the early years of the twentieth century, parts of Glamorgan and Monmouthshire apparently had small populations of nightingales in the river valleys (as far west as Bridgend and Port Talbot, the region of Brin Eos). Perhaps, then, some of the names really did refer to the actual bird. The enigma of *eos* persists.

I am lucky when it comes to nightingales. They are, almost literally, on my doorstep. Even in the shut-down days of winter, the places where I find nightingales in spring feel as though they hold on to a last gasp of summer in breath-held anticipation of the birds' return. Here in the Weald, I'm in prime nightingale territory. They can turn up anywhere there is good territory round here. Some years ago, living on the border of Sussex at the time, near Glydwish, I heard a nightingale from bed one night. It sang the next night too. Lured into the street, I followed the sirenic notes, tracked them down a third of a mile from my house to a tiny patch of bramble right by the A21. The bird sang for several nights more before, presumably, flying on to try new territory, perhaps disconcerted at the competition from passing traffic. Last year I heard one on my local patch in Headcorn – a large oaky common just across the street. This one sang from a roadside hedgerow for weeks.

My nightingale place is very old. Dering Wood has been around since before the Norman Conquest, and may even predate the arrival of Germanic-speaking peoples in this land of the *Cantii*, the original folk of Kent. It is a special wood in that regard, much used, worked, altered, and enjoyed over the centuries in different ways, but there remains today a distinctive medieval feel to its network of wood banks and ditches and assarted edges (woodland cut away to create fields). No doubt some of this antiquity encourages its modern reputation as the 'screaming wood' – it is purportedly the most haunted village in England. There are no trees of serious age now, but there is much evidence of historic coppicing, a practice that would have once been common and extensive right across the Weald, now carried out specifically for nightingales at Dering by the Woodland Trust. It's one important reason why nightingales like it so much here in the Weald. It's not the trees *per se*, but what is produced *underneath* the trees by patterns of coppicing: clearings in the canopy where light can penetrate to the floor and allow scrub to grow into thick knots and tangles. However it is, or was historically, created (humans, foraging herbivores, fire, storm), it is this understorey that nightingales need for nesting. It's why you will also find nightingales outside of woods, in open, thicket-rich scrubland.

The medieval Weald must have provided lots of ideal habitat, with its woodland pastures and pig pannage 'dens', and sustainable, rotational coppicing for charcoal and timber. Medieval *wuda* were not silent and primeval; they were peopled, busy, working places for much of the year, smoky with colliers' fires, ringing and rasping to the axe and billhook and saw. Nightingales thrived on this fundamental of medieval life and economy. If our ancestors

knew the nightingale's song well, it is because they knew
and managed their woods well too.

This evening I am in Dering with my younger daughter.
As in most years, I've been visiting the site as often as
possible since the beginning of April. I can never know
for sure that I've heard the very first male of the season
back on Dering turf, but the hope is to catch their
arrival — that ecstatic moment when the woods are
startled and stunned. It's Harriet's birthday. Yesterday was
mine. We were both born (37 years and 20 minutes
apart) in the primrose brilliance and dalliance of spring,
and the time of nightingales. We have come for a birthday
blessing.

Later in the season there is no waiting and no guessing.
In May I will hear the song as soon as I open the car door
and it will reel me into the woods' interior. This birthday
evening, I lead Harriet to my usual spot down paths off
paths until we reach one especially narrow track that is
nearly always thick with squelching clay, whatever the
season. Tall, well-spaced oaks tower over a dense growth
of hornbeam and birch saplings, with a low, dense
understorey of bramble and honeysuckle. Nightingale
Alley, I call it.

I wander slowly, listening, pausing every few metres.
Several times I think I've got one, fooled by phantom
refrains from song thrushes. The evening dims. We wait
on (or I do at least; Harriet is more distracted by leaves
and puddles). Thrushes. Robins. Wrens. And then,
immediately loud and on cue as I pass by its hiding place,
one sings, as though it had every devious intention to
startle me. Harriet hears it too and looks up. The evening

is split by a cleaving, moon-bright note. The heart swells.
The woods grow.

Nightingales have that ability like no other British bird.
However briefly heard, however often heard, the song is a
force, a genesis, as every medieval love poet knew well, for
'the wodes waxen grene', as one English lyric states, 'when
the nyhtegale singes', or, as Geoffrey Chaucer puts it in
The Parliament of Fowls, the song 'clepith (calls) forth the
grene leuys (leaves) newe'. You couldn't move for
nightingales in the rarefied worlds of medieval romance,
debates and dream-visions. Even then the bird had
transcended its own poetic fame, as it continued to do,
fervently, for centuries to come. If you wander through a
wood or grove or blossom-fringed meadow in spring and
hear a nightingale, whether you realise it or not, you are
inside a medieval poem, transported out of time and
yourself to play the solitary wanderer happening upon or
contemplating love in some leafy, secluded dell.

It's how the best of medieval nightingale poems begins
(which happens to be the best medieval owl poem too).
The Owl and the Nightingale, written at the height of
fashion for avian songsters in vernal scenes, takes place *in
one sumere dale / In one supe diȝele hale* (hard-to-find nook).
These secretive places do curious things in medieval
poems; they are portals to other worlds, discoveries,
revelations, like the nightingale's song itself.

Nightingale alley is my *diȝele hale*. It is the best spot in
the wood for nightingales. From year to year, I can usually
count several birds defending their territories along a
track 100 paces in length. There are good numbers
elsewhere in Dering, but this is the site claimed by the
biggest number of males, and for six brief weeks it
becomes a nightingale echo chamber. The birds are often
very close to the path, though no easier to see for that.

Even when they sing in more open or higher spaces (as they sometimes do earlier on in the season, retreating progressively into thicker depths as the weeks go by), the close lattice of branches still makes it very difficult to pinpoint the source of the song.

The Owl and the Nightingale poet understood these difficulties. One of the defining and memorable qualities of the poem, what makes it a first in English literature, is that its nightingale is richly informed by ornithological realities as well as conventions of genre. The comedy of the poem often results from this incongruity: a nightingale who, although female because it was long believed (even by John Clare, apparently) that the female bird did the singing, is self-consciously aware of her species' mythical status in human culture and plays (or denies) it to full advantage in arguing her case. The poet knowingly and repeatedly includes naturalistic aspects of the nightingale's appearance or habits that clash with the romanticised figurative qualities of her celebrated poetic persona. To the owl, her opponent is a 'dim' and 'foul' colour, just a *lutel soti clowe* 'little sooty ball', which isn't too far from the truth. Right from the start, the bird is located in real nightingale habitat in *ore vaste þicke hegge / Imeind mid spire & grene segge* 'one impenetrable, thick hedge / Intermingled with reeds and green sedge'. She conducts nearly the entire debate, unseen, from the middle of dense scrub, much to the irritation of the owl, who later insults the nightingale for living *Þar þornes boþ & ris idraȝe* 'where thorns and twigs are tangled', *Among þe wode* (weeds), *among þe netle*, the sorts of undesirable, untidy places where *men worpeþ hore bihinde* 'people thrust out their backsides' to do *hore node* 'their business'.

Tonight, one sudden song is my lot. But it's enough. It means they are here and it has all begun. Harriet is asleep

on me now. What has she really heard? She's three today
and won't remember this evening, but I want to think that
a song so loud and sensational will find its way to the edges
of her subconscious somehow and nestle there. Remember
this, I want to say. I don't know how much longer it will
keep singing, but you heard it here. Remember that.

Why are there no nightingale place names in England?
This was a species that resonated with great power and
beauty in the medieval poetic imagination – peerless bird
of the age, 'immortal Bird!' long before Keats called it so
– that was assuredly present, abundant and widespread
across its range in the hedgerowed pastures and coppiced
woodlands of medieval England; that, like a cuckoo, must
surely have been a familiar, easily heard sound, a song of
spring; that has an unparalleled vocal capacity to affect
place in the most sensational way; and yet it is nowhere
to be seen in the names of England's towns and villages.
It is silent.

It is a conspicuous and strange absence, as though the
bird were wryly repeating its own famed invisibility,
refusing to emerge. I've heard it said that nightingales
were just too abundant – there were so many that to call
a place after a nightingale wouldn't sufficiently differentiate
it from another nightingale place. Perhaps, but this doesn't
stop, for instance, crows turning up in place names, as
we'll see in chapter ten. Was it that the old name itself,
nihtegale (pronounced with four syllables: '*nicht-uh-
gahl-uh*'), was just too much of a mouthful? Or was it that
nightingale, old as the name is, and familiar as it is now to
everyone whether they've heard one or not, wasn't
actually the term used by the ordinary person?

The last possibility is an argument that has been suggested, on the basis that there is, in one Old English glossary, a possible alternative for nightingale: *hearpe*, 'the harper'. If this was true, then it's feasible (though impossible to prove) that the various 'harp' names to be found in numerous counties in England are nothing to do with human harpers, but actually places where nightingales were heard. Think of that, should you happen to live in Harpsden in Oxfordshire, Harpham in Yorkshire, Harcourt in Shropshire, Harpenden in Hertfordshire, or Harpley in Norfolk. These places might just be the few, obscure, long-lost survivors of a name that was once used all over the country to describe the harp-sweet notes of the nightingale.

Despite these invisibilities and silences, there is one aspect of place that is always very apparent when it comes to British nightingales. In the most literal, straightforward sense of place as location, nightingales make themselves markedly present or absent through their choice to breed, almost entirely, in only one of Britain and Ireland's four countries, and even then confining themselves largely to the more southerly half of that country. Limits and demarcations are and always have been a characteristic part of this bird's story in Britain, the far north-western outpost of their Eurasian range. At the edges of the nightingale's territories (such as in the Welsh Marches) this effect is intensified, and especially so because the species' outermost limits present a bold border across England, as though nightingales had some grand architectural oversight in determining their range. Traditionally speaking, this boundary is said to reach between the Humber and Severn rivers, stretching diagonally north-east to south-west like an invisible glacier, or some Roman wall beyond which nightingales have rarely dared to go for fear of the natives.

These questions about where one may encounter or may not encounter nightingales are very old. People have been aware of the basic facts for many centuries. Gerald of Wales, as well as remarking that nightingales steered clear of his own country, wrote that they could not be found in Ireland either; a contemporary author, Alexander Neckam, reported that the species 'abhors those places made unpleasant by the great cold'. *The Owl and the Nightingale*, in typical witty fashion, turns this received wisdom to comic use. The owl berates the nightingale for not travelling to countries where song is much needed because life is hard: 'why do you never sing in Ireland or Scotland, or Norway or Galloway?' The nightingale provides an explanation, echoing hostile attitudes of the time towards Irish and Scottish populations: 'It's all wilderness and wasteland there', and the people wild animals'. 'What on earth would I do there with my song?' she exclaims spitefully.

It was these thicket edgelands of the nightingale that commanded my attention more and more, for it seemed to me that these were the places where the nightingale paradox might be most concentrated. Borders have that sort of intensifying effect; liminal spaces where the difference between one thing and another are most obvious by way of immediate proximity, but where the differences can also become unclear, so that what ought to clearly distinguish actually ends up blurring. I wanted to find these frontiers, to understand how listening to nightingales in such places might be different, how the birds maybe inhabit these places differently to those I know in the nightingale capital of Britain. How, too, were places on the edge where nightingales once were, but have now gone, affected for those who knew their former presence?

I knew that our nightingale populations have been dwindling for some time (since the 1960s), but I hadn't appreciated how fast it seems to be happening. Far from pushing further north as other species are doing in our warming climate, nightingales are doing the opposite in Britain, and, in keeping with this enigmatic bird, no one is entirely sure why. Their movements are producing a strange, simultaneous advance–and–retreat, whereby they fly north from Africa in spring, reaching our shores and establishing breeding territories across England within their traditional range, but slowly, like spring in reverse, that progress is also moving further and further south.

In the spring of 2023, a week after Harriet and I listened to our birthday bird in Dering Wood, I travelled to Lincoln. Here, so I thought, was the most northerly outpost for English nightingales, on a Wildlife Trusts reserve near the city, not so far south of the old Humber-to-Severn line in the sand. But the map of nightingale places in England needs redrawing.

Grahame Hopwood was waiting at the door of his workshop when I arrived. He shook my hand enthusiastically and welcomed me in with big smiles. He wore battered work boots and, despite the cool temperatures so far that spring, was in shorts. The day was certainly warm, the first gloriously spring-bright day of the season in fact, but I couldn't help feeling that Grahame was the sort of person to embrace shorts all winter long – a man driven by a perpetual optimism, a deep love of the outdoors, and an urge to spend as little time as possible indoors. Born in Stockport, he has worked in conservation all his life, joining the RSPB straight from school, then working in various jobs in Scotland for much of his career, before arriving at Whisby Nature Park in 2004. From that moment on, for the last 20 years, it's all been about nightingales, here at what he calls his 'spiritual home' for the bird.

'Nightingales have been here since 1985, so I've never not known them at Whisby. Back then, Lincolnshire had a good population. If you look at the county reports for that decade' – he quickly pulled a small pamphlet from a shelf of neatly labelled and dated nightingale scientific literature – 'you can see there's only one or two sentences for the species: there was no need to write anything more – doing fine, move on!

'The birds here probably colonised from a patch of woods east of the city called the Limewoods. They've not been there for years, but this place scrubbed up after the gravel pits were decommissioned and produced a great alternative. It became a reserve in 1989. When I turned up as assistant warden in 2004 I asked my boss if I could start doing more with the suitable nightingale habitat, and that's what I've been doing ever since – I'll show you how when we get out there. I can't prove it of course, but I'm sure the work we were doing here at that time contributed to the increase in our population. If you look at this –'

I glanced quickly at the data on his computer screen: 12 singing birds in 2005, up from 7 the previous year, and then 15 by 2012. Grahame talked on, pulling out more scientific papers while he spoke about the reserve's ecology (studies on the impact of deer, on the importance of scrub-woodland, surveys for specific years), skipping from one topic to the next while I scribbled notes as fast as I could. He delighted in the minutiae of nightingale conservation. One hand-drawn survey from 2013 had immaculate red annotations on a map of a section the reserve, not only recording the exact dates when he heard individuals singing, but tracking with neat, dashed lines the birds he heard singing simultaneously from specific locations. It was a beautiful document. You could construct a chronological soundscape map in your head, charting the nightingale event over the course of one spring – the arrivals, the sequences, the proximities and competitions.

'Synchronised registration, that's what it's called. It's the only way to be sure of how many birds are on site; you have to hear individuals singing at the same time, otherwise you can end up with a completely inaccurate picture: just because one sings in front of you and then a minute later one sings behind you doesn't mean it's not the same bird. Anyway, look, shall we head out? Let me show you the nightingale's spiritual home.'

As we walked, I asked Grahame more about his attachments to this place and its nightingales. He stopped.

'You know what they call me? The nightingale man of Whisby,' he said, with a smile that was half dead proud and half self-mocking. 'The two are inseparable for me. Whisby is synonymous with nightingales. You can't have one without the other.'

I'd noticed throughout our conversations that Grahame spoke about nightingales in the present tense, describing them and this place as though the marriage were still intact. It isn't. Grahame had sombrely informed me when I first contacted him about Whisby that nightingales had failed to return in 2022, after 37 years breeding on the site. They did not turn up in 2023 either. Grahame wasn't ignoring the absence, or denying it, but it was as though he couldn't get out of the habit of talking about them as if they were still here, or believing somehow that if he keeps them here in the present tense of his own words that maybe they will return.

'I really hope they will. I think they will. There's some evidence that the birds further south are holding their ground now, even increasing in numbers, so you just have to hope that those places will be the nurseries, if you like – the birds will start to recolonise old territories further north in coming years. Some people will think that's pie-in-the-sky, and maybe they're right, but I have to be optimistic. There's no other way to be in this game, otherwise what's the point?

'But there's no doubt last year was a very sad year for me when the nightingales didn't come back. A little bit of me died.' He looked at me earnestly for the first time that morning. 'Other people feel the same, I know. From all around, counties where the birds were decades ago but not now, this is where people came. I'm getting calls even now, from people who don't know the birds aren't here any more, or who are hoping they've returned, to ask, are they here? Have they arrived yet? People want to hear the bird. And why wouldn't you? Me, I love coming at night, about one in the morning. You ever done that? It's fine hearing them in the day, but there's nothing like nightingales in the dead of night. Something to do with sound travelling better at night, and the fact that most other things are silent. Now, this is perfect habitat. It's one of our hotspots.'

We stopped at a crossroad of paths, busy with dogwalkers and amblers. In one of the quadrants there was thick undergrowth of bramble, rose, hawthorn – all the expected plants. Above was a small oak, a good perch for a singing male. 'A few years ago we had a female nesting right there, just a few metres off the path; it was really popular with photographers. She didn't seem to care a bit. It's one of the reasons I have to be really strict with dogwalkers though – you just can't have dogs going off the paths in a place like this. The birds don't seem to mind humans, but then we're not rummaging about in the bushes; a dog is basically just a wolf. Too many dog owners don't understand the unseen damage that can be caused when their pets are off the leads and in the undergrowth.

'Now,' Grahame said, a little further along the path around the lake, 'can you see through there?'

'Yes,' I said.

'Exactly. You can see through. It's getting leggy. Come next winter I'll have my eye on a space like that as somewhere to coppice. You can see how the scrub has started to shrink back and there's more and more open ground. Some of that is good; nightingales need open patches alongside scrub to forage for insects. But as it stands now, that's probably no good for them: these ashes have got too tall and there's not enough light getting in.'

I thought of Dering Wood, of the Weald, of all the woodlands across the country in the Middle Ages that were coppiced like this. The difference, of course, was that Grahame was doing it specifically for nightingales, but the systems are the same, and Grahame's work at Whisby was the legacy of the Norman *copeiz* (copse) and the early English *graf* (grove). All around Coot Lake, there were woodland stretches in different stages of coppiced regeneration; some ready for cutting back again, some in perfect condition right now, and some that will achieve perfection in a few years. Grahame took me through a gate marked 'Sanctuary, no entry', to see a newly coppiced patch.

'We've just finished up here this winter gone.' It looked like outright deforestation, but on closer inspection you could see the great care behind the work. The trees right down to the ground, all the trunks and branches sectioned, sized and piled. 'We had broad-leaved helleborines come up here when we first cut it back; that's one of the lovely things you find when you coppice, the dormant seedbank of plants that's been underneath all the scrub just waiting to come up. Amazing.' Already you could see the seedling scrub plants starting to push up through the earth. Grahame bent down to pull up a tiny sycamore.

'It will take eight to twelve years before it's ready, but it will be here for them when they come back.' He might have been talking of a child who'd recently flown the nest, with all the complicated feelings that come to any parent dealing with that moment in their life. Keeping a room ready and waiting is one way of coping, of keeping a home homed.

I'd originally intended to visit Whisby on the hunt for Britain's most northerly nightingales; that place where I could get a sense of the nightingale's half-presences and near-absences, put one leg either side of the border, as it were. In one, rather sad sense, I'd achieved that. In Grahame's words there was still a lingering half-presence of nightingales. And here on the spot of what was for some time the proud, most northerly place for the species, their recent departure had thrown into sharp focus what it meant for nightingales to be or not be in a place. Before I left Grahame that morning I asked him if he knew where the most northerly location for the birds now is.

'That honour goes to a place called Castor Hanglands. It's to the west of Peterborough, about an hour's drive from here. Give it a go there.' He shouted after me as I left, 'And go at night.'

If there's one place that perhaps deserves more than any other to bear the new title of most northerly site of nightingales on the north-west frontier of Eurasia, somewhere in the far top corner of Cambridgeshire where it borders with Northamptonshire and Lincolnshire is a top contender. This part of England is, after all, Clare country, and if there's one English poet to be eternally associated with the nightingale other than Keats, it has to be his contemporary, John Clare. As exquisite as Keats' ode might be, to any naturalist Clare's exact, in-the-moment description of discovering a nightingale's nest while on hands and knees among brambles is the more thrilling of the two, for the simple fact that Clare, to use his own words against Keats' inexperience, has 'witnessed the things he describes'.

Castor Hanglands nature reserve is in the heart of John Clare country, right by Helpston, the village where the peasant poet grew up and lived for much of his life, across the road from Swaddywell (Clare's Swordy Well), and containing as part of the reserve, alongside ancient woodland perhaps as old as Dering, Ailsworth Heath (Clare's beloved Emmonsales). There's every chance that Clare may have heard and seen nightingales on these very sites. Certainly, he would have known them in the general surrounding area, because they formed part of the little sphere of local living that was so profoundly important to him; he knew all things in his Helpston world intimately. These things are the subjects of his poems. To leave this vicinity was, for him, to be 'out of my knowledge', and, tragically, out of his mind (he ended his days in an asylum). Clare lived, as most did, a way of life largely unchanged since the Middle Ages, but right on the border of change in his time.

This, then, was where my search to know the places of nightingales ended up, nowhere near as far north as I'd intended (even Lincoln was some way south of where I'd originally imagined I'd find myself), and only 12 miles from where I'd contemplated cuckoos on the edge of Yaxley in winter. Driving home from Whisby, I thought of what the sudden loss of that site for nightingales in 2022 means on a national scale. I visualised a map of what the nightingale border looks like now, beginning somewhere on the Suffolk coast and proceeding uncertainly to south-west Norfolk, through Cambridgeshire and Northamptonshire (just), and steadily down by Oxfordshire and Berkshire way until it reaches the Severn at the traditional western end point. In most of the counties south of this line, remaining populations are sparse and declining. Now, not only the Humber but the Wash too is north of the wavering limit of nightingale land. In this diffuse and erratic arc that continually closes in on England's south-east stronghold, Castor Hanglands is an outlying site on a frail finger of land that reaches towards Lincolnshire, as though pointing ruefully towards former territories.

Go at night, Grahame said. It's in the name, after all. Very little altered from Old English *nihtegale*, the 'night singer' is another of those ancient Germanic names found in the earliest records. Like the owl, it was clearly a bird that was experienced as part of the nocturnal biophony, and it must have pervaded people's feelings for place powerfully. Predictably, the poet of *The Owl and the Nightingale* turns the songster cliché on its head: as far as the owl is concerned, there is nothing to her opponent *bute chatering* – 'once you've done twittering you're out of all talent!' She even jokes on the name, stating that it should more accurately be *galegale* (which we might translate in the owl's invective as 'blabberblabber'!) The nightingale's tendency to sing ceaselessly for long periods – the great outpourings of passion in poetic terms – is little more than an irritation to the owl, who argues that the nightingale has far too much to say for herself.

Other treatments take the famed nocturnal voice more seriously. There is an Exeter Book nightingale riddle. And the thing it emphasises more than anything else is the tremendous, ever-changing song:

> I speak through the mouth with many voices,
> sing with modulations, frequently switch to
> my head-voice, holler loudly,
> keep up my customs, do not hold back from cries.
> Old evening-poet, I bring to noblemen
> bliss in the towns when I bellow
> with bending voice; still in their homes
> they sit silently. Say what I am called,
> who, like an actress, the jester's song
> loudly apes, announces to men
> many greetings with my voice.

The giveaway here is 'evening-poet', a heavy nudge in the direction of 'night-singer' (early poets *were* singers, in the true oral tradition). The other clincher is the sheer volume of words for sound and voice, as though the composer of this riddle wanted to overwhelm the reader or listener with vocabulary as the nightingale does with its diverse vocalisations. It is not so apparent in translation, but the accumulating Old English words (repeatedly given as just 'voice' above) dominate the description: *reord, singe, cirm, hleoþre, stefn, styrme, sceanwendwise, woþ.* This poetic excess is really no excess at all. Nightingales do possess an extraordinary level of complex richness in their songs and calls – more than 1,000 discrete sounds, it has been shown, through combining different units from a vast repertoire

– so it doesn't seem too far-fetched at all to see them as performers.

All that vocal dexterity is nicely captured in the riddle too, particularly through the Old English words *wrenc* 'modulation' and *wrixle* 'vary'. Both these words appear in one line in the riddle, and the alliteration on that *wr* sound pinpoints for us the idea of change: the root of both words come from a much older term that carries the sense of twisting and turning (hence 'wrench' and 'wrist' in modern English). Another meaning of *wrenc*, in fact, is 'trick', so in its own way the nightingale, like the cuckoo, is a trickster. Here, again, we have a bird beguiling us with transformations – the untraceable paths of a nightingale's ever-changing song.

Despite all that, I realised I'd never actually heard nightingales at night. At dawn and dusk, yes, but not in the dead of night as Grahame had keenly recommended. That, then, was the plan. I would wait it out till dark, and then find nightingales at Castor Hanglands, as late as I could force myself to stay up; go out of my knowledge, as I'd done with owls, into estranging and transforming night.

In the end, I was there long before dusk. I couldn't resist the usual temptation to try and see the bird that is everywhere and nowhere, and I'd run out of ways to hold off my impatience that afternoon. I heard them immediately. They were singing well, perhaps encouraged by the welcome and sudden warmth of the day after a cold spring. Following one song off the path through glades between scrub to an ash arbour, I saw the bird with staggering ease – no squinting and ducking or stretching and straining as usual. It was high on a hawthorn, plain as a blackbird on a roof. The nightingale was, for once, unquestionably there. I thought of Clare 'creeping on

hands and knees' to see his bird somewhere not far from
here, as I crouched in thick beds of dog's mercury by a
decaying elder to watch mine.

This bird, for all its persistence and gusto, probably
wasn't singing for a mate, but rather to warn off competitors.
Usually, only unpaired males sing in the small hours,
because the demands and risks of such nocturnal efforts
are a virile demonstration of potency. This day-singer, at
any rate, didn't seem to mind my presence at all. Just as the
riddle says, it kept up its ways, did not hold back. I'd caught
it at full pelt, launching those climactic, brimming refrains
that come at the pinnacle of performance, like a guitarist
peaking a knockout solo on a wailing, string-bending
note. It is nightingale blarney, delivered with a machine-
gun staccato. Through binoculars I could see perfectly its
thrown-back head, the wide, convulsing beak, and below
that, a gulping, bull-frog throat that throbbed as though it
were the engine of life. A long, preposterous tongue might
have emerged at any second.

When I returned hours later for more of the same,
there was no singing. Parked up some distance away, I
leaned on my car and listened. That afternoon in between
visits I'd read up on what Grahame had said about sound
at night. It's true. Sound does behave differently at night.
It travels better on the warm air up high, which refracts
sound waves down to earth, rather than up into the sky
as it does during the day when the air temperature is
cooler. No wonder a place could feel so affected by this
bird: the wrench of a song under spell at night's sleight of
wrist, the wrixling dark that twists and turns like a
nightingale's song the properties of sense and the sensable,
even sound itself.

This much was true for Peterborough's human nightlife
at least, and the roar of traffic south of Castor on the main

carriageway to Leicester. I'd not noticed it earlier at all, but now I could hear it as clear and loud as if it were only a field's distance from me. It wasn't ideal, the tarmac roar and city boom, but back in the woods the sound was muffled and my attention framed by the trees' cover.

I passed through the gate on the Hanglands' north-west edge ('Hush! Let the woodgate softly clap', Clare writes), turning off my torch as I re-entered. No light this time. No seeing. I stood and listened, ready for one to strike up any second and to follow its trail into the glades. I waited. The last ticks of late-to-bed blackbirds, a muntjac coughing, but that was it. And then nothing at all.

All that operatic exuberance this afternoon! If a nightingale could give itself so freely to song by day, I thought, then others – lone males in want of mates in the dead of night – would surpass even this display of machismo. The turn of April into May should mark the beginning of the crescendo of nightingale song season. Surely the birds couldn't all be paired yet? More likely, the birds were held back by the prolonged April cold, particularly at night when temperatures had often struggled to get above freezing – the same conditions that Grahame fears did for the Whisby nightingales. In a complete circuit of Castor's wood pastures, an hour or so of wandering, I heard nothing more than the occasional, briefest snatches, each one luring me towards it for seconds and then disappointing, silent the moment I changed direction. I gave up on the night and traipsed back towards the car.

Then, as I passed through the gate at the wood's boundary and turned on my torch to light my way across the fields, the blackness immediately by my unexpecting right ear exploded. I looked at my torch, quickly and instinctively switched it off, momentarily confused by the remarkable timing; it was as though I'd flicked some detonation and the torch were wired to some invisible fuse. Perhaps I had startled the poor thing, and now it vented its tiny nightingale spleen at me in tremendous ire. My first nightingale of the year had been like this, another practical joker jumping its song upon Harriet and me in Dering Wood. That moment had surprised me too, but this time had the split-second force of miracle about it – all that volume and power bursting from the black silence and space.

The bird didn't make it into full song. Instead, it raved briefly between long intervals, expelling and giving everything in seconds at a time, and then, no less suddenly, gulping back down its own jack-in-the-box song. I imagined the bird's beak going at it in the dark, then trapping shut, then sprung again a minute later to release whole caverns of sound to the gaping night. How does a nightingale occupy a place? Like this, I thought. Like this. It does not suffuse gently, as the curlew does, or faintly and distantly with echoic repetition, like a cuckoo. It does not lend its voice, like the birds of the marsh. With a nightingale, it is not the place that has the song, but the song that has the place. It seizes, devours, wholly and instantly – a sudden, huge song that leaps and recoils from the subterranean depths of something far smaller than itself.

I stood an arm's length from the bird, willing each last fit of nightingale splendour from the long pauses. I imagined the arc of notes, issuing from a small, dim bird in a thicket by a gate on the edge of a wood, sent up to sing down night-migrating females, then travelling on and fast, down again, to be heard somewhere not far from here by someone else, an unintended listener on the edge of the nightingale's northernmost place in Britain. I hoped they knew just what they were hearing.

Hawk in the Wood

Wroxton, Oxfordshire ~ Hawkhurst and the Weald, Kent

You'd never guess the meaning of Wroxton in a lifetime of guessing. As with Yaxley, the name remains firmly hitched to the past, well removed from anything that makes sense in modern English. Neat and perfect Wroxton, just west of Banbury in Oxfordshire, is what we like to call a quintessential English village. It is all traditional thatch and local stone the colour of heather honey. There is, as you'd guess, a duck pond (with a thatched duck house), and a church built of the same ochre ironstone as the cottages.

On the day I visited, on a muggy day in August, the place was a strange contradiction of busy trade and curious desertion. I saw few people. There were more red kites, almost one for every time I glanced up. All Saints Church, dusky walls darkened more by rain, had a glossy bush of deadly nightshade at its porch. The cottages' thatch was in various states of repair and disrepair, like the moulting mallards on the pond. One roof was mid re-thatching just that morning – men up precarious ladders with sheaves of reeds ready for the laying. Others were dark and dank with age in the rain, and others brightly smart with recent replacement, including the North Arms, one of two pubs in the village that have both long been closed. I wiped one street-front window and peered through cobwebbed glass to make out a sad wooden table by a vacant inglenook wanting light and warmth, just as the table's dusty forms were missing the comfort of a backside or two. You get the best view from the other side of the building. One of the attic windows is from where, in 1852, William Kalabergo jumped three storeys to escape police after he'd murdered his uncle, but broke his leg on landing, was captured, tried, and hanged.

Not far from the North Arms, just across the road from the church, there is a splendid, not-so-little Jacobean pile behind high, gated walls and concealing trees. It was built on the foundations of a medieval Augustinian priory, and for the last 60 years has been the UK campus of an American university (little rural Wroxton, home to hundreds of American students).

What I really wanted to find, though, was just outside the village. At the end of Main Street and west to the junction at the old road to Stratford and Birmingham, there is a stone guide-post, sculpted and erected in the same century as the mansion. I went to find it in the drizzle because it pointed me towards the very best and most obscure of all Wroxton's treasures: the name itself, hidden behind strange, concealing words.

Wroxton means 'the buzzards' stone'. Take one *wrocc*, a buzzard, take more – that's *wrocca* – then add a *stan*, and put them together: *wrocca stan*. What was this stone? Something ritual? Just a prominent stand of rock, or a waymarker of some sort, much like its modern counterpart on the corner of the A422, perhaps also directing travelling traders east along the old routeways? It's easy to imagine a buzzard taking up familiar residence on a perch such as that, as we often see them now; totems on telegraph poles, mud-clumps mid-field. Unlike some birds, buzzards seem very sensible place identifiers to me. Almost as reliable as stone itself. When they're not sat, visible, contemplating the livelong day, they're soaring, often in twos or threes – turning slow, steady gyres above the higher reaches and ridges of land, which are attractive to us too because they are obvious and shapely landmarks. Buzzards' circular flights describe the contours of land beneath them, spiralling those geographies upwards into the regions of sky.

That typical soaring action of many raptors is, to my thinking, one reason why you'll find so many in place names. Except that, as at Wroxton, you often don't realise they're there. Look behind the wall and you'll discover more. Once you know a *wrocc* for what it is, you'll notice the Wroxalls, Wraxalls and Roxhill (all meaning the buzzards' nook or valley) in the Isle of Wight, Warwickshire, Dorset, Somerset, Wiltshire and Bedfordshire. There's more. Besides the eagles, Old English had lots of names for other raptors, nearly all of which seem to have been variously applied generalist terms for 'bird of prey' (no doubt changing or adapting in sense from place to place). A buzzard, for instance, could also be a *tysca*. Then there's *cyta*, the word that eventually produced modern 'kite' (you'll find that in Kidbrooke, south London), but that word too could refer to a buzzard. And both these species could also be a *putta* or *pyttel*, as could a harrier, a name that is preserved in places such as Putley, Putney or Pitshanger. *Wrocc, tysca, cyta, putta* or *pyttel* – there is no doubt, at least, that raptors ranged as widely as their names over the horizons of people's homes and imaginations.

And then, of course, there are the hawks. Old English *hafoc* – *hafoc* of the ridge in the charterlands of Berkshire, in Somerset and Buckinghamshire too, *hafoc* of the hill in Northumberland, *hafoc* of the lea in Hampshire. *Hafoc* (the 'f' is pronounced 'v') became hawk, and hawk became the standard English term the world over, and it is used, in the same way our medieval predecessors apparently did, in both very loose and very specific senses. *Hafoc* could include falcons as well, which means, all in all, that raptors are very well represented in our place names.

This chapter is about one *hafoc* in particular. A true hawk. Its scientific name, although comparatively modern in origin, speaks straight to a medieval identity: *Accipter gentilis.*[1] Noble hawk. Hawk gentil. There cannot be another point in history when goshawks were so apparent in human interests and fashions. And yet, unlike breeze-easy, scavenging kites and buzzards, in the wild this hawk is, nearly all the time, virtually impossible to see.

I was 36 when I saw my first goshawk. It happened as all the best encounters do, entirely of its own accord, not in any of the goshawk-likely spots in Britain to which I've travelled in hope over the years, to where I knew they could be seen on spring mornings when the breeze and your luck is right, but one Sunday in March in 2019 as I pushed baby Islay in a pram through a wood near Cranbrook on another mission to soothe her to sleep. It wasn't working – she was defiantly awake – and then, a goshawk. It surged towards us along the ride where I'd ended up and wasn't entirely sure where I was, and for a second or two it was right above us: an immature bird, autumn colours in spring, neat bronze arrowheads all down its breast and concentric stripes along its wings repeating in waves from its carpals down to the tip of its long, barred tail. Time rippled, radiating beyond the stone-drop centre of a hawk that had the spinning, magnetic power of its own glaring eye.

That was my first. Blessed at last at 36. Islay was one. She saw it, I'm sure, reclined skyward in her buggy when

I'd stopped short and stared up. I turned to her afterwards, as if for confirmation from the only other person around. The thin, mercurial flight of a goshawk's life had crossed briefly with ours. The moment was part of our bond, just as the owls had been the year before. My first goshawk, right there with my one-year-old for whom all things were firsts in the beauty and chance of the world.

I went back two days later. I desperately wanted to see the bird again, and as it turned out I wasn't the only person with a goshawk secret. That same Sunday afternoon I'd called my friend Stephen, a birdwatcher who lives nearby. He'd seen it too, and not just one.

'I saw a pair earlier this week. One chased the other into the trees just below where you were on the ridge.' We didn't say it, but we knew what this might mean.

I was there at daybreak, marching as fast as I could up an owl-dark track, anxiously hoping the birds would be calling dawn courtship through the trees so that I could track them. I needn't have worried. I heard them long before I reached the location: piercing, sharp notes, urgent, alarming, but deliberate and steady. I followed the sound – *kek kek kek kek kek* – straight to the very same triangular wedge of larch where my bird had soared overhead on Sunday. I saw them, not well, but there were two, certainly. The trees were well spaced, so that while the foreground was still benighted, dawn appeared broad between the thin verticals of black pines on the far side. I followed the birds quickly and quietly, catching brief views of smoky, vaporous shapes, visible for less than seconds across dawn spaces as they flew between night and day.

The sky was luminous that morning, golden as the gilded pages of a missal. I remember it so well because there are few times when familiar places have been so estranged as to become unknown again. I realised, days later, that the location of those first goshawk encounters was not a new part of the forest to me at all, but I'd arrived via different paths and not recognised where I was. And then goshawks appeared. There were hawks in the wood. And the sky was on fire. A change in light can have that effect: the way a room can appear and feel so different at different times of day, or when fog or snow come down and transform your well-known world. Your whole mood can be affected. That morning in the forest was a dreamlike, dream-altered moment, when time and space were distorted in new arrangements. The birds and the place were mine alone, and only I and one other person knew anything about them.

Suddenly I had a goshawk place in my life, but in a way such a place had already existed for me for years. Four miles down the road from Cranbrook is the village of Hawkhurst. As with other seemingly straightforward place names, you can't immediately assume any hawk-named place in England is a safe bet: Hawk was a personal name in the Middle Ages, so sometimes, as in Hawkshead or Hawkswick, some chief's territory is memorialised rather than a bird's habitat. But Hawkhurst means what it says: this is a place where you can expect to find hawks. No misunderstanding; just follow the name. It's there in Domesday Book, one of the few settlements in the Weald interior that had become substantial enough by 1086 to be named separately as an independent village.

The Weald is full of hursts. The region of Hawkhurst, on the border of Kent and Sussex, must be the highest concentration of hursts in the whole country – Sissinghurst, Lamberhurst, Ticehurst, Wadhurst, Staplehurst, Chainhurst,

Speldhurst, Sandhurst, Goudhurst, and so on. Hurst means 'wooded hill'. It is just one term reminding us that the Wealden counties were once – and, relatively speaking, still are – wood specialists, thick with vocabularies of arboreal nuance. The language of wood is rooted deep, word and wood entwined and engrained like the warped Wealden timbers in our Cranbrook house. In the Germanic runic alphabet (still in use in early England), there were tree-letters; quite literally letters that signified different tree species. Some of these managed to survive for many centuries to come: Þ 'thorn' and 'ash', the rune name transferred to the letter Æ, were prickly hangers-on, knotty interlopers in the newfangled Roman alphabet ushered in with Christianity.

Just as early English had rich topographical vocabularies for marsh or hill, so it had for woodland. *Weald* itself describes extensive or ancient woodland, a *holt* is a single-species wood, and *fyrhth* (*frith* in modern English spelling) refers to 'land overgrown with scrub on woodland edge'. Then there's *sceaga* (shaw), meaning a 'strip of wood', *bearu* 'small wood' or *graf* (grove) 'coppiced woodland', and *hangra* (hanger) for 'wood on a gentle slope'.[2] Another speciality is *denn* (*fold* in Sussex), the woodland pastures where swine were grazed in autumn. These, too, are part of the dendro-ecology, clearings in the Weald that eventually became settlements in their own right: Benenden, Frittenden, Biddenden, Marden, Rolvenden to name a few. And then there are the trees themselves: Salehurst, 'the wooded hill with sallow trees', Ewhurst Green (yew), Elmley, Boxley, Ash, Appledore ('apple tree'), Oakleigh, Perry (pear) and Birchington.

Hawkhurst is a good hurst: a long, steady up-and-over approaching from south or north where the long climb on either side crests the ridge quickly at the busy crossroads. My father lived in a cottage on the hurst for the last ten years of his life, moving there in the same year I got my teaching post in Cranbrook. I have a memory for every contour of that hill, every approach and angle. I got stuck going up it once, not long after Dad had moved there, trying foolishly to make it home in a blizzard. The hurst had me. I reverse-slid the car back to level, ditched it, and battled up the hill on foot, stopping the night and next day at Dad's until it was possible to retrieve my car.

The main village of Hawkhurst, mostly Victorian in origin, occupies the top of the hill, where for a great many years a dark-stoned church with a bent weathervane stood deserted and boarded, but since converted to housing, like much of the land on every side of the hurst in recent years. The other village site, known as the Moor, is located at the bottom of the hill around a green, next to a far older, medieval church, and this is where the first Hawkhursters were probably located. They saw, knew and named their hurst and its hawks from the south, looking up and north.

Exactly *which* hawk is uncertain. England has several hawk towns and villages. Hawkley, Hawkhill, the various Hawkwells, Hawkinge, Hawkes End, and the Hawkridges (including the one in Berkshire where I went boundary hunting); all refer to hawks of one kind or another. Both true hawks to be found in Britain take their names directly from Old English: the *spearhafoc*, named well for the size of bird on which it typically preys, and *goshafoc*, the goose-hawk, which may also refer to its potential size of prey, or perhaps to its own brutish proportions (it is the largest Accipitrinae species in the world). Modern Hawkhursters cover all bases: approach from the west and you'll find a painted kestrel on their village sign, but come from the south, down where the original settlement was, and there's a fine wrought-iron silhouette of a hunting sparrowhawk.

Whatever species those first folk saw and named, these hills in the old Weald rich in woods and woody words were surely home to the true hawks, masters of the full-leaved, thick-forest chase, to be seen riding thermals on glorious days of warm promise. I like to think that my father's cottage on the very top of the hurst is built on former prime territory. In the long winter after he died, I spent a lot of time there alone, sat in his chair at his table by the fire, writing drafts of some of the early chapters of this book. When spring came and I went out again onto his tiny rooftop balcony on the roof of Hawkhurst, there was the Weald. On bright blue days at that time of year − the tantalisingly short window of opportunity when it's possible, though still difficult, to see goshawks − I could stand there and easily imagine a pair in extravagant display above me where land is closest to sky, the birds launching from their perch and soaring clear of the hurst horizon.

The number of times I've seen a sparrowhawk or a goshawk in full, still, and up close, is very few. They don't do in full, still, and up close. You see them in flashes and parts. Even sparrowhawks, numerous and seen quite commonly (I see them most weeks), are often only glimpsed in sheering horizontal strafes, sensed at the tilting up-and-over moment into hedgerow ambush. They are always on the cusp, at the in between of everything. Even more so for goshawks, which most people will never see once, or realise they have seen. Imagine looking at a bird lodged in the geometry of a thicket, the infinite angles slicing the thing into jigsaw pieces. The bird moves, moves again, and slowly you can say you've probably viewed enough different components to claim you've seen the whole by assembling it in your imagination. It's like that with hawks, except you might only piece together the whole from collected hawk parts over many years. You may never manage it in a lifetime.

I have, just once, seen a young, female sparrowhawk up close. One humdrum Monday she materialised on the fire escape balcony of the third-storey flat in which I lived at the time. I missed her arrival, though I'd been by the window the whole time. I could only surmise: a chance fly-by sighting too good to miss, shift and acceleration towards the next second, straddling the instant like the poor-bastard dove she shafted from the iron railing only moments before I looked down and saw her. She was there for a full half hour at her meal, plucking and tearing, just a couple of feet away on the other side of the glass, me on my stomach, face up against the pane watching a vision of hawk completeness.

I went back to the wood exactly one week after my first sighting. This time, my fifth visit, they weren't there. Everything was quiet. Stephen and I had been confident all week that they were setting up home on this western edge. It looked good: the trees here were larch, a favoured nesting tree of goshawks in coniferous forests, and the birds had been around for days, calling and chasing each other in the shadows. Had they gone? Was that it? Then, as if in answer, from some distance away – *kek kek kek kek kek*. I hunted the sound down to a large, rectangular block of Scots pines nearer the northern edge of the forest where the trees were packed in tightly and it was barely possible to see sky out the other side. I watched the birds

appear and disappear between trunks, then walked the
perimeter, hoping for better, closer views, but they
remained in the dense heart of the trees, well away from
the paths.

For the next two weeks I returned to the new block as
often as I could. I heard them always, saw them sometimes.
Occasionally, just occasionally, I'd turn a corner and a
pine-bark goshawk left off its pine-bark perch and slipped
away ahead of me. Once, the rasping alarms of jays drew
my attention into the interior and for a few seconds I
managed to get an irate goshawk in my sights before the
mobsters succeeded in driving it off. And then there was
the damp morning when I stood on one corner of the
plantation, tossing up which path to take, distracted by a
party of crossbills high in the pine-needle tops, when one
of the goshawks, the female by its size, landed right damn
in front of me. I froze, tried to pretend I wasn't there. She
froze. We looked directly at each other, each unsure who
should make the first move. She was wet, and her breast
looked stained with dark, oily drops of rain. Her eyes
burned deep yellow, the colour of autumn birch leaves. In
her beak, I saw, was a long twig. So she was nest-building,
or at least going through the motions. My hands were in
my pockets. Did I risk raising my binoculars? What a
view that would be. I inched out one hand, lifted it to my
chest, moving in painfully slow stages. The bird tolerated
me for a while, but as my fingers closed over one binocular
barrel she launched with wings like a cape and was gone.

By mid-April, both birds were silent, and the sightings
diminished. There was still the occasional intimation, the
sense that I'd missed something that had just happened
behind me, a sign that registered just enough to count.
But the birds had gone into the pine depths, and the brief
time of goshawk visibility was over.

Strangely enough, it was that period of waiting that
most noticeably affected my new connection to that
wood – a wood I'd known and walked in for years before
even the suggestion of a goshawk slipped into my head
and the forest fringes. They were there all right, but, like
nightingales, it was an absent presence. This is how it is
nearly all the time with goshawks. They are, in this way,
our top predator: fiercely secretive, rarely seen haunters,
cloak-and-talon hunters. In the absence of mammalian
predators such as lynx and wolf that once stalked British
woodlands, goshawks can still give us that tiniest feeling
of unnerving wildness that would have been a far more
real and serious prospect in our early ancestors' lives.[3]
Minacious, mad-eyed, nerves wired to lightning and fire,
tiger-striped. The comparison is not far-fetched. Like
tigers, goshawks might seem uncamouflaged, but the
stripes and bars across their plumage are highly effective
at breaking up and confusing outlines, as well as mimicking
the shades of shifting, broken light filtered through leaves.
And as with tigers, it's often only the behaviours of other
creatures that will alert you to their invisible presence.
With goshawks it's usually corvids, frequent prey birds as
well as keen-eyed, intolerant mobbers, sounding the alarm
in their torn voices. To me that spring, it was a frayed
savagery that crept into the rows of neatly planted pines.
It was an undoing, the narrow, tame corridors made wide
and wild.

Place in the grip of fear and fierceness. Of all avian
predators, the goshawk has the fiercest reputation.
Bloody-taloned and bloody-minded – an outright
lunatic, T. H. White suggests in *The Goshawk*, or

intransigent psychopath, as Helen Macdonald describes in *H is for Hawk*; the terror of its prey and the bane of any human who seeks to tame it, capable of reducing veteran falconers to traumatised, grey-haired wrecks through stubborn belligerence. It is a very old reputation, and like many of our old, still-surviving cultural perceptions and traditions, it is rooted, or achieves its most repeated and powerful expression, in the Middle Ages, crystallised into something like fact or dogma over more than a thousand years of history.

Bloody violence is central in the cluster of words in Indo-European languages that define birds of prey. *Accipiter*, raptor and hawk, all deriving from or akin to a group of Latin and Germanic words describing the actions of seizing, taking and holding, go back to very ancient *★kap*, meaning 'to grasp'.[4] It was not the eye – the piercing, orange eye – that gripped old imaginations when it came to articulating impressions of these birds; it was the clutching talons. *Hafoc* essentially means 'seizer' or 'grasper', and those other generalist raptor terms in use in early English, *putta* and *pyttel*, mean something like 'swoop' or 'throw down' (connected to the action of 'putting').

Of all the terms available in medieval Britain though, it was *raptour* that proved most influential to writers on the subject. In the late Middle Ages it became a popular and useful alternative to *hafoc*.[5] You can see its appeal when you look at the various words in modern English derived from Latin *raptus*: rapture, rapt, rape, rapacious, and so on, as well as closely related ravish, ravage and ravenous. All have something, again, to do with seizing, snatching, stealing, taking. At the root of this lexical knot is aggression, lust and violence, still very present in our sense of rape, for instance, but lost to more winningly romantic associations of 'ravish'. Middle English *raptour*

meant both 'bird of prey' and 'robber', and more than
one writer enjoyed playing with that double meaning.
The vicious plunderer-hawk is clearly present in
Bartholomew the Englishman's description of a goshawk
in his *Properties of Things*:

> *The goshawk is a real foul and is i-armed more with boldenesse*
> *than with clawes. And as moche as kynde [nature] bynemeth*
> *[defines] hir in quantite of body, he rewardeth hire in boldnesse*
> *of herte … heo [she] is a coveytous foul to take other foules, and*
> *for the takynge of other foules for pray heo is iclepid [called]*
> *aucipiter 'a raptour and a ravyschere'.*

Two giants of fourteenth-century English literature make
use of this reputation for rapacious ferocity. Geoffrey
Chaucer, in his Trojan War epic about the tragic love
affair between Troilus and Criseyde, features the
sparrowhawk in his description of the lovers' first, sexual
embrace. He poses a sinister rhetorical question to his
readers, which asks us to think of these human characters
as prey and predator: 'What myghte or may the sely
[innocent] larke seye / Whan that the sperhauk hath it in
his foot?' Instinctive killing and sexual desire are equated
very closely here. In reading those words we might well
think of the fact that there can, in truth, be a disturbingly
fine line between violence and arousal (though with
goshawks, as often with raptors and other predatory
creatures, the roles between sexes are reversed). As any
breeder of goshawks knows, male sexual display to a
female before she is ready may well result in fatality
(which is why in captive breeding programmes they are
kept in adjoining but separate aviaries until the right
moment). In the wild, there's a good reason why the
smaller male goshawk generally keeps clear of his mate,

dropping food to the nest with lightning speed, or calling for his partner to collect deliveries from a designated nearby post.

The other writer, and Chaucer's friend, John Gower, takes the *raptour* associations between sex, death and violence even further. In his retelling of the famous Greek myth of Tereus and Philomela – in which Philomela transforms into a nightingale to escape Tereus's rage – Gower, in an echo of Chaucer's portrayal of Troilus and Criseyde, depicts Tereus's rape of his sister-in-law explicitly as a raptor's predation. Metaphorically, Tereus becomes a goshawk:

> *[He] hield hire under in such wise [a way]*
> *That sche ne myhte noghte arise [could not get up]*
> *Bot lay oppressed and desesed [tormented]*
> *As if a goshawk hadde sesed [seized]*
> *A brid, which dorste [dares] not for fere*
> *Remue [escape]: and thus this tirant there*
> *Berafte hire …*

Tereus is a 'tirant raviner' in every sense, dramatically and gruesomely depicted by Gower as hawks are in many manuscript illuminations of his age: a granite, barred, muscled, clenching beast, pinning a duck or some other terrified bird to the ground, sometimes at its feast even while the creature is still alive. I think of my balcony sparrowhawk, me rapt at that furious bird intimately astride its ravaged prey.

Early in May, when I thought I'd probably seen the last of my goshawks, Stephen rang to say he'd found the nest, and that if I wanted to see it I should meet him at the location marked on the map he'd sent by email. There was that thrill again – the promise of more goshawk sightings, covert operations, the knowledge that we had this secret to ourselves. I made my excuses with the family and set off that very afternoon.

I'd half expected Stephen to blindfold me when I arrived at our rendezvous, spin me around several times, and then uncover my eyes when he'd led me to the site. The birds had nested where we'd hoped they might, right in the middle of the Scots pine block. It was a clever move on their part. The larch planation where we'd originally found them was small and sparsely planted, with no undergrowth to speak of. Any nest would not have been hard to find. By contrast, the Scots pine location had a thick understorey of birch and sweet chestnut, with tall, dense bracken beneath that, which made finding your way inside the block or getting to the other side practically impossible (I tried once, that August when the young had both fledged, and not only quickly lost my bearings, but then spent an embarrassingly long time escaping back to the path).

When we arrived at one corner of an adjacent plantation some way off from where I'd expected to end up, Stephen glanced, then walked up and down all nearby tracks to check we were alone. When he was sure no one was likely to pass by, he manoeuvred me into place behind a shield of sapling chestnut trees off the path.

'That's it. Just a little to the left, by that stick I've laid down there. OK, now through that gap there, look across into the trees. See where there are two growing close together, there, the ones in the sun at the moment? And then further back, behind them, there's a thick, shaded trunk, with a kink in it and a fork above that?'

'Got it.'

'Well not that one, but look through the fork, and sort of squint your eyes through the branches behind. You see?'

I didn't, and I was amazed that Stephen had found the nest at all, from that distance, from that angle. It took another few minutes before I finally found what Stephen was describing, and it appeared to me then with all the sudden magic of the goshawks themselves – a dark knot of branches, like a supersized squirrel's drey, wedged with seemingly careless and precarious haste in the top of a pine, and which seemed to me now impossible *not* to see. But, with typical goshawk evasion, it disappeared repeatedly behind a curtain of needled branches every time a breeze shifted them and the high, spindly pine tops swayed. When I lowered my binoculars, I had to retrace my steps according to Stephen's instructions each time, repeating the routine like some initiation: two sunlit trees close together, larger tree behind with a kink and a fork, look through the fork ...

'Here,' Stephen said, having set up his telescope, 'That's on full magnification; take a look.'

What I saw was eye, all eye – one giant, saturnine eye. I swore. 'That's what I said!' Stephen laughed.

It was goshawk parts again, disassembled elements that had so recently and unexpectedly come together for me. As if viewing the bird in a broken mirror. Most times it was a fragment of tail, shard of wing, back of the head – I usually couldn't tell, only knew that some piece of a tremendous bird was brooding and breathing up there, and that I was able to watch it. Just sometimes, at the right moment, the angle of the bird and the light and the movement of the branches were right, and I met that eye again. Despite the distance between us, it felt as though she was locking onto mine in a double voyeur's gaze. For the next month or so, this was how I saw the forest: a hawk's view of a hawk staring straight back at me down the wrong end of a telescope. Everything was condensed into that yellow eye.

My goshawks, though wild and wildly stunning, were only youngsters, first-time breeders not yet fully out of juvenile raiment. When I finally saw an adult, a full-grown female up close, it was like discovering goshawks for the first time all over again. Even from a distance I couldn't miss her. She was huge and magnificent, and as I approached she seized the space and me like a sharp change in the wind. She was a big and bloody maturity of hawk, and nothing about her disappointed.

She was Ellah, and she belongs to Emma and Mike Raphael, one of Britain's premier falconry display teams. As husband-and-wife duo they have been exhibiting their birds and talents up and down the country for decades, most especially for English Heritage. In season, there is not a single weekend when they are not at some venue and event flying raptors for the crowds.

It mattered not a bit to me that Ellah was a captive bird. The effect was quite the same, and anyway, when else would I ever get up *this* close to a goshawk? I'd seen her distantly earlier that day, flying to Mike's gloved fist, swinging her talons up in the final split seconds to devour the hand that fed her. The weather was warm and sultry, but she was an icy splinter. And now, right in from of me, even tethered to a bow perch, wild and wired instinct still raged inside her. Storm-dark, hoodlum-hunched, pyromaniac stare. Every inch and feather of her was the picture of goshawk, like the one in my childhood

Ladybird book: imperious pose against a red sky, haughty
as a church elder, with an eye, not yellow like my birds,
but the colour of best bitter viewed through glass in
winter sun.

She was perched forefront and centre, surrounded by
falcons – lanner, saker, merlin, peregrines, even a hoary
arctic gyrfalcon, the most prized of all falcons in the
Middle Ages, and the only bird on display to match Ellah's
size. It was a truly medieval line-up. These species were
the 'must have' noble accessories in the great, unparalleled
age of falconry. Like coveted coats of arms, they were
emblems of grand status. The literature of that age reveals
the reputation and grandeur of goshawks, 'iloved of hire
[their] lordes', as Bartholomew the Englishman says.
Besides Gower's accipitrine Tereus, Chaucer has one in
his *Parliament of Fowls*, with 'fetheres donne [dun] / And
grey', and Sir Thopas in *The Canterbury Tales* has a 'grey
goshauk on honde'. The twelfth-century Anglo-Norman
poet, Marie de France, has her knightly hero in *Yonec*
shapeshift into 'that noble bird' – a mature male of 'five or
six moultings' – and in a French retelling of Tereus and
Philomela contemporary with Gower's, the heroine has a
medieval noblewoman's knowledge of goshawks, falconry
terminology, and moult patterns. To look upon a goshawk
like Ellah is to be transported to the time and place of
these medieval writers.

'Superb, isn't she?' A woman dressed head to toe in
medieval attire – gaberdine, wimple, worsted stockings
– appeared by my side. 'Those eyes are mesmerising.
She's nine years old and they keep getting darker. They'll
go red eventually. She could live another decade yet,
fingers crossed.'

I smiled at her get-up. This was Emma. I'd arranged
to meet her and Mike at Battle Abbey near Hastings, to

see them fly Ellah over the grassy slopes where that famous event of 1066 reputedly took place, and to talk to them about medieval goshawks. The couple specialise in historical displays, and own a whole wardrobe of costumes ranging right through British history from the Romans onwards. Both of them share extensive experience of falconry as well as knowledge about the sport's history, but they have specified roles for their events. Mike is the practitioner. I only saw him from afar that day, a medieval austringer with his black labrador; silent, stern and as focused as his birds. Emma is the voice of the team, the entertaining – and not a little humorous – public face. ('Ellah is after only one thing ladies and gentlemen, and it's the same thing hubby wants from me. Food, ladies and gentlemen, pure and simple.')

'She seems so unbothered by everything,' I said, unsure whether I ought to be surprised or not that Ellah appeared totally unfazed by gawping onlookers.

'It's funny, she's completely comfortable at these events. She'll happily preen and bathe in front of crowds, but at home she's not like that at all. She's much more difficult – much more your typical goshawk. She's confident with her territory there and it makes her bolshy and impatient, like a stroppy teenager. Goshawks are naturally solitary, nervous birds, so they're not all that suited to public displays. For ages we put off having one because everyone said it just wasn't possible – don't even go there, they said! But then along came Ellah. She was three by the time we got her and already socially imprinted – that's how most falconry birds are reared these days – so a lot of the work had already been done. She was manned too – that's what we call habituating the birds to humans – which is also why she and the other birds you see here aren't unhappy around strange humans. Mike had hunted before with a goshawk, so he knew exactly what to do with Ellah, but it's true what they say about them: they are bad-tempered and highly strung, even when they're trained. You can easily have a collection of falcons, but one goshawk will take up every bit of time and patience you have. It can break you! Never the other way around — it will die rather than give in to force.'

The process of manning was comical to me. I'd read about it in White's *Goshawk*, when he walked his bird to Buckingham and nervous mothers wheeled their prams across the road. I'd seen it in action in David Cobham's 1980s television adaptation of White's book, in which the trainer sits in a pub with his pint in one hand and a hawk on the other, surrounded by old men and the fug of tobacco smoke. These moments seem ridiculous, alluringly eccentric. It struck me, though, that this wasn't the case for medieval people. Such was the popularity of falconry that many must have been familiar with birds of prey in the run of everyday things. In a time when humans and non-humans customarily and familiarly lived much closer together, coming across a hawk being manned cannot have been that unusual. What an enviable thing! Among the host of domestic and wild species that mixed and interacted with us in the busy, lively markets and public spaces of towns and cities in the Middle Ages, you might brush up against a peregrine one day, and a goshawk the next. These birds, too, were part of an experience of place that is foreign to us now.

I told Emma about my goshawks, about the nest, and, by now, the tufty young birds, two of them, clutching and flapping clumsily on perches nearby.

'What we call branchers. Every stage of development has a name in falconry because in history birds would have been taken from the wild, not born in captivity. A chick in the nest is an eyas, then there's a brancher, like your two – a juvenile that's left the nest but can't yet fly; then a sore hawk, which means it's in its first year but not yet moulted. Sores caught on migration are called passagers, and if they're caught at any time after the first moult then they are known as haggards. It makes a big difference *when* you catch a wild bird for training – a haggard is going to take a lot longer to condition, and will be more defiant. But then you skip out the intensive rearing stage with chicks. Medieval hawks caught for falconry were mostly passagers or haggards.'

I imagined lithe medieval boys shinning up trees in my local wood to bring down the branchers. It's possible that they did. It's an old wood, established well enough in the sixteenth century to appear prominently on Christopher Saxton's 1579 atlas of England and Wales. My birds actually might have been the first breeding goshawks there since the species was shot to extinction in Britain in the nineteenth century. It seems astonishing that the species could have suffered such a dramatic change of fortune, to be so despised and vilified, when once they were prized and protected right across the land. Medieval kings coveted hawks, and the shires of England were obliged to provide them, as gifts, fines or rent.

'Not all the birds came from England,' Emma continued. 'Plenty came from the continent. German hawks were popular, and Scandinavian ones too (Ellah is a Finnish–German cross, now that I mention it). Big gosses from the northern countries were most popular. They still are. Especially the pale Siberian ones, like the white gyrfalcons – look up how expensive they are on the internet!'

There is a lovely symmetry to this. Continental goshawks, coveted and imported by the kings of England, were also responsible for the recovery of a British population in the 1960s and '70s. A merry band of falconers made secret releases in woodlands up and down the country (so it is said), and the birds simply made themselves at home with no help whatsoever. The falconers, no doubt, hoped to keep a sustainable trade in operation by taking a chick or two once the birds had bred, rather as their medieval forbears did. Over the decades the population grew and spread, although most people are completely unaware that they ever disappeared, or that now they're back, silently and invisibly ensuring that some of our wooded places are gripped by wildness. It's likely that my goshawks were born somewhere in Sussex, and that their parents would have been part of the gradual easterly progress the species has been making from further west in southern Britain over the decades of my lifetime.

'People released goshawks into woods in the past as well. That was probably common – a sort of wild management. You let your trained goshawk go at the end of winter, it looked after itself, bred, and then you took up the young at the end of the season, and round it goes. A perfect system really. And it wasn't just a bird for royalty. More lowly folk flew hawks too – fowlers, hunters, keepers – which also helps explain why you might choose to let your birds go after winter: you don't have the expense and bother of feeding them all year round. Hawks aren't birds that can be flown for display, like falcons, because they just don't do that. They only fly to hunt. And they're birds of woodland, where you can't see them a lot of the time, so there's no exhilarating chase to watch. In the past, you trained and flew goshawks to

kill. For some, it put food on the table. When we fly Ellah
we have to stimulate that hunting impulse – we use an
electronic pheasant lure flushed out by our dog, Cosmic,
for her to chase.'

What all this meant was that goshawks held an unusual
and double status for medieval royals. On the one hand,
these birds were intimately associated with the elite, as
indicated by the goshawk's modern scientific name. Royal
households captured, bought and trained hawks
specifically, just as they did falcon species. But goshawks
didn't have the exclusivity and prestige of a peregrine or
gyrfalcon, which could be flown conspicuously, in front
of others, for display and sport. Hawking was something a
king or his austringers did privately, for the thrill of
martial stealth and strike: it was secretive, solitary and
silent work, like the bird itself.

It also meant that the place and presence of raptors in
the woodlands of England's medieval past was more
varied and alive than I'd ever considered. The *hafoc*
names of our places give us clues to the ways people
perceived habitats and ecosystems, to how they observed
and imagined the places around them, but those names
very probably also signpost sites where the birds had
become part of economies associated with the sport of
falconry, which required complex, local knowledge of
ecologies and countryside management in order to
sustain those incomes and practices. In some cases, our
hawk places are a legacy of one of medieval Europe's
most enduring and captivating cultural obsessions. They
are the places in which wild and released birds hunted
and bred, in which they could be watched and caught,
their eyries protected and monitored, in which a great
king or a lowly fowler might cast off their hawk to
catch and kill. Whatever the purpose or design, place

and hunter alike were charged with the thrill and speed
of the raptor's chase.

I saw my goshawks one last time that summer. When the
chicks from my pair had become fully fledged sores, and I
thought, not for the first time, that the show was long
over, one morning, as I was walking right by the old
spying spot, I saw one of the two youngsters perched and
casually observing the world just metres above me. The
nest was empty, the parents gone into the quietness and
secrecy of late summer hush, and there was a feeling of
abandonment.

At first I assumed it hadn't seen me because it was
ridiculous and implausible that a wild goshawk would be
comfortably perched so close to me on the bare edge of
all that forest. This bird, only months old and still with a
few downy, pillow-fight feathers to lose, was yet to learn a
fear of us and the art of invisibility.

I watched it for several minutes, and then two women
on horseback came along the path, chatting, bright and
loud in their high-vis jackets and laughter. Before they
saw me, I vanished into the sweet chestnuts where I'd
spent all that time in previous months watching the nest.
They trotted nearer. I kept still. They passed by me and
right under that bird, right under it, and the only thing it
did was to lower its head and watch them slowly move on
as I watched it watching them, who saw nothing. I wanted
to launch out and point and shout – 'Look, look what it
is!' – but didn't dare, of course, didn't dare for fear of
looking suspicious, for fear that the hawk would fly, that
the game would be up, that my goshawks would no
longer be a secret.

When I was sure the women were gone and no one else was around, I came out onto the path. The hawk did not move. It inclined its head and regarded me the way it had those women high on their horses. I thought of them, elsewhere in the forest now, unaware of what they'd missed, of what that spectacular bird meant to this old wood, to England's goshawks, to me and Stephen. It clutched one branch tightly in its left foot, the other raised but clutching air as though in idle hours it instinctively satisfied that need to seize and hold.

I did not see the birds again. The time now was for invisible terror. Bated quietness, alert alarms, that same edginess I'd felt in the periods between sightings earlier in the year.

'You can feel it when goshawks are still around. Things change when they move in and out,' Stephen said in December when we took a winter walk around the site. 'The female goes further afield in winter, but the male stays on territory. He's still here. It just feels, well, goshawky. If both birds are gone you feel that too. Don't ask me how.'

The air is drawn and held. It strains and creaks in the wind. The wood is strung. We wait for spring.

Crow Hill

Crackpot, Yorkshire Dales ~ Headcorn, Kent ~ Upper Beeding, Sussex ~ Lapford, Devon

Crackpot is the most perfect place I have ever visited for a name. I went one spring on my way west over the Pennines, tempted half by the name's false suggestions of lunatics and junkies, and half by the truth. I had never heard of Swaledale, the beauty spot where the village is situated, had only been to the Yorkshire Dales once before (as a boy in a binbag-coat on a wet school trip) and had no particular expectations beyond the thought that a place called Crackpot must be worth a visit.

I found it up and down the quiet and narrow stone-walled lanes, a little hamlet of a village on the south fellside above the River Swale, which cuts a fast-flowing, sinuous valley west to east through the limestone heights, and all along its length are trout becks and luminous meadows with neat, squat barns, and where curlews call and breed.

The real meaning of Crackpot, of course, has nothing to do with any modern associations attached to that word. It is coincidence alone that a Victorian slang expression is identical to the spelling of a place name that has remained virtually unchanged in centuries. It's Norse, as you might expect in this northern part of the country, and means something like 'rift or hole where there are crows'. Crackpot is at once unique and commonplace. For while

you won't find another Crackpot anywhere, you will find
other corvid places everywhere. As if to prove that point,
you need only follow the Swale 20 miles west of Crackpot
into Cumbria, and you'll find Ravenstonedale, and then
eight miles north of there you'll find Rookby, and go just
half a mile north-west for Kaber – the jackdaw hill. I
found all these places that day. In just one morning, I had
breakfast on the bridge at Crackpot watching carrion
crows and a raven, and finished for lunch beside a
methodist chapel on Kaber's hilltop, looking across to a
magnificent stone barn with bright red doors and a black
flurry of jackdaws. There were rooks at Rookby, too.

This book began with cranes. It ends with crows, the
only birds to boast, collectively, an even greater record in
our place names. *Corvus* was hailed above all in the name
of place.

People have probably been thinking as the crow flies,
determining time and space and fate by big black birds,
for as long as we have coexisted.[1] In one version of the
foundational story of King Edwin of Northumbria's
conversion to Christianity in the seventh century, a raven
or carrion crow threatens to overturn the decision when
it croaks inauspiciously from a particular region of the sky
and causes the royal crowd to reject the newfangled
religion, until someone fires an arrow at the bird and kills
it.[2] But these auguries and superstitions are by no means
exclusive to England and English. Prehistoric and
medieval communities in Britain, Ireland and, indeed, all
across the northern hemisphere exalted and feared corvids,
especially the godly raven, in ritual and myth and the rites
of names in the old languages. While we cannot know

just how early some of the corvid place names in Irish, Scots, Cornish and Welsh may be, the many examples today strongly suggest that preliterate tribes and clans living millennia ago marked and invoked their own places of the crow as much as anyone.

By the time medieval English people were bestowing names upon the villages that survive with us to this day, a reverence for ravens and other corvid species had clearly existed for a while in Britannia, as it had in the Germanic motherlands of the proto-English tribes. The broad sweep of corvid place names across languages in these lands reveals how extensively and particularly these birds had achieved a special relevance in ancient minds, but the staggering number of surviving examples in English takes some beating. Crow species appear in England's names so frequently and repeatedly that there is probably no county that does not have at least one centuries-old, corvid place name, and most have more. Most of the seven British species are recorded, but as you might expect it's the widespread black foursome – raven, crow, rook and jackdaw – that turn up most often.[3]

Take crow. In my south-eastern part of the country, there is Crowborough in East Sussex, Crawley in West Sussex and Hampshire, and Crowhurst in Surrey. Beyond, there is Croydon in Cambridgeshire, Crowfield, Crowell, Crowmarsh and Cranoe in more central counties, Crowton, Crawcrook and Craster further north, and to the south-west there's Creacombe and Crowcombe. As for the other three species, there's Rookley and Rookhope, Rockland and Rockbeare, Rochford and Ruckinge, even, possibly, the town of Rugby. Jackdaws are at Caber, Cabourne, Cawood and Cavil, and both Norse and English words for raven appear in Ramsgate to Ranskill, Ramsbury and Ramsdean, Ravenfield,

Ravenscar, Ravensworth and Ravenshead. This is the briefest of surveys. When you consider that there are umpteen other examples, teeming too in other languages from one end of the British Isles to the other – Celtic *bran* and *fitheach* and *préachán* and *feannog* – the count is dizzying, running to several hundred at the least. Crow surrounds us.

Medieval English had lots of names for Corvidae (the crow family to which these birds belong), a further indication, perhaps, of how firmly these common birds caught people's attention. Tellingly, as we've come to expect, the names imitate or signal sound, as well befits such a loud, garrulous, chattering bunch. Besides the four already discussed, there was *agu* for magpie, and *higera* for jay. A word of caution, however. Dealing with old crow names seems straightforward, because so many survive to match the number of species we have in Britain, and most translate with neat ease into their modern counterparts. Somewhat confusingly though, we cannot assume that the names were applied just as they are today. *Higera*, for instance, seems to have referred to the magpie as well as the jay, and possibly the green woodpecker too (which perhaps isn't so surprising, given that bird's mocking laugh and its jay-like moustache), and it seems possible that these two crow species weren't even recognised as corvids. The evidence, such as it is, implies that early people may have treated the smaller black corvids as diminutives of the giant raven, and that the names *hrefn*, *hroc* and *crawe* were variously interchangeable and suited, depending on, say, what call a particular bird uttered, where and when it was heard, what it was seen to be doing, whether it was on its own or part of a group, as well as by whom it was seen in what part of the country. In short, although we can make reasonable guesses about what crow species are identified in particular place names, we cannot be sure, because the transferability of crow names masks more precise species distinctions that might (or might not) have been made.

Corvids are everywhere. I began with that simple fact. Simple, that is, when you are actually looking for crows, but the point was I hadn't been looking. With the exception of choughs and ravens (more common than they once were, but still rare enough to raise excitement), and the occasional jay with its exquisite blue wing-band and stark white backside, I was shamefully uninterested in the commoner species. I was not alone in this neglect. Mark Cocker, author of *Crow Country*, a book all about how corvids − rooks specifically − are at the heart of his relationship with the Yare Valley in Norfolk, notes that while they eventually became his 'route into the landscape', for a long time he gave them 'less thought' than any other bird. They were just 'so commonplace'.

If that is our modern reaction to the everydayness of crows, it wasn't always the case. You might reasonably assume that such ubiquity, and the perennial reputation as pest, would make these birds unhelpful and undesirable when it came to distinguishing features of place. How would anyone know one crow hill from another, this rooky wood from that rooky wood? But perhaps the corvine allure to placemaking sensibilities was that very dependability; a conspicuous and routine presence contributing to one's deep familiarity with a very localised home radius.

That, at least, was how I saw it in my own recently determined interest. Crows taught me to look again at what is already and obviously right in front of me. Crows took me to new places in old places I would have never thought to seek were it not for allowing myself to be led by the simple fact that the birds were there. I stopped along paths where there was no immediate reason to stop other than watch crows, and drove roads that I'd never driven before. Crows were my new guiding principle. It felt like starting all over.

Jackdaws were first. For many of us they are the species most easy to see: common, noisy socialites, inhabiting rural and urban areas with equal ease and opportunity, and told apart up close from the other three possible confusables by their smaller size, ashen head and neck and, unusually for birds, piercing pale eyes. Depending on your mood, there is either something dapper about them, or ghoulishly crematorial.

There are always jackdaws on Headcorn's village green. When not pecking through the cropped grass for food, they can be found in small gangs in the oak trees, some fidgeting in mischievous squabbles, others still and shut-eyed – grey-naped nappers too old for all that. My daughters chase the grass-strutters, putting them to cackling flight. I examine their smart colours – the charcoal spectrum of the head, the sharp, rakishly black forehead cap in striking contrast to the white eyes, and, something I'd never noticed before, the trim square of feathers growing neatly down the upper mandible of the bill, like a vintage spat on a polished shoe.

A little further into town, I find them at the church tower. Jackdaws are reliable church-goers; lovers of crenellations and thick-wall cavities that make good nesting substitutes for cliff crevices. They seem permanently in the eddy of a sudden breeze, gusting and spiralling up together like bonfire ash. In the high street there are more, a clattering of birds perched on roof ridges and chimney tops, dropping their calls like stones down the shafts. They shift unpredictably and comically between taking things easy, and then bursting up in bother, as though intent on something vital that is forgotten no less quickly.

Always, jackdaws accompany themselves with perpetual chatter, a combination of two knapped notes that form a cluster of metallic sparks around the flock, and which are recalled in the bird's name. *Jack-daw*! It's not bad, as onomatopoeic names go, but early English was there first. The one that turns up in place names is *ca*, which presumably recalled the same sound as *daw* did to later speakers (Cah! Cah!) There's *ceo*, too, which for us now is better suited to the chough's Italianate farewell, but which was probably used for both birds where their territories overlapped, and we know was used for the jackdaw first. Like *ca*, *ceo* mimics the second, longer note of jackdaws, as does *ceahhe* ('*chair-huh*'), which became *chowgh* by the fourteenth century (pronounced 'chuff' by Shakespeare's time).

Next, it was *hrocas*. Rooks. It's a favourite Old English word of mine. It sounds so innately and immediately ancestral. *Hrrr-aw-k*. Something about the back-of-the-mouth, throaty vowel and the gargling *rrs* coming off that initial *h*. I've heard it said that the name does nothing to evoke the actual sounds of rooks, which are better suggested by a more generic 'caw'. Not in my book. To me, *hroc* conveys very well that distinctly coarse, abrupt, guttural note that rooks make alongside and beneath all that top-level cawing, somewhere between a carrion crow and a raven in pitch. It feels wrenched from the throat, like something said in anger.

Rooks expanded my ventures to the outlying farmland where they spend their days in flocks probing the fields along the River Beult, which are routinely flooded in winter. Unlike jackdaws, you won't find rooks in urban centres, although you will find their rookeries – those messy stick bundles that look like blood clots in arterial branches – close by to our settlements; very often right on the edges of villages, roads, service stations, municipal roundabouts, wherever there is access to soft-soiled, short-grassed spaces. I like to think this cohabitative aspect of rook behaviour registered easily with villagers wherever the birds constructed their very obvious nests on the outskirts of towns. There is more than a little sense of homemaking to it all.

The spot I spent most time watching rooks was a crossroads I have approached hundreds of times on my way to and from work. In that winter of crows, I came to know it not as the place where I need to be extra careful of fast traffic on the last stretch to Headcorn, but as my own rook corner. They were often there, up to 20 or 30, picking through pats and stabbing for grubs. A convenient bare-earth layby meant that I could pull up and watch them at very close quarters. Just metres from the 60-miles-per-rush-hour traffic headed to Maidstone and a queue of motorists waiting to join the flow, I sat watching rooks through a hole in a hedge – no doubt to the bemusement of anyone who glanced my way to see a man apparently involved in some bizarre stakeout. I could see and admire the nacreous slick on the birds' black coats, the huge, outsized bill like antique sheep shears, and even individual warty patterns on that characteristic bare skin at the bill's base, akin to a turkey's wattle, but shrivelled and death-grey.

Watching the birds in this way felt like a new devotion to place. What I really wanted, though, was a roost, one of those great dusk gatherings of company-seeking corvids in their thousands that are the defining spectacle of these birds' social tendencies, and which I was sure – though I'd never actually seen one – must confer something transformative on a landscape. I'd read about the really big roosts in Britain, especially the one at Buckenham Carrs (the site of Cocker's *Crow Country*), which attracts tens of thousands of rooks, making it one of the biggest roosts in Europe. But I knew this wouldn't do. Crows were now firmly about homing in on home. The trouble was that we were already well into a very mild February, and before long the roosts would be breaking up. I probably had two weeks at best.

St Peter's, on a hill in Upper Beeding near Steyning in Sussex, is the family church. Marriages, funerals, baptisms – they've all happened there. My great-grandmother is buried in the graveyard (she who wandered Sellindge at night in her grief, from whence she was brought to Sussex for the last years of her life). The whole horizon viewable from there is permeated and marked by our family. Literally. My grandparents are buried in nearby St Botolph's, my parents' names are etched in a giant beech leading up to Chanctonbury Ring, and my father's ashes had a chalky burial beneath an oak sapling on a downland slope at Steyning Bowl.

Steyning, just over the hill from Worthing, is where my brothers and I spent much of our childhood, where our grandparents lived, and now my mother does in the very same house; the house where big Christmases happened, and still do, from where we ran down the twitten to the brooks with empty jam jars to fish in the clear streams, and where a pair of swans guarded their cygnets every summer. We know the route across the brook and the Adur, up the knoll to St Peter's, with charter-like precision: to stickleback stream (minus the sticklebacks these days), from the stream to the bridge, from the bridge by the thorny scrub to kingfisher dyke where we once saw a pike, from the dyke up the steps, and from there to the church.

St Peter's and its landscape is, therefore, one of the oldest and most familiar places of any in my life. It is also a place of jackdaws, and it was them I'd come to see. I had not seen them for years, and was unsure to what extent my hazy recollection was confused or merged with other memories, but I had a notion they've been gathering to roost above the church for at least the span of my life, and probably far longer. (In my uncle's time as a child in Lower Beeding, rooks were there too, nesting in big elm trees that have long since fallen to disease.)

When I met my brother at the church one afternoon in mid-February an hour before sunset, the arrival was already underway.

'I've been watching them for ten minutes,' Richard said. 'I reckon there's a hundred now, but they keep coming.' He pointed behind him. A steady train of jackdaws flew from the west, homing to one tall beech immediately by the church, until they numbered some 300 birds. Their flight was so straight and purposeful it seemed as though they responded to some magnetism in the hill, drawn by a pulsing energy in the earth's ore.

The light was going fast. The birds grew quieter. We intended to stay until dark, at which time we would leave the birds to it, chattering away like my daughters after lights out. What we hadn't expected was that, in a single moment that seemed to us totally without warning or preparation, they would all take off, with immediate volume, as though every one of them suddenly panicked at the gunshot of their own collective squawk. They flew east, towards the next ridge of downs, dropping down out of sight somewhere in a fold between hills.

So this wasn't a roost. I'd assumed in ignorance all those years. St Peter's was, correctly, what I now know to be a pre-roost gathering. All across this part of the Adur valley where the river slices between the Downs, jackdaws were assembling in similar, small parties before moving on to the night's main event. But where had they gone? They weren't far, we knew that much, but it was too dark now to do anything else. Tomorrow, we determined, tomorrow we would be ready.

We came from the Devil's Dyke the following morning, over the brow of the long hill, sea to our left, the counties of England to our right. Start far east and far up, we'd reckoned beerily the previous night in the pub. That way we can't miss them – we'll meet them coming the other way.

The omens were good. Cloud was down, so on the high tops we were in the damp and the whiteout, and early mists brewed in the cauldron depressions. Viewed from below, this stretch of the South Downs has a wildness and magnitude about it that I find missing from more westerly lengths on the other side of the River Adur. It is steeper, harder, with more trees and rough vegetation, less denuded or smoothed by the plough's action. You could almost think yourself in Wales or Scotland when the clouds hide the summits and the sharp folds of the hills look as if they soar to mountains.

A landscape in those conditions, shrouded in mists and mysticism, must have appealed to people living in the region thousands of years ago. There are, indeed, the remains of an Iron-Age fort right on the edge of the Dyke's 30-metre-deep dry valley (the longest, deepest and widest in Britain). We walked its ramparts before we set off west. There were already signs of spring in the February gloom – blackthorn blossom, celandines, sprightly skylarks, an optimistic ice-cream van. In other respects, winter stuck fast. Hunched trees bore the worst up here, absorbing so much wetness from another flooded season that they seemed to ooze rain from the inside out. Water hung in fat drops from every branch and twig.

Inside the fort there was a single crow on a thorn bush, and then unseen, from somewhere to the west, a raven's hard rasp, like a heavy spade on concrete, or a car crunching gears, except that a raven's utterance has nothing of that mundanity. It is a command, a resounding imperative to harken. There are few things more portentous than a carrion crow's five-times *caw* coming out of obscure air, and a raven's gutturals even more so. Two ravens appeared over the fort, and then descended back into cloud as they banked into the Dyke.

These king corvids have not long returned to more southerly counties after decades of persecution, but there's no doubting that they were here when ancient Britons were constructing their panoramic hilltop forts all along the South Downs – among the first bird species to colonise newly ice-free territories in the early Holocene. There is little doubt, too, that these birds would have meant something special to those people. Although there is no linguistic evidence surviving to reveal what part these birds played in Iron-Age cultures, archaeological excavations have turned up a remarkable number of raven inhumations (as well as rooks and carrion crows) in pits and shafts.[4] The most recent thinking on these burials is that they are clearly ritual, even sacrificial, hinting at something chthonic in pagan practices: a connection to a realm beneath and in earth that bridges this world with others, and extends our imaginings to a very different sort of place.

Walking west along the white spine of the down, Richard and I spoke of crows in high places. Corvids at summits and peaks. In place names, crows are often associated with these geographies; hills, cliffs, valleys, and trees too − heights in their own way − crowned with significance by solitary black birds with unpropitious coughs. Somewhere east of us, perhaps even within sight on a clear day, there was Crowborough and Crowhurst, 12 miles apart in Wealden country, close to the borders of Surrey, Sussex and Kent. These places mean, literally, crow hill. There are many others.

Was there something in this? Did crows exalt and bewitch these elevated topographies just by their presence? Certainly, to witness a gathering of those birds at dusk, as we hoped to discover again that evening, is to feel that such a place, already characterised by dint of height above the level, is somehow bestowed with further powers towards which the birds in tremendous numbers gravitate as though under some spell. Or, instead perhaps, that the birds themselves are the source of powers wrought upon the land by their visitations. The sight, at any rate, is unmissable as a flaming beacon.

We talked, too, of the more grisly associations that might connect corvids with hilltops − their iconic predilection for carrion (and other easy pickings). The reality is that most species, even the so-called carrion crow, spend far more time eating invertebrates than anything else, but they are also supreme opportunists, so the crow, looking like a little raven, and sometimes attending carrion alongside its larger cousins, will have been caught up in traditions that stubbornly persist, independent of ecological truth. This reputation lies behind the most famous of early English corvid portraits, in which the raven appears alongside wolf and eagle in the beasts-of-battle motif that features in almost any Old English poem with slain bodies. Battlefields aside, people may also have encountered corvids at corpses from public executions (as we might disturb them from roadkill today), and this perhaps encouraged a general association between crows and cadavers hung high in prominent locations as conspicuous deterrents to other would-be malefactors. There is a folk tale connected with the Downs not far from where my father is interred, about a highwayman who haunts the old track across that way, near to where he was hanged and buried, and where the farm there still bears the title Lychpole, which likely means 'corpse pole'. References to gibbets and gallows in place names are not uncommon, and are even directly connected with corvids, such as one charter boundary 'crow-post' at Uplyme in Devon, which, if it wasn't a site for hanging vermin, might have been a gibbet.

The catholic diets of crows that sometimes brings them in contact with the human dead makes them, for us, literally and figuratively, hangers-on, attendants of death. Those connections, the result of our own morbid obsessions, can be reverently transcendental in our imaginations, making the birds emissaries of the afterlife (as was probably the case with the Iron-Age pit burials). But such associations also made these death-black, death-summoning birds creatures of ill omen and macabre repute, in league with evil, sinners and the supernatural. I had begun to wonder whether places bearing the crow name might sometimes be imbued with those superstitions too. Not literally places of death, as the gallows or graves or battlefields are, but at which crows bestow an indefinable but palpable sense of the uncanny, or exercise some preternatural knowing for the weird and frightful in a place. In times past, a feeling for the spectral and occult wouldn't have been unusual, but you don't need a belief in apparitions or demons to experience such things. Some places are just spooky as hell.

This region of the South Downs has its fair share of ghostly folklore, as the name, Devil's Dyke, indicates. In just the four-mile stretch between the Dyke and Beeding there are plenty enough lost villages and ruinous settlements for any number of hauntings. It is, in the words of early twentieth-century, Sussex-born author, George Aitchison, a 'devil-ridden district' where you cannot 'doubt what manner of gods once ruled on the heights' or feel 'an ever-brooding presence that watches you'. If it was ghostly we wanted, we'd come to the right place.

The cloud dispersed by afternoon and the day brightened. At Truleigh Hill, approaching the down's western end, we stopped to look north onto the flooded fields below, which appeared like lakes. We could see for miles now, right to the Surrey Hills on the distant horizon, and all across the Low Weald in every direction between, with Beeding and its outlying villages – the tower of St Peter's visible – immediately to our west. All that remained now was to find our roost in this devil district. The plan was to climb inside that place at dark, an idea, I admit, that wasn't entirely free of hesitation. It's one thing to spend a night in a wood, but when that wood is home to thousands of demon-black birds making all manner of fearsome noises, that's another order of creepy.

Tottington Woods is small, but is nonetheless the largest patch of woodland in the Adur valley between Steyning and Henfield. It is semi-ancient, predominantly oak, well used by dogwalkers by day, part managed by a group of volunteers, and largely owned by private individuals who tend to their plots and make pleasant camp in summer. We, in winter, trespassed as far as we could from the paths in the heart of the wood and pegged our tarpaulin between two trees over wet leaves. We stowed our bags in the hollow of one oak and ran for the southern boundary of trees as the sun set, where the hills bear down on the villages of Edburton and Fulking.

In the end there had been no wild crow chase, no haphazard drive across the countryside. By half past four that afternoon we knew where to go from the vanguard pairs of jackdaws making their way towards the area of Small Dole with a compass-straight, head-down directionality. We saw them land in roadside shaws and farmland copses, and down at sea level in the village they were unmissable, steadily gathering in number and noise and impatience for something to happen. A few outlying flocks, we noticed, were already moving to the trees at Tottington.

Dusk was spectacular that evening – electric pink, clouds like something molten. It backlit the trees and hills, and scorched those black birds blacker. From the edge of the wood we watched several hundred chattering jackdaws come in to the pre-roost sites on the outskirts of Small Dole, later joined by screeching rooks, and when the trees could hold no more the whole lot of them burst onto the fields. More jackdaws, more rooks, claimed the vacant trees. Sound and movement were inseparable in the pullulating mass, so that all the elements of the roost complex were various, mirroring iterations of a singular crowness. On the ground, the birds formed a long, higgledy hedge line, and then they condensed into one corner of the field so that the green land furred over with black crow blight. Still more birds joined from the west. We were all waiting.

They stayed down until it was very nearly dark. The final moment came when another, equally large flock surprised us from somewhere out of view to the east and stirred above the woods like a bad-weather warning. That was it. The field crows went up as one body in a sea-surging roar, and all were in the air at once, brewing chaos at twilight. Then the wood, by now a gaping door in the dark of the wider landscape, was theirs. It was inside the crows, and now we were inside the wood, listening to the din as though from inside the sound itself – the shriek and clamour of some 4,000 birds. They did not settle at once, but kept up a restless vigil for an hour or so after their arrival, battering the dusk over our heads. Even when we could no longer see them, their agitations still accompanied our tasks until we fell asleep in the unquiet wood.

Rain did come that night. I woke several times to its pelting, and a cold wind through the open ends of our tent. There was a paleness to the sky, as if cast by a pallid lunar light, though no moon was visible. I found it more unnerving than the darkness I'd expected inside a wood, for against its wan illumination the entangled

trees were darkly visible, their branches like so many
clutching hands and fingers that cracked and creaked
in the wind. The red warning lamp of the radio mast
on Truleigh Hill cast a fractured light through the trees.
An occasional yelp or croak came from one bird or
another dreaming corvid dreams. I was glad not to
be alone.

Next morning, we struck camp in the rain at first light.
The crows were already heading out. We'd arrived with
the birds, and we would leave with them too. Twilight
entrances and exits.

The jackdaws and rooks twisted out above us in a long,
extending rope that reached into the still-dark west. It put
me in mind of bats I'd once watched pour into a tunnel
of air from a belltower in Wales. The birds go with greater
determination by morning. There is no waiting around.
Whatever force had arrived with their hoards last night,
now it went as though under instruction, released like
curses upon the world by day, then recalled each night to
the same den of witchy power.

By night, Tottington is the wood of crows. There are,
like crow hills, crow woods all over Britain. In fact, along
with Rookery, Crow Wood is probably the single most
recurring bird place name in England.[5] If it's possible for
crows to be lumbered with our omens and persecutions
for so many centuries, it doesn't seem far-fetched to
suggest that some of those places that carry the birds'
names may have shared those associations – some
unfavourable, and some, perhaps, just spectacular. In
Beowulf, one of the final, foreshadowing moments before
the eponymous hero's death is the account of the Battle
of Ravenswood. The setting for this tale, prominently
pairing ravens and a wood, with trees as ready-made
gallows for the defeated warriors, and the threat of

swinging bodies as raven food, makes for an unnerving
combination of bird and place. Centuries later,
Shakespeare's Macbeth, plotting Banquo's murder, longs
for the 'agents' of 'seeling night' presaged by the 'crow'
making 'wing to the rooky wood' – a 'night-rook', we
might say, as one medieval monk names the obscure
nocturnal bird more commonly known in early
ornithology as the 'night-raven'. In the old lands where
superstitions were real and died hard, where elves, gods,
goblins, dragons, wolves and snakes all possess places,[6]
crows, too, must have sometimes set the local imagination
racing for a topographical tale or two. *In Crow Wood they
say the souls of the unbaptised and the devil hi'self scream there
a' night ...*

There is always something oracular about corvids en
masse. Every stage and component of the event – the
anticipation, the pre-roost gatherings, the roost itself,
arrivals, departures, the increase and progress of it all –
conveys an uncanny foresight, as though the birds are
aware of something coming over the hill. There are no
medieval records of corvid flocks as omens (they tended
to involve single ravens or carrion crows), but the sheer
spectacle of the 'mingled swarthy crowd', as Clare
memorably puts it, 'Rook, crow and jackdaw, noising
loud', makes you appreciate emphatically why some
species were important in the practice of augury for pre-
modern people.
      Modern science has begun to explain the intricate
workings of corvid roosts, although there is still much
we don't know. It has been recently argued that the
jackdaws' departures to and from the roost are triggered

by the birds' contact calls, which crescendo until the hubbub reaches a particular volume and intensity. As in murmuration flights, so the research states, the individual and the group are tightly synchronised, so that the detonated confusion of noise and wings at take-off is actually the outcome of communication and consensus. That level of group cooperation is also behind the tendency to congregate in such huge numbers in the first place. The current thinking is that roosts function variously and diversely as information centres for the dissemination of knowledge about food sources.

Displays of corvine intelligence that look to us like prophecy do have a scientific basis. We know that some crow species, with comparatively large forebrains densely packed with neurons, can perform complex cognitive tasks, such as processing, prediction and tool-using. It seems that jackdaws, uniquely among birds as far as we know at the moment, can communicate with their eyes (one explanation for the unusual white colouration), and are capable of interpreting human ocular signals.

Knowledge about these sorts of ingenuities is nothing new. People living centuries ago may not have had the empirical evidence of modern science, but they observed and intuited corvid brilliance nonetheless. Some species' knack for mimicry, in particular, has proved enduringly popular and fascinating to us, especially when that mimicry includes the human voice.

There is no shortage of medieval talking crows. Writers readily drew upon examples from classical literature, such as the Roman poet Martial's epigram, which has a magpie state, 'if you did not see me, you would deny that I am a bird'. There is a similarly mischievous magpie or jay flaunting its vocal transformations in one of the Exeter

Book riddles. It mimics other creatures in clever onomatopoeia (jays have been observed imitating everything from natural sounds to lawnmowers and motorbikes in the modern world), and is the only riddle in the whole collection to provide an answer, in the form of runes which must be decoded and rearranged to spell out *higera*.[7] Centuries later, Chaucer included a talking crow in 'The Manciple's Tale', the last story to appear in his longest, last and best-known work, *The Canterbury Tales*. A white crow spies his master's wife at adultery and tells all. Furious, Phoebus kills his wife and then turns on the messenger, damning the white crow black and speechless forevermore, except for a tuneless croak. This is a dark lesson about the abuses and dangers of speech and speaking, the fine lines between fiction and truth, the ethics of telling tales itself.

The medieval crow who knows and says too much could be threatening in more real ways. Human 'trouble-makers' – women, peasant rebels such as Wat Tyler – were frequently depicted as chattering magpies or jays, a comparison that denounces corvid abilities as superficial and deceiving. Medieval theologians required a similar tactic because it was a necessary task for them to prove the elevated status of human beings – the one species created in the image of God and who alone among earthly creatures will inherit the kingdom of heaven. Some churchmen sought to be definite on the subject (with all the indefinite certainty of those who protest too much): birds like crows only *appear* to be intelligent, but we should not be fooled, they tell us. There was too much at stake for it to be otherwise. As one theologian put it, if 'crows had the dictates of reason … how many cities and castles could they not burn down?' Aelred of Rievaulx's point is that should non-humans be granted the privilege of rationality, well, then human exceptionalism would be undone.

I am on a hillside again, at the advent of night and a new year. Beneath the cold ground where I am sat with a flask of single malt for warmth are the foundations of two Roman forts, and perhaps earlier settlements beneath that. The medieval addition to this historical sedimentation is above ground just behind me, still upright and intact. Bury Barton is a working farm, built around an ancient and traditional cob-walled courtyard, with a deconsecrated but intact fifteenth-century chapel on the roadside. (I hopped the gate and snuck inside the chapel once, disturbing a barn owl, and thought about how W. G. Hoskins, father of landscape history and proud Devonian, was there marvelling in 1966, as I would do half a century later.) Bury, recorded in Domesday, is from *burh*, Old English for 'fortification'; perhaps the Anglo-Saxon landowners paid homage to all that history beneath their feet as much as they labelled their own battlements in the name.

The views from here extend clear in a broad sweep west to east across the Yeo Valley. Nine miles south-west of here is Exbourne, where I went in search of cuckoo spirits some springs ago, and 15 miles south-east is Exeter cathedral (a certain bishop of which once owned Bury Barton. That Leofric again). Directly north of me, bright on the opposite horizon with Christmas illuminations and a star above the church tower, is the village of Lapford (near Crediton town, which as it happens is a possible origin site for the Exeter Book). It is Boxing Day, the shortest day has passed, and the old year – it always astonishes me – revolves already towards next year's midsummer. For some time to come though, you won't notice that slow changing of light, and by mid-afternoon I'm already waiting on Bury hillside in the gloom.

I have found, just this day, a new pre-roost party of crows in this green valley between Exmoor and Dartmoor. We're in Lapford for Christmas.[8] Devon has been a part of Ginny's life since childhood. At one time, her Victorian paternal forbears held considerable distinction in the county: they owned and ran a school in Lapford, and others were timber merchants in Totnes. Any wealth to speak of has long since gone, and now my father-in-law, the last of his family in Devon, holds down the ancestral seat in a two-bedroomed, tumbledown cottage (once part of the old school), in the lee of the church and a graveyard rookery. If his stories are to be believed – implausible, incredible, but which nearly always turn out to be true – then that same rookery has kept up its commotion since at least the days of the family's earliest residency in the village. Rooks, Ginny has often said, are the singular and defining sound; wherever she hears rooks they are Lapford to her, and all the complicated emotions that have buried their way into her lifelong relationship with this place.

This morning, we listened from bed to the rooks *a-hrocing* and *a-craaing*. They arrive at first light, taking up their lookouts in the various taller trees at the village centre, including the ash tree immediately outside our bedroom window. Even this much, simply listening with purpose, was already more than the sum of my interactions with the Lapford rooks in ten years of visits. Today though, I watched them hourly, recording when and for how long they were away feeding somewhere, and again when they returned to their church-side posts, breaking off from whatever activity or conversation I was engaged

in whenever I heard the rooks leave or return. At a
quarter to four, they departed for the final time that day
and made for the other side of the valley, where they
joined dozens more and spiralled up over the old forts. I
slipped on coat and boots, left everyone dozing in front
of Christmas television, and ran down to the river Yeo
under the flights of crows.

This gathering, unlike the one at Sussex, is composed of
many more rooks than jackdaws, but both are present, and
carrion crows too.[9] As I sit beneath them, dozens have
become hundreds, then a thousand or more, in a single,
threading gyre over Bury Barton hill. More come still from
the north and east and west across the valley, which has
sunk deep into itself, as though that hollow space between
the horizons were the increase and matter of dusk, or the
Yeo were suddenly the widest of English rivers, broad and
black and treacherous. Just above, like a fluttering bat over
water, a woodcock rodes up the valley sides.

The crows fly towards me with that same intuition of
one-track purpose and prescience I've so often felt
watching them on their roost journeys: envoys of the
world, a thousand Huginns and Muninns returning to
Odin with news picked and scavenged from abroad. A
thousand omens for the Roman augur.

This is not the roost. That final assembly is still to
come, somewhere I have not yet discovered. This much
is obvious when part of the flock tears away and heads
south towards Dartmoor. It is gone from view and does
not return. Then most of the group, leaving just 20 or so
birds at Bury, suddenly fly back across the valley. They are
restless, ranging swiftly west to east, east to west, along
the ridge, back and forth like the woodcock I can no
longer see, or a cloud blown between two mischievous
wind gods.

Such is the endless movement of birds in this quick and constant twilight change, it feels as though I am witnessing a creation and destruction all at once. The night and the land are one. Crows have done this. Crows pluck and weave the filaments of day's end and last light, are black vectors describing the sheer being of this place. They are hardly visible to me now, just particles of night. I watch them until I can make out nothing at all. I hear them though. They do not stop. I step back into the valley, led up the hill and home by Lapford's lights and the sound of 800 crows in the dark.

Epilogue

Why We Need the Medieval

Shortly before I finished writing this book, we moved to Essex. Only two and a half years after the up sticks from Cranbrook to Headcorn, there we were again, moving on and moving homes. We swapped Kent's white horses for three cutlasses on a new county escutcheon. Essex, now, was our country. We had discussed the possibility of this relocation countless times over the years, but that was it; no concrete plans, just imagined futures. So when the moment came and we took the chance, it felt like no less a surprise and upheaval than if we'd never considered the idea. Within two weeks Ginny had applied for a new job, interviewed, and accepted. The reality of leaving Kent behind, where I'd spent over a third of my life and our children had begun theirs, of selling the house and buying another, of finding the girls new schools and me work, and the stress of trying to ensure that all that went smoothly in the time we had available (it didn't), was much harder than either of us could have imagined. Our Kentish ties were rooted deep.

We were thrilled as much as daunted. God knows a new life in Essex was an exciting prospect. One of our beloved homes from home became, simply, home. I began getting Essex earth under my nails straightaway, months before we arrived, learning local names in vicinities close to marsh where we thought we might settle, buying maps to research and track possible new localities with charter-like detail: Roman roads, the nearest patches of local woodland (rather less than we had in Kent, but still); a small River Blackwater flowing right past our eventual new house, and the Chelmer, after which Chelmsford takes its name – hometown of J. A. Baker, where I found myself another teaching job – both rivers eventually flowing out into saltmarsh at Maldon. I began making discoveries too about my East Anglian ancestors in Polstead, Boxford, Woodham Walter and, lastly, Little Baddow, from which my great-grandfather, Henry John, went to London in search of a better life.

What the move did for us, wrenching our emotions between extremes, was bring into question everything we thought was, or took for granted as, unquestionable. A change of place was a dramatic change in us too, in what we assumed was comfortable and certain and secure. For me, undoubtedly, it was the most trying period yet of my 42 years. I worried lots. I lost weight. We both suffered sleepless nights. In our new house, a neglected thing in need of love, bought at a bargain price so we could afford more space, we battled damp and rats. At least there were owls, which called to me on my first, solitary night in the empty house when I went ahead of the family to collect the keys. That was something. The whole affair focused the hard extent to which we, as individuals and as a couple with children, are affected and formed by *where* we are. It can make or break happiness. In the year of our move from Kent to Essex, we were placed and placeless, often troubled by the bewildering and unsettling sensation of both identifications at once. Even now, we have moments of doubt that we've made the right decision.

We were up against some serious questions about the very idea of place itself; about how it is defined, how we relate to it, why and how it matters. More than ever, we understood that the place we choose to call *our place* matters a great deal to us. In our own ways, we were confronted with the sorts of enquiries that academics have pondered, debated and categorised in formal theoretical terms. Much of this, of course, was unconscious and instinctive. We just felt these proverbials at some visceral level: that home is a state of mind, not just a place; that to be at all is always to be in place; that to live in any true way is to be rooted and immersed in place. But I also returned very intentionally to those writers who had taught me to think about place, rereading passages from their works over and over, as though to rehearse their ideas were a consoling and essential part of my adjustment to everything.

There was another reason, I realised, why these geographers and philosophers of place so seized my attention at this time. It was because their words, repeatedly, recalled the medieval world I had spent so long recovering and inhabiting on my journeys for this book. Reading Edward Casey, who declared that 'To live is to live locally, and to know is first of all to know the place one is in', and Yi-Fu Tuan, who wrote that the feel of place 'is made up of experiences ... repeated day after day and over the span of years', or Arturo Escobar, who identified place (in contrast to the abstractness and emptiness of 'space') as 'the particular, the limited, the local and the bounded' – I saw in all these articulations the places I'd visited and imagined with their particular and local worlds, the experiences and the bounds of the Anglo-Saxon charter descriptions, and all those birds in the names that played their role in the day-to-day and the span of years that go to making a feel for and a knowledge of place.

It's a connection that Tuan makes himself – that is, between the medieval and what he deems to be authentic place. In his book *Topophilia*, he makes the point that for most of human existence our perceptions and distances have been what he calls 'vertical', directed not outwards across geographical terrain, but upwards to gods and heavens from the relatively limited circumference of home ground; whereas in the modern, largely secular age we have been instead orientated along the 'horizontal', ever since colonial explorations led to brave new worlds overseas, and, we could add, industrial globalisation took hold with rapid and destructive force. What Tuan argues is that the transition between the Middle Ages and the Early Modern era (broadly speaking, the sixteenth century in Europe) marked the beginning of a radical shift in how people thought about and related to place. Significantly, given the emphasis Tuan and other humanistic geographers put on rootedness and authentic living, the implication is that the time before modernity is to be desired and preferred. The time, that is, when the 'affective bond between people and place' was a more natural and readily apparent aspect of human existence.

Tuan is dealing in generalisations, and there are, of course, plenty of very good reasons why we certainly wouldn't want to rewind the historical clock (servitude and plague, for starters). Nor should we fabricate some sort of absurd, romanticised 'Deep England' nostalgia for a past that didn't exist. But there are, I think Tuan would agree, valuable lessons to be learned if each of us were to adopt and carry with us a little of the medieval spirit. Lessons that might make us happier. The Middle Ages, that long span of years in which so many of our named places and names for our fauna and flora came to be, has a special role in reminding us of the profound importance of celebrating, protecting and connecting with place.

In twenty-first-century Britain, as much as, or more than, anywhere in the Western world, we have a problem with place. On one level, it might be that too few of us think about our relationships with place at all any more, and therein lies the problem (as suggested by a 2022 survey by the Office for National Statistics, which reported that around half of UK citizens feel no particular sense of connection to their neighbourhoods). But a great many of us are aware, and – without any idea what to do about it – would likely agree that we are disconnected more than we are connected, and that thinking about our places, local and national, is just as likely to induce anxiety and dismay as anything else. Why is that?

One answer is that we are constantly and increasingly at risk of *losing* place, at a frighteningly unprecedented rate and scale. Place, even some of those places supposedly protected by law, is under perpetual threat from every angle and, it seems at least, forever disappearing. The problem is epidemic: intense competition between the need for new houses and a need for nature; big industry and corporate enterprises claiming 'economic growth'; climate change jeopardising coasts and other fragile habitats; monoculture farming relying on too many chemicals and water companies degrading and polluting ecosystems; a countryside throughout most of Britain and Ireland that is almost entirely privately owned and provides welcome but, nonetheless, very restricted access (Scotland is the exception). Under such circumstances it is little wonder that our relationships with place are under strain or cut loose.

Perhaps the problem is that we have strayed too far from the medieval. Limitations are not always limiting. In the relentless drive towards globalisation, expanding the horizontal further and further, we have gone so far beyond our bounds that we have lost ourselves. It's a familiar enough idea: that hypermodernity with its global reach of fast and virtual communications, its focus on consumerism and mobility, its need and desire for locations that some have called 'placeless places' – airports, retail parks, highways, fast-food chains – erodes appreciation of the unique identities of particular places, and prevents the possibility of 'authentic' living.

The rewards of the placeless lifestyle are tremendously irresistible to us, and nearly all of us to some degree celebrate and appreciate these mobile new ways of thinking about what place is. We want and demand modernity's convenience, its immediacy, its expansiveness and interconnectedness. But all of these privileges, unavoidably and undeniably, change what place means to us, and they come at a price. Our material culture – what globalisation delivers to us so easily now – is profoundly and intentionally ephemeral, so often produced for us somewhere on the other side of the world (like much of our food). That detachment has a knock-on effect; it detaches us from places too, because when we pass on the doing of all this to someone else somewhere else, however convenient this might be, and when our priorities are quantity, cheapness and speed, what we lose is investment, care, responsibility, and the natural longevity of creation and process. As Rebecca Solnit puts it, catching beautifully a sense of the medieval:

> There was a time not so long ago when everything was recognizable not just as a cup or a coat, but as a cup made by so-and-so out of clay from this bank on the local river or a coat woven by the guy in that house out of wool from the sheep visible on the hills.

Birds are the way in which I find and know the boundedness of place. Boundedness in the sense I have used it above, not as inhibiting restriction, but as exactness and particularity. Places without birds are, indeed, placeless to me, however beautiful the view. Birds are intricately and richly part of the dimensions and totality of everything as, are the other non-human lives that are no less the breath and shape and movement of place, and that are included implicitly in the general spirit of this book. Medieval people knew the bounds of their worlds by all life, as the names show us.

There was for most medieval people simply living by their daily agrarian routines no disconnection between them and us, between human and non-human. As landscape historian Richard Jones states, our pre-modern ancestors 'accepted their total absorption in their environment and readily acknowledged that they were shaped by it'. In the medieval world view, humankind was part of everything else, affected very literally by planetary and meteorological influences as much as the failure of a harvest or the divination of a single high-flying crow. What medieval people knew instinctively was that the make-up of their own bodies, their very identities, were hitched to polyrhythmic systems that determined the proper workings of all things in the harmonious, steady turning of the universe's spheres. They observed and understood the multitude of lives and elements other than our own, and knew that this was all part of what we mean by place.

It is hard for us now to conceive this level of immersion, but the holistic way of seeing and doing things is embedded firmly in the language we commonly and glibly use to describe all things 'eco'. 'Eco' words have become trendy and subject to hackneyed, meaningless greenwashing, but follow the roots back and you'll discover that Greek *oikos* meant simply 'house' or 'social unit'. Follow the roots deeper and you'll find Indo-European *ueik, which described concepts of settling and neighbours (and so, too, related to the 'dwelling' origin of many place names with *wick* in them, including Wicken Fen). Hidden in our modern stock of eco-words is the profound and poignant reminder, if we would only take the hint, that nature is *us*. It is our house, our true place of dwelling and neighbourhood. Biodiversity and place cannot, or rather should not, be separated, because place is made and sustained by the intertwining narratives of *all* cohabiting lives and elements. To diminish life is to diminish place itself, and in our time we have radically diminished both. Our place names are a guide to those old, intuitive cohabitations. They are a tool for the first steps that Right to Roam activists Nick Hayes and Jon Moses propose in *Wild Service* towards 'restoring communities to the beating heart of the natural world'. If our aim is a vital, 'mass reconnection to the land', then let us begin with the signposts from our medieval past.

For one of the same reasons that many birds likely appealed to early place-namers – that they are easily seen – birds have become handy indicators of this ecological disconnection. In their modern plight, species such as the cuckoo expose the gap between 'then and now' that is perhaps the most defining and disconcerting aspect of our twenty-first-century ecological circumstances. So, too, do the names. Those places in which formerly present species have disappeared are solemnly displaced, in the truest sense of that word. We can witness that displacement in the sprawl of modern suburban environments too, which, with a certain grim irony, fashionably assign bird nomenclatures to roads and residential spaces (Sandpiper Drive, Nightingale Way, Lark Rise, Goldcrest Mews …) where the species named are nowhere to be seen and probably never were present. In the midst of the current place-making frenzy in England to build 300,000 new homes a year (which at the time of writing looks set to intensify exponentially), such examples are everywhere.[1] For medieval people, there was no such disconnect between name and place. The birds in the names really existed; they were part of specific places that human inhabitants knew intimately, probably all their lives, and the names grew organically out of those experiences.

One especially grave and intensive loss of birdlife occurred while I was writing *The Cuckoo's Lea*. In the summer of 2021, the most recent, and ongoing, outbreak of avian flu (H5N1 to be precise) began decimating wild birds, drastically altering the very essence of those birds' habitats and homes. I saw the impact of this for myself in 2022 when I joined Brian Hodgson on the Solway Firth to see the wintering population of Svalbard barnacle geese, but many other species all over Britain, and indeed globally, have been devastated in their thousands. Seabirds have been particularly affected, killed in numbers that have probably reduced some populations to lower than they have ever been. In 2022 and 2023, the Farne Islands were closed to visitors because H5N1 was so virulent among their internationally important seabird populations, and this after closures in 2020 and 2021 because of another pandemic, Covid-19. The winter of 2023/24 brought some welcome relief for British birds, but there were severe outbreaks elsewhere, and the virus spread for the first time to the Antarctic. The catastrophe is not over.

Avian flu gives us further cause to reflect upon our relationships with place. The uncomfortable truth is that the mutation and spread of such diseases can be directly traced to modern intensive farming systems (H5N1 began with poultry and transferred to wild birds). Yes, pandemics have always happened – the most famous of all, of course, the Black Death, was a medieval killer – but the way we have come to manage environments in response to global human populations has radically assisted the evolution and circulation of deadly pathogens that, as Covid-19 showed, can infect us as much as any other animal. Research into zoonoses (diseases passed from non-humans to humans) is revealing more and more that it is humans' exploitation of ecosystems worldwide that is contributing dramatically to the problem. Our abuses of land and resources damage and disrupt the evolved relationships between communities of animals (including us), causing unnatural contacts, imbalances, weaknesses and degradations in so-called 'sick landscapes' that massively increase the chance and risk of new, deadly diseases.

The devastations of avian flu and other such diseases show us, in essence, what happens when our relationships with place go wrong. They are, to borrow Edward Relph's words, 'what results from an insensitivity to the significance of place' – the consequence of mismanaging ecosystems in ways that are categorically unlike pre-modern holism. They are a product of divisionist thinking, which perceives humans as separate, different, and exceptional to everything else. The lessons to be learned by us are a timely echo of the old verities: we must rediscover and relearn our connections to the intricate networks of place; seek less to shape and more to be shaped by our environments and the communities to which these environments are also home.

Ecological restoration in all its forms is now widely recognised as a crucial effort in the fight against future pandemics, as well as climate change and extinction. We live in an age that is increasingly fixed on restorative aims. That unassuming prefix *re* (directly from Latin, meaning 'back, again') has become a common and defining word stem in modern ecological discussions: we reforest, regenerate, reintroduce and rewild, *re*placing what has been *dis*placed. We are acknowledging, slowly, that to restore ourselves we must restore our places. Each of the many recent reintroduction and wilding schemes in the UK and elsewhere is, as environmental historian Dolly Jørgensen reminds us, 'by necessity a practice that looks to the past' – and a medieval past at that, because our place names and the species they mention are often central evidence in these aspirations.[2]

Our futures, in this sense, depend upon that past. Looking back to the bountiful forms and possibilities of dwelling that once shaped how people perceived and interacted with their local worlds, restorations can heal severed relationships that were once crucial to meaningful connections and identities, and could be again – a common inheritance of natural heritage. They reinvest belonging where it should be; not only because this or that creature belongs in this or that place, but because our own untethered belonging is at stake and needs rescuing too. We must find meaning in place again, through birds and all wild lives, if we are to ensure our own physical and emotional survival. We need these spirits of place.

Acknowledgements

The Cuckoo's Lea has been many years in the making, which means that the encouragement and guidance of a great many people is bound up in every word of it. Thank you to everyone over the years who has supported me in any way. My former tutors and colleagues at Royal Holloway University are some of the first people I must thank for their support, particularly the late Ruth Kennedy, who supervised and enthused about everything I wrote on birds in medieval literature. Thanks, too, must go to my mentors, Isabel Davis and Mike Bintley, at Birkbeck College during the tenure of my honorary research fellowship; their advice and belief were central to the development of this book. To Mike, specifically, thanks for the years of support, friendship and talk about the medieval non-human over pints of good beer in Canterbury.

This book would never have seen the light of day if it were not for my friends and colleagues at New Networks for Nature, a charity for which I was proud to chair the steering group for a time. From 2009–2024, New Networks provided an influential and inspiring forum for a tremendous variety of people involved in every aspect of wildlife and conservation, from art, poetry and music to science, geology and political activism. The conversations and connections that came out of the charity's annual events established and helped many careers and projects. Thanks in particular go to Amy-Jane Beer, Tim Birkhead, Mary Colwell, John Fanshawe, Ben Hoare, Harriet Mead and Jeremy Mynott.

Mary and Jeremy both feature in this book, and I offer them extra thanks for meeting with me in the field along the way of my travels. For the same reason, I also thank Brian Hodgson, Nicola Chester and Grahame Hopwood. Of all my guides and fellow walkers, I owe a special and deep debt of gratitude to Nick Acheson. He has been a much-valued friend for some years, giving generously of his time and knowledge and reading every part of every draft of this book (sometimes several times). Nick's ecological expertise and personal experiences of local place have been invaluable to me.

I must also thank various friends and colleagues at Cranbrook School and in the wider local area. Cranbrook was, quite literally, the first place of this book; a book which is, in part, a paean to fifteen years living and working in that town and the county of Kent. So many acquaintances have contributed to and influenced my writing, but to Stephen Message and Simon Penny, who will remain lifelong friends and fellow birdwatchers, I owe particular thanks (and very probably a pint or two, which gives me, as if I need an excuse, one very good reason to keep returning to Kent).

I have been fortunate that so many people were willing to discuss topics and details in this book over the six years it took me to write it, and to read chapter drafts. The ideas and advice of these people have been invaluable and essential in making *The Cuckoo's Lea* what it finally is; my deepest gratitude goes out to all of you. Many of you are mentioned above, but I must also mention John Baker, Mark Cocker, Richard Cox, Aengus Finnegan, Harry Jenkinson, Richard Jones and Stephen Rutt.

Many thanks go to Jim Martin at Bloomsbury for being so enthusiastic about this project from the very start. When I sent my proposal to him in 2022 he insisted it would be published by hook or by crook and was instrumental in getting the sales team to see its vision and potential. Thanks also to everyone else at Bloomsbury involved in the book too, most especially to my editor, Heather Bradbury, who has made the whole process so enjoyable and straightforward and with whom I hope to work on many more books to come, my copyeditor Elizabeth Peters, and Julie Bailey, who was significantly involved early on. I have greatly appreciated how optimistic everyone has been about my ideas and decisions at every stage, not least in the keen support for my suggestion that Matt Johnson design the cover. Thank you, Matt, for your beautiful design, which will be the reason anyone picks this book up in the first place.

To the generosity and support of everyone in my immediate and extended family, I owe so much, but especially to my brothers, Richard and Philip, for sharing a lifelong love of nature with me, and to Richard additionally for accompanying some of the journeys for this book, reading drafts (and for shrewdly managing my expectations about the likelihood of ever getting published!). Thanks to my parents: my late father, to whom this book is dedicated, and even more so Mum, for choosing to educate her boys in the great British outdoors, allowing us to run free and explore, and for never failing to believe in me. Finally, to my girls, to whom I owe every happiness: my daughters Islay and Hattie, who I'm immensely proud to say are shaping up to be quite the little naturalists (who cares what else your children know if they can identify herb-robert and nightingales before the age of six ...), and my wife, Ginny, for humouring me, for always encouraging, for sharing in my adventures, and for turning up at Cranbrook School in 2013. I cannot say or do enough to repay you for making this book and my career as a writer possible.

Birds in English Place Names: A Glossary

This is a selective list. For more birds, place name examples, discussion and references, please see *The Birds and Place Project: Discovering the Birds of England's Place-Names* (birdsandplace.co.uk).

The taxonomic sequence below follows that found in most British field guides where possible.

Bird – *brid, cocc, fugel, hana*
Birdbrook, Essex (brook of the young birds); Birdwood, Gloucestershire (bird wood); Cockfield, Durham (cocks' open land), Foulden, Norfolk (bird hill); Fowlmere, Cambridgeshire (wild birds' mere); Henley, Shropshire (hens' wood or clearing); Henstead, Suffolk (hens' place)

Swan – *elfetu, swan*
Elvet, County Durham (swan island or swan river); Elvetham, Hampshire (swan water-meadow or flatland in a river bend where swans are); Swanbourne, Berkshire (swans' stream)

Goose – *gos*
Gooseham, Cornwall (goose meadow); Goosey, Oxfordshire (goose island); Gosfield, Essex (goose open land); Gosforth, Northumberland (geese's ford)

Duck – *duce, ened*
Doughton, Gloucestershire (duck farm); Dukinfield, Cheshire (ducks' open land); Enford, Wiltshire (duck ford); Enmore, Somerset (duck pond)

Bittern – *pur*

Purbeck, Dorset (hill ridge shaped like a bittern's beak); Purleigh, Essex and Purley, Berkshire (bittern clearing)

Heron – *hragra*

Rawerholt, Cambridgeshire (heron wood); Rawreth, Essex (heron stream)

Stork – *storc*

Storrington, West Sussex (storks' farm)

Eagle – *erne*

Arley, Warwickshire and Earnley, West Sussex (eagle wood or clearing); Arnold, Nottinghamshire, 'eagles' nook', Yarnscombe, Devon (eagle's coomb)

Kite – *cyta*, *glida*

Gledhow, Yorkshire (kite hill); Gledwish, Sussex (kite marshy meadow); Kidbrooke, London (kite brook)

Buzzard – **wrocc*

Wroxall, Isle of Wight (buzzard's nook); Wroxton, Oxfordshire (buzzard's stone)

Hawk and other raptors – *hafoc*, *puttoc*, *pytell*

Hawkhope, Northumberland (hawk remote valley); Hawkridge, Somerset (hawk ridge); Hawkhurst, Kent (hawk's wooded hill); Pitshanger, London (raptor's wooded slope); Pudlestone, Herefordshire (raptor's hill); Putney, London (raptor landing-place)

Crane – *cran*, *trani*

Cranbrook, Kent (cranes' stream or bog); Cranmore, Isle of Wight (cranes' marsh); Cransford, Suffolk (cranes' ford);

Tranmere, Merseyside (crane sandbank); Tranwell, Northumberland (cranes' spring)

Plover/lapwing – *gifete, hleapewince, *tewhit
Iffley, Oxfordshire (plover clearing); Lapford, Devon (lapwing ford); Tivetshall, Norfolk (lapwing's nook)

Sandpiper/wagtail/dipper – *stint*
Stinchcombe, Gloucestershire (sandpiper's valley); Stinsford, Dorset (sandpiper's ford)

Snipe – *snite*
Snitter, Northumberland (snipe shieling); Snitterfield, Warwickshire (snipes' open land); Snydale, Yorkshire (snipe hollow or haugh)

Woodcock – *wuducocc*
Cock Beck, Yorkshire (woodcock stream); Cockshutt, Shropshire (place where woodcock can be caught)

Dove/pigeon – *culfre, cuscote, dufe*
Culverstone, Kent (originally Culversole – pigeons' boggy place); Duffield, Derbyshire (open land of doves); Shotley, Suffolk (pigeon wood)

Cuckoo – *cucu, geac*
Coxwold, Yorkshire (cuckoo wood); Cuckfield, Sussex (open land with cuckoos); Yaxham, Norfolk (cuckoo's promontory); Yaxley, Cambridgeshire (cuckoo's lea)

Owl – *ufe, ule*
Ousden, Suffolk (owl's valley); Oldcotes, Nottinghamshire (owl cottages); Ulcombe, Kent (owls' coomb), Ulgham, Northumberland (owl nook); Ullenwood,

Gloucestershire (owls' wood); Ulley, Yorkshire (owl wood or clearing)

Woodpecker – *fin, speot*
Finborough, Suffolk (woodpecker hill); Finmere, Oxfordshire (woodpecker pool); Spexhall (woodpecker's hollow)

Lark – *lawerce*
Larkbeare, Devon (lark hill); Larkton, Cheshire (lark down); Laverstock, Wiltshire (farm frequented by larks); Laverton, Gloucestershire (estate with larks)

Swallow – *swealwe*
Swalecliffe, Kent; Swalcliffe, Oxfordshire; Swallowcliffe, Wiltshire (swallow cliff)

Wren – *wrenna*
Warmfield, Yorkshire (wren's open land); Wrenbury, Cheshire (fort associated with wrens); Wreningham, Norfolk (promontory at the wren place)

Dunnock – *dunnoc*
Dunkeswell, Devon (dunnock's spring); Dunnockshaw, Lancashire (dunnock copse)

Thrush – *osle, throstle, thrysce, scric*
Ossett, Yorkshire (the dwelling or fold frequented by thrushes); Owslebury, Hampshire (blackbird fort); Shrigley, Cheshire (thrush glade [although, possibly shrike]); Thrushelton, Devon (farm frequented by thrushes)

Tit – *mase, *tite/titel*
Masongill, Yorkshire (titmouse ravine); Titley, Herefordshire (tit wood)

Jackdaw – *ca, ka*
Cabourne, Lincolnshire (jackdaw stream); Cavill, Yorkshire (jackdaw open land); Kaber, Cumbria (jackdaw hill); Kigbeare, Devon (jackdaw grove)

Crow – *crawe, kraka*
Crackpot, Yorkshire (limestone rift frequented by crows); Crawcrook, Durham (crow nook); Crawley, West Sussex (crow wood or clearing); Creacombe, Devon (crow valley)

Raven – *hrafn, hrefn, hremn*
Ramsgate, Kent (raven's pass); Renscombe, Dorset (raven's combe); Ravensdale, Derbyshire (raven's valley); Ravenshead, Nottinghamshire (raven's headland)

Sparrow, or some such small bird – *succa, sucga*
Suckley, Worcestershire (sparrow clearing); Sugnall, Staffordshire (sparrow hill); (Stretton) Sugwas, Herefordshire (sparrow-frequented floodland)

Finch – *finc*
Finchale, Durham (nook of land in a river bend frequented by finches); Finchampstead, Berkshire (homestead frequented by finches); Finchley, London (finch wood or clearing)

Bunting – *amer, bunting*
Amberley, West Sussex and Ombersley, Worcestershire (bunting wood or clearing); Buntingford, Hertfordshire (buntings' ford)

Permissions

The extract from *Nature Cure* by Richard Mabey on page 38 is © Little Toller, 2021. It is reproduced by permission of Richard Mabey.

The extract from *The Moth Snowstorm* by Michael McCarthy on page 49 is © John Murray, 2015. It is reproduced by permission of Michael McCarthy.

The extract from *Rebirding* by Benedict Macdonald on page 52 is © Pelagic, 2019. It is reproduced by permission of Benedict Macdonald.

The extract from *Landmarks* by Robert MacFarlane on page 103 is © Penguin Random House, 2015. It is reproduced by permission of Robert MacFarlane.

The extract from *The Seafarers* by Stephen Rutt on page 172 is © Elliott and Thompson, 2019. It is reproduced by permission of Stephen Rutt.

The extract from *Storming the Gates of Paradise* by Rebecca Solnit on page 264 first printed by the University of California Press June 2007. Reprinted by permission of Aragi Inc on behalf of Rebecca Solnit. Any use of the material without the correct copyright credit will be illegal.

Notes

Prologue

1 The word 'place' is Middle English, from Old French. Old English had a number of place terms, such as *stoc, stede, stow* or *worþ* (all of which appear in place names). *Ing*, a common element in place names, meaning 'the people or descendants of', could also mean just 'place' in some names ([Market] Deeping, for instance). Precise dating of *when* English places began is a complex matter. Farmsteads and hamlets existed from very early on (the [now reconstructed] Anglo-Saxon village at West Stowe originated in the fifth century), but the village as a larger, consciously planned (e.g. nucleated) site with an open-field system is thought to have appeared and developed between the ninth and twelfth centuries, in what has been termed the second revolution in the history of the English landscape (the first came in the Bronze Age with large-scale reclamation and clearance). More places originated or were developed during the twelfth century, when there was an intensification of town planning and growth. The names of some of these places may descend back much earlier, borrowed and inherited as settlements emerged, developed and changed sites within vicinities.

2 Mudford and Wetwood mean exactly what the names suggest, and Shitterton relates to foul-smelling effluence – probably a farm or village next to a sewer of some sort (the Old English verb *scitan* means 'to defecate'). Braintree means 'Branca's tree'; Bitchfield, Bil's open land'; Scratchbury, via an Old English word for the devil (*scratta*), 'the haunted fort'; and Frostenden is 'frog valley'.

3 The truth about exactly how Germanic peoples settled in lowland Britain (in what numbers, over how long, and with what particular intentions) and what happened to Brittonic

tribes is one of the great conundrums of British history. It is now widely accepted that the traditional *adventus* described by early historians such as Gildas and Bede, in which Germanic hoards invaded and pushed out or vanquished the Britons, is inaccurate. It is far more likely that there was considerable multilingualism, exchange, and a great deal of continuity for the Britons during this time.

4 This is the combined result of the wealth of surviving documentary evidence in England (most significantly William the Conqueror's Domesday survey) and the extensive research undertaken and published by the English Place-Name Society since 1923, which is still ongoing. No other country in Britain and Ireland has the same history and body of research. As the authors of the latest and most authoritative dictionary of Welsh place-names remark, 'In Wales, progress has been much slower' than in England. Many Irish names including birds, such as townland and minor place names, are only recorded in more modern times. It is difficult, therefore, to make accurate comparisons between the numbers of birds in different countries' place names that might have once existed, or might be very old. On the surviving evidence, however, it is true enough to say that England's record of birds in old names, both in terms of species mentioned and the number of individual examples, is remarkable.

Chapter 1

1 In *Totemism*, Lévi-Strauss states that 'natural species' are totemic to humans not so much because they are *bonnes à manger* 'good to eat', but rather because they are *bonnes à penser* 'good to think with'. Elsewhere, he speculates that it is birds most of all that occur to us as a 'metaphorical human society' (*The Savage Mind*).

2 Mark Cocker remarks in *Birds and People* that 'If we ever had to vote for a family to serve for the entire 10,500 species of

bird and even whole panoply of life on Earth, then cranes would probably make the shortlist'.

3 This list could be extended to Scotland, where there are also *cran* and *trani* place names, and further to include Brittonic *garan* in Cornish examples. Gaelic *corr* (crane, as well as heron) turns up frequently in Irish place names.

Chapter 2

1 Even by the time of the Conquest, the voiceless form of *g* (pronounced *y*) was already sometimes being written with a *j*, *i* or *y*.

2 When Old French *cucu* arrived with the Normans, new place names using the new word apparently sprung up quickly, such as Cuckfield in East Sussex, which is possibly recorded as early as 1087. The alternative explanation is that there existed an unrecorded Old English *cucu* pre-dating the Conquest.

3 Dogs bark *ham ham* in Albanian, or *gong gong* in Malay. Cockerels call *quiquiriquí* in Spanish, but *o o o* in Mandarin.

4 *Gaukaz* and *cucu/kuku*, according to linguists' reconstructions, although it is thought that not all *cucu*-sounding monikers for the bird in Indo-European languages have a common source, despite the striking similarity between so many of the names. *Cucu*, then, if it did exist in Old English independent of the Norman influence (see above), found its way virtually unchanged all the way into Middle English.

5 There is another place, down on the Fens itself, where this connection between summer fen-living and cuckoos must have been even more apparent: the name of a farmland road, 'Euximoor Drove', east of March near Christchurch. *Eux* descends from *geac* in a similar way to Exbourne. Its full name was at one time Yekeswellemoor (1431), 'the marshy ground by the cuckoo's spring'.

6 The reed warbler is one of the commonest host species for cuckoos in Britain. In other habitats, species such as meadow

pipit are the chosen hosts (as on Dartmoor). The cuckoo host race specialising in pipits has, like its reed warbler counterpart, evolved to produce eggs that closely mimic its host's.

Chapter 3

1 There is a single possible swift place name: a reference to *swiftan beorg* 'swift's hill' in an Anglo-Saxon charter dated to the ninth century. This might, however, involve an unrecorded personal name.
2 In the Middle Ages, as in the classical world, it seems highly likely that swifts were not distinguished from hirundines, and that swifts and swallows were sometimes confused or treated as variations of the same species.
3 There are plenty of goose place names in England, but unsurprisingly they refer to domestic birds (e.g. Gosforth, 'goose-ford'). There are some that may pertain to wild geese, such as Gosfield in Essex, but it is impossible to know for sure.

Chapter 4

1 The hedge bank in question is, in fact, still visible in one or two locations, but not anywhere I had thought to look. After I'd made my visit with Nicola, I discovered a paper published in *Berkshire Archaeological Journal* by Dick Greenaway, in which he proposes the correct boundaries of the granted woodland at Hawkridge, not at the modern named site on the ridge at all, but in fact down by the village east of Bucklebury, at Stanford Dingley, which he identifies as the site of Cuthwulf's hamlet.
2 The word *landscip* existed in Old English, but meant simply 'region, area of land'. The sense we are familiar with today relating to art and the idea of transforming the land's features for aesthetic purposes came about in the seventeenth century, from closely related Dutch *landschap*.
3 Charters were not exclusive to England. There are the Llandaff charters of Wales, for instance, preserved in a twelfth-century manuscript, but these contain few birds.

4 These are all prominent landmarks in the boundary clauses
   and, fortunately, easily identified today. Stoke Orchard was
   simply *stoce* a thousand years ago (a general term for an
   outlying farm or settlement, as well, simply, place); Cockbury,
   which survives as nearby Cockbury Court, was *coccan burh*,
   then and for a long time before a fortification on the adjacent
   hill to Cleeve (but now named Nottingham Hill); and the
   ealden or *grena weg* now seems to be part of the Winchcombe
   way, which cuts right over Nottingham Hill and heads south
   towards Cleeve Common.

5 The foremost scholar of English toponyms was Margaret
   Gelling, whose books, *Place-Names in the Landscape* and *The
   Landscape of Place Names* (the latter with Ann Cole), are
   essential reading for anyone interested in the topic.

6 It is feasible, perhaps, that Moorstock *is* the old site of Ulaham,
   but I say this based purely on the fact that the latter seems to
   have been located broadly in the same vicinity as Moorstock.
   Kent is yet to be represented in the English Place-Name
   Society's county-by-county volumes, and to my knowledge,
   there has been no archaeological research into lost Ulaham.

Chapter 5

1 In modern taxonomy, *Nycticorax* is the genus name for night-
   herons, which do have coarse, crow-like calls and are
   characteristically nocturnal in their feeding habits.

2 This depiction was very commonplace in a range of religious
   and scholarly texts, but the best-known examples are those in
   the bestiaries. These were immensely popular among the elite
   literary classes in the later Middle Ages and are perhaps best
   described as moralised natural histories. The texts feature animals
   naturalistically (or as the authors found them 'naturalistically'
   described in previous bestiaries or encyclopaedias, anyway), then
   attach a moral to each one so that readers might learn neat
   lessons about their own behaviours by paying attention to the
   'book of nature'. For a beautiful example of a bestiary, visit
   abdn.ac.uk/bestiary.

3 This is changing. Warming global temperatures, diminishing snow in northern countries year on year, are slowly doing away with the grey morph tawny, as reported in research from southern Finland.

4 The Brittonic term *cumbo has become Modern Welsh *cwm*. *Cumb* might have also been influenced by another Old English *cumb*, meaning 'cup or bowl'.

5 'Hall' often derives from *halh*, which denotes a variety of land features broadly and loosely related to 'nook': recess, hollow, sunken land, projecting land, hemmed-in land, and so on.

6 It was common practice in pre-modern times to divide the night into a 'first' and 'second' sleep, with a short period awake and active in between.

Chapter 6

1 Fulstow is 'the meeting place of birds' (a migration point perhaps), east of the Wolds in Lincolnshire and still described as a 'marsh village'. Fowlmere is 'the wild birds' mere', near Cambridgeshire and close to what once would have been fenland. Fowley is the name of an island in Chichester Harbour, and another west of Faversham on the north Kent coast.

2 From Old English *sumpt, which itself derives from the same root as 'swamp', and from which we get our word 'sump'.

3 It is not certain that *pur* exclusively meant bittern because it also translates other bird names in early medieval glossaries, including, as it happens, the snipe. In the fens of medieval Cambridgeshire, however, there was a *purfenne* and a *snytfenne*. The presence of both bird names in this location seems a good indication that *pur* did indeed mean bittern, even if it was used for, or later transferred to, other species.

4 Irish Gaelic for snipe is *naosgach* and bittern is *bunnán*. In Cornish, the word is *kiogh*, hence the minor place name Boquio (snipe's dwelling) in Cornwall.

5 *Huilpe,* cognate with the Dutch name for curlew, *wulp,* is the root of *whaup,* a term for curlew in Scotland and northern England, hence Whauphill in Wigtownshire in Scotland, and Whaupmoor Burn near Alnwick in Northumbria. As with *pur* for bittern, we cannot be sure that *huilpe* only referred to curlew in medieval England.

Chapter 7

1 Most famous of all is Saint Columba's association with Iona, but consider also Saint Enda and Inishmore, Saint Molaise and Inishmurray, Senan and Scattery, Féichín and High Island, Colmán and Inishbofin, Blane and Bute, Cattan and Gigha, Cormac and Eilean Mor, Brendan and Eileach an Naoimh.
2 Archaeological evidence, along with some place names and accounts in the Icelandic sagas, suggests that early medieval monastics from Britain and Ireland may have been present in Iceland and Greenland before the Viking settlement of these northerly locations.
3 Avian flu has taken its toll in more recent years, but in 2019, of Britain's 53,000 or so pairs of Arctic terns, over 2000 bred on the Farnes.

Chapter 8

1 Some of the nightingales in place names are attached to a Welsh word for tavern, which implies a nickname for singers with impressive and renowned voices.

Chapter 9

1 Following a 2019 genetic study, many sources now accept the recent proposed change for the Eurasian goshawk's genus from *Accipter* to *Astur* (also meaning hawk).
2 My definitions are from Margaret Gelling and Ann Cole's *The Landscape of Place-Names* (a revised version of Gelling's

Place-Names in the Landscape). Gelling did more than anyone to demonstrate how fundamental topography was to medieval concepts of place and the practice of place-naming.

3 These mammalian predators are recorded in our place-names. Wolves are not uncommon, as in the Norse Cumbrian name Ullock, meaning 'place where wolves play', although *wulf*, like *hafoc*, was a personal name too. Lynx might be remembered in Lostford, Shropshire.

4 There is more than one theory about the etymology of *Accipiter*, but one thought is that it is influenced by Latin *accipere*, 'to take', and thus, like raptor and hawk, it ultimately derives from Indo-European *★kap*.

5 *Raptor* did exist in the Anglo-Saxon vocabulary as an alternative Latin word for *accipiter*, but it had not yet made it into the English language itself. Predominantly, the word was used to mean 'thief'.

Chapter 10

1 It has been said that the proverbial flying crow may be a precise reference to the straight-aimed, evening flights of rooks to their roosts. In this chapter, as in the adage, I use the term *crow* in the generic sense when referring to family Corvidae or the *Corvus* genus, and *carrion crow* when specifically describing *Corvus corone*.

2 This story is famously told by Bede in his *Ecclesiastical History of the English People*, but with a different bird, a sparrow, which becomes a metaphor for the Christian human soul when it flies from the stormy winter's night into a firelit hall.

3 There are eight species: raven, carrion crow, rook, jackdaw, jay, chough, magpie and hooded crow. The last was previously considered a subspecies of carrion crow, but has been designated independent status. There is no way of knowing whether medieval people differentiated the two or not. The

Old English terms for the birds we now call raven, crow, rook, jackdaw, jay and magpie all turn up in place names (*higera*, magpie or jay, appears only once, in a charter reference). We don't know if any of the medieval words for jackdaw from which comes the modern word for chough were applied to that species (*Pyrrhocorax pyrrhocorax*) in medieval times, and therefore it is impossible to say if the chough is intended in any place names. *Agu*, magpie, doesn't appear at all, although Tardebigge in Worcestershire may be Celtic for 'hill of the magpie'.

4 Danesbury Fort in Hampshire is the best-known site for these raven pit burials. Some 80 percent of nearly 2,000 bones excavated between 1969 and 1988 belonged to corvid species, predominantly ravens.

5 Both these particular corvid place names, it should be said, are modern. It is possible that they do descend from older pre-existing names, but as far as I can discover there is not a single early-attested Crow Wood (*crawe* + *wudu*) in the records. There are, however, many *crawe* place names attached to other Old English terms for wood (holt, shaw, hurst etc).

6 All of these appear in place-names. Elveden, in Suffolk, probably means 'elf valley'; Drakelow (Cheshire) is the 'dragon's tumulus'; and Shobrooke (Devon) is the 'haunted brook' (Old English *sceocca* means 'demon').

7 Riddle 24: I am a wondrous creature. I vary my voice: sometimes bark like a dog, sometimes bleat like a goat, sometimes honk like a goose, sometimes yell like a hawk. Sometimes I mimic the ashy eagle – cry of the warbird – sometimes the kite's voice I speak with my mouth, sometimes the gull's song, where I sit gladly. G they name me, also Æ and R. O helps, H and I. Now I am called as these six letters clearly indicate.

8 Lapford, incidentally, may mean 'lapwing ford', although it could also refer to an unrecorded personal name, *Hlappa*.

9 When I returned to the site the following Christmas, I couldn't find the birds, for two nights. On the third, a raven banked over the ridge and flew south, calling as it went. Below its flight path, there was the flock, a huge black stain on a field about half a mile away.

Epilogue

1 At the time we left Kent in 2024, there were two in Headcorn, three on the edge of Cranbrook, and no village between those two places that didn't have development underway. In the Essex village we moved to there are two halfway through development right on our road, one in the next village north, and plans for more in the area.
2 Particular examples are the use of place-name evidence to justify reintroducing white-tailed eagles (see chapter 7) or storks (e.g. Storrington) to Britain.

The * symbol at the beginning of words in this book denotes reconstructed words; that is 'missing' words for which we have no written evidence. All Proto-Indo-European words are reconstructed, for instance, because PIE is a prehistoric common ancestor language which can only be recreated by comparing related vocabularies in related modern languages and working backwards from there.

Further Reading and References

General

Cameron, Kenneth. 1996. *English Place-Names*. B. T. Batsford Ltd, London.

Cox, Richard. 2002. *The Settlement Names of Lewis*. Clann Tuirc, Ceann Drochaid.

Gelling, Margaret. 1984. *Place-Names in the Landscape*. Dent, London.

Gelling, Margaret and Ann Cole. 2014. *The Landscape of Place-Names*. Shaun Tyas, Donington.

Joyce, P. W. 1910 and 1920. *The Origin and History of Irish Names of Places*. 3 vols. Longmans, Green and Co., London.

Nicolaisen, W. F. H. 2001. *Scottish Place-Names*. John Donald, Edinburgh.

Oosthuizen, Susan. 2019. *The Emergence of the English*. Arc Humanities Press, Leeds.

Owen, Hywel Wyn and Richard Morgan. 2007. *Dictionary of the Place-Names of Wales*. Gomer Press, Ceredigion.

Rackham, Oliver. 2020. *The History of the English Countryside*. Weidenfeld and Nicolson, London.

Watt, Victor. 2004. *The Cambridge Dictionary of English Place-Names*. Cambridge University Press, Cambridge.

Yalden, D. W. and U. Albarella. 2009. *The History of British Birds*. Oxford University Press, Oxford.

Websites

Survey of English Place-Names: epns.nottingham.ac.uk (The most comprehensive online site for English place names, as thorough a resource as you can get on the subject without consulting the many weighty volumes of the English Place-Name Society's publications themselves.)
Also, Key to English Place-Names: kepn.nottingham.ac.uk

The Exeter Book

Most of the medieval texts cited and discussed in this book are from the Exeter Book, a single manuscript containing most surviving Old English poetry. For these poems in the original, see theexeterbook.exeter.ac.uk and theriddleages.bham.ac.uk. This book uses my own translations, but for more of the Exeter Riddles in modern English, see Kevin Crossley-Holland's 2008 book, *The Exeter Book Riddles*, or the Riddles Ages website mentioned above.

Chapter 1: An Antiquity of Cranes

Boisseau, S. and D. W. Yalden. 1998. The Former Status of the Crane *Grus grus* in Britain. *Ibis* 140: 482–500.
Buxton, John and Chris Durdin. 2011. *The Norfolk Cranes' Story*. Wren Publishing, Sheringham.
Cocker, Mark. 2013. *Birds and People*. Jonathan Cape, London.
Leopold, Aldo. 1949. *A Sand County Almanac*. Oxford University Press, Oxford.
Lévi-Strauss, Claude. 1966. *The Savage Mind*. Weidenfeld and Nicolson, London.
Lévi-Strauss, Claude. 1964. *Totemism*. Merlin Press, London.

Chapter 2: The Cuckoo's Lea

Colgrave, Bertram (ed. and trans.). 1956. *Felix's Life of Saint Guthlac*. Cambridge University Press, Cambridge.

Davies, Nick, *Cuckoo*. 2015. Bloomsbury, London.

Jefferies, Richard. 2012. *Nature Near London*. Collins, London.

Macdonald, Benedict. 2020. *Rebirding: Restoring Britain's Wildlife*. Pelagic, Exeter.

McCarthy, Michael. 2015. *The Moth Snowstorm*. John Murray, London.

Pryor, Francis. 2019. *The Fens: Discovering England's Depths*. Head of Zeus, London.

Wordsworth, William. 2008. 'To the Cuckoo' in *The Major Works*. Oxford University Press, Oxford.

Chapter 3: Pathless Ways

Backhouse, Janet. 2001. *Medieval Birds in the Sherborne Missal*. British Library Publishing, London.

Boswell, James. 2008. *The Life of Samuel Johnson*. Penguin, London.

Gerald of Wales. 1982. *The History and Topography of Ireland*, trans. John O'Meara. Penguin, London.

Gladstone, Hugh. 1910. *The Birds of Dumfriesshire*. Witherby and Co., London.

Hudson, W. H. 2016. *A Shepherd's Life*. Little Toller, Beaminster.

Isidore of Seville. *The Etymologies of Isidore of Seville,* trans. Stephen A. Barney. Cambridge University Press, Cambridge.

Leopold, Aldo. 1949. *A Sand County Almanac*. Oxford University Press, Oxford.

Pliny. 1938–1962. *Natural History*, trans. H. R. Rackham. Vol 1 of 10. Harvard University Press, Cambridge, MA.

Trevisa, John (trans). 1975. *On the Properties of Things: John Trevisa's Translation of Bartholomaeus Anglicus, De proprietatibus rerum*. Vol. 1 of 3. Clarendon Press, Oxford.

Chapter 4: Charterlands

Bond, Michael. 2021. *Wayfinding*. Picador, London.

Chester, Nicola. 2021. On *Gallows Down*. Chelsea Green, London.

Greenaway, Dick. 2016. Locating 'Hawkridge Wood':
    Interpreting the Bucklebury Charter of AD 956. *Berkshire
    Archaeological Journal* 82: 101–107.

Hooke, Della. 2015. 'Beasts, Birds and Other Creatures in
    Charters and Place-Names' in *Representing Beasts in Early
    Medieval England and Scandinavia*: 253–282. Boydell and
    Brewer, Woodbridge.

Hoskins, W. G. 2013. *The Making of the English Landscape*. Little
    Toller, Beaminster.

Hoskins, W. G. and Christopher Taylor (ed.). 1988. *The Making
    of the English Landscape*. Hodder and Stoughton, Sevenoaks.

ihti.ca (Inuit Place-Names)

langscape.org.uk (Glossed texts of the Anglo-Saxon charter
    boundaries.)

Macfarlane, Robert. 2015. *Landmarks*. Hamish Hamilton,
    London.

newyorker.com/culture/the-new-yorker-interview/going-
    home-with-wendell-berry (Amanda Petrusich, an interview
    with Wendell Berry).

Chapter 5: An Owl's Cry

Ambrose, Saint. 1961. Hexameron, Paradise, and Cain and Abel,
    trans. John J. Savage. Catholic University America Press,
    Washington, DC.

Baker, J. A. 2015. *The Peregrine, The Hill of Summer & Diaries*.
    HarperCollins, London.

Cartlidge, Neil (ed.). 2001. *The Owl and the Nightingale*. Exeter
    University Press, Exeter.

Swanton, Michael (trans.). 1996. *The Anglo-Saxon Chronicles*.
    J. M. Dent, London.

Thomas, Edward. 2004. 'The Owl' in *Collected Poems*. Faber and
    Faber, London.

Vitalis, Orderic. 1968-1980. *The Ecclesiastical History of Orderic
    Vitalis*, 6 vols. Clarendon Press, Oxford.

Chapter 6: The Marsh Dwellers

Chaucer, Geoffrey. 2018. 'The Prologue and Tale of the Wife of Bath' in *The Canterbury Tales*. W. W. Norton and Co., New York, NY.

Clare, John. 2004. 'To the Snipe' in *Selected Poems*, ed. Paul Farley. Faber and Faber, London.

Colwell, Mary. 2019. *Curlew Moon*. HarperCollins, London.

Dale, Johanna (ed.). 2023. *St Peter-on-the-Wall: Landscape and Heritage on the Essex Coast*. University College London Press, London.

Defoe, Daniel, 1978. *A Tour Through the Whole Island of Great Britain*. Penguin, London.

Dickens, Charles. 2003. *Great Expectations*. Penguin, London.

Heaney, Seamus (trans.). 1999. *Beowulf*. Faber and Faber, London.

Gordon, Ida (ed.). 1979. *The Seafarer*. University of Exeter Press, Exeter.

Johns, C. A. 1868. *British Birds and Their Haunts*. Society for Publication of Christian Knowledge, London.

map-of-essex.uk (John Chapman and Peter André's 1777 map of Essex.)

Poole, Kristopher and Eric Lacey. 2014. Avian Aurality in Anglo-Saxon England. *World Archaeology* 46: 400–415.

Svensson, Lars. 2023. *Collins Bird Guide*. HarperCollins Publishers, London.

Chapter 7: The Gull's Home

Augustine, Saint. 1952. *City of God, Books VIII–XVI*, trans. Gerald G. Walsh and Grace Monahan. Catholic University of America, Washington, DC.

Bede. 1999 *Ecclesiastical History of the English People*, ed. Judith McClure and Roger Collins. Oxford University Press, Oxford.

Evans, R. J., L. O'Toole and P. Whitfield. 2012. The History of Eagles in Britain and Ireland. *Bird Study* 59: 335–349.

Leslie, Roy F. (ed.). 1985. *The Wanderer*. University of Exeter Press, Exeter.

Melville, Herman. 1992. *Moby Dick*. Wordsworth Editions, Ware.

Moffat, Alistair. 2022. *Islands of the Evening: Journeys to the Edge of the World*. Birlinn, Edinburgh.

Nicolson, Adam. 2004. *Sea Room*. HarperCollins, London.

Riordan, Maurice (ed.). 2014. *The Finest Music: Early Irish Lyrics*. Faber and Faber, London.

Rutt, Stephen. 2019. *The Seafarers*. Elliott and Thompson Limited, London.

Swanton, Michael (trans.). 1996. *The Battle of Brunanburh* in *The Anglo-Saxon Chronicles*. J. M. Dent, London.

Webb, J. F. and D. H. Farmer (trans. and ed.). 1965. *The Age of Bede*. Penguin, London.

Chapter 8: Everywhere and Nowhere

Cartlidge, Neil (ed.). 2001. *The Owl and the Nightingale*. Exeter University Press, Exeter.

Chaucer, Geoffrey. 1972. *The Parliament of Fowls*. Manchester University Press, Manchester.

Clare, John. 2004. 'The Nightingale's Nest' in *Selected Poems*. Faber and Faber, London.

Gerald of Wales. 1978. *The Journey Through Wales and The Description of Wales*, trans. Lewis Thorpe. Penguin, London.

Hewson, Chris M. *et al*. 2018. Estimating National Population Sizes: Methodological Challenges and Applications Illustrated in the Common Nightingale, a Declining Songbird in the UK. *Journal of Applied Ecology* 55: 2008–2018.

Hough, Caroline. 1997–98. Place-Name Evidence for Old English Bird-Names. *The English Place-Name Society* 30: 60–76.

Keats, John. 2008. 'Ode to a Nightingale' in *The Major Works*. Oxford University Press, Oxford.

Luria, Maxwell S. and Richard L. Hoffman (eds). 1974. *Middle English Lyrics*. W. W. Norton and Co., New York, NY.

Neckam, Alexander. 2012. *On the Nature of Things*. Cambridge University Press, Cambridge.

Ticehurst, N. F. and F. C. R. Jourdain. 1911. On the Distribution of the Nightingale During the Breeding Season in Great Britain. *British Birds* 5: 2–21.

Chapter 9: Hawk in the Wood

Chaucer, Geoffrey. 1972. *The Parliament of Fowls*. Manchester University Press, Manchester.

Chaucer, Geoffrey. 2018. 'The Prologue and Tale of Sir Thopas' in *The Canterbury Tales*. W. W. Norton and Co., New York, NY.

Chaucer, Geoffrey. *Troilus and Criseyde*. 2006. W. W. Norton and Company, New York, NY.

Gower, John. 1980. *Confessio Amantis*. University of Toronto Press, Toronto.

Macdonald, Helen. 2014. *H is for Hawk*. Jonathan Cape, London.

Marie de France. 1999. *Yonec* in *The Lais of Marie de France*, trans. Glyn Burgess. Penguin, London.

Murray, K. Sarah-Jane and Matthieu Boyd (ed. and trans.). 2023. *The Medieval French* Ovid moralisé. Boydell and Brewer, Woodbridge.

Oggins, Robin. 2004. *The Kings and Their Hawks: Falconry in Medieval England*. Yale University Press, New Haven, CT.

Trevisa, John. 1975. *On the Properties of Things: John Trevisa's Translation of Bartholomaeus Anglicus, De proprietatibus rerum*. Vol. 1 of 3. Clarendon Press, Oxford.

White, T. H. 2007. *The Goshawk*. New York Review of Books, New York, NY.

Chapter 10: Crow Hill

Aelred of Rievaulx. 1981. *Dialogue on the Soul*, trans. Charles H. Talbot. Cistercian Publications, Kalamazoo, MI.

Aitchison, George. 1936. *Sussex*. A. and C. Black Ltd, London.

Chaucer, Geoffrey. 2018. 'The Prologue and Tale of the Manciple' in *The Canterbury Tales*. W. W. Norton and Co., New York, NY.

Clare, John. 2014. 'January' in *The Shepherd's Calendar*. Oxford University Press, Oxford.

Cocker, Mark. 2008. *Crow Country*. Vintage, London.

Davidson, Gabrielle L. *et al.* 2014. Salient Eyes Deter Conspecific Nest Intruders in Wild Jackdaws. *Biology Letters* 10: 20131077.

Dibnah, Alex J. *et al.* 2022. Vocally Mediated Consensus Decisions Govern Mass Departure from Jackdaw Roosts. *Current Biology* 32: 467–469.

Lacey, Eric. 2015. 'When Is a Hroc Not a Hroc? When It Is a Crawe or a Hrefn! A Case Study in Recovering Old English Folk-Taxonomies' in *The Art, Literature and Material Culture of the Medieval World*. Four Courts, Dublin.

Moore, P. G. 2002. Ravens (*Corvus corax corax* L.) in the British Landscape: A Thousand Years of Ecological Biogeography in Place-Names. *Journal of Biogeography* 29: 1039–1054.

Serjeantson, D., and J. Morris. 2011. Ravens and Crows in Iron Age and Roman Britain. *Oxford Journal of Archaeology* 30: 85–107.

Simpson, Jacqueline. 2009. *Folklore of Sussex*. The History Press, Stroud.

Epilogue

Casey, Edward S. 1996. 'How to Get from Space to Place in a Fairly Short Stretch of Time' in *Senses of Place*. Santa Fe School of American Research of Minnesota Press, South Minneapolis, MN.

Cresswell, Tim. 2004. *Place: A Short Introduction*. Black Publishing, Oxford.

Fox, Michael Allen. 2016. *Home: A Very Short Introduction*. Oxford University Press, Oxford.

Hayes, Nick and John Moses. 2024. *Wild Service: Why Nature Needs You*. Bloomsbury, London.

Jørgensen, Dolly. 2019. *Recovering Lost Species in the Modern Age*. The MIT Press, Cambridge, MA.

Office for National Statistics. Estimates on relationships with others, volunteering, sense of belonging to a neighbourhood, and say in what the government does, Great Britain: 22 June to 17 July 2022.

Solnit, Rebecca. 2008. 'The Silence of the Lambswool Cardigan' in *Storming the Gates of Paradise: Landscapes for Politics*. University of California Press, Berkeley, CA.

Tuan, Yi-Fu. 1974. *Topophilia: A Study of Environmental Perception, Attitudes and Values*. Prentice Hall Inc., Englewood Cliffs, NJ.

Index

Acheson, Nick   28–31, 33–9, 98
Aelred of Rievaulx (*Dialogue on the
      Soul*)   253–4
Aidan, Saint   165
Æthelred, King   108
Æthelwold, Abbot   93
Alfred, King   101
Ambrose, Saint (*Hexameron*)   117, 122
Anglo-Saxon charters   88–9, 91–7, 100,
      101–5, 107–8, 246, 261, 283–4
Anglo-Saxon Chronicles, The   112
Arctic tern   103, 169, 171–74, 177
Aristotle   68
Ashford   15
Augustine, Saint (*City of God*)   175
avian flu (H5N1)   82–4, 267–8, 286

barnacle goose   75, 76–85, 267
barn owl   29, 109, 112–3, 122, 130–1,
      254
Bartholomew the Englishman   68–9,
      70, 220, 225
Battle Abbey   225–6
Battle of Brunanburh, The   179
Bede, The Venerable   (*Ecclesiastical
      History*)   168, 180, 281, 287
Beowulf   143, 250
Berkshire   89–91, 97–100, 102, 179,
      201, 209, 214, 283
bestiaries   113, 284
birds; *see also individual species entries*
      migration   27, 63–5, 67–9, 75–8, 80,
            84, 173–4, 228
      names in Gaelic   148, 160–1, 177,
            179, 236, 282, 285
      names in medieval English and
            Norse   27–8, 42–4, 113, 117, 118,
            147, 148, 191, 201, 208–10, 214,
            219–20, 236, 239, 287
      sounds and songs of   43, 59, 60–2,
            116–20, 122–3, 127, 129, 131, 145,
            146–150, 151, 155, 188–91, 196,
            201–6, 236, 239, 244, 249, 252–4,
            255, 257
Birds of Dumfriesshire (Hugh
      Gladstone)   77–8
Bishop's Cleeve   88–9, 100–3, 284

Bishopstone   152
bittern   146–7
blackbird   44, 203
blackcap   185
black-headed gull   178
Blackwater (river and estuary)   139–43,
      147, 150, 154, 259
Bosham   178–9
Brenhilda, Saint   167
brent goose   134
Brin Eos   184–6
British Trust for Ornithology   183
Broads, The Norfolk   31–9
Bucklebury   98–100, 283
buntings   16, 96, 102
Bury Barton   254–5, 256
buzzard   82, 119, 208–210
Byrhtnoth, Ealdorman   139

Caldy (Calders)   14, 103
Cambridgeshire   42, 52–62, 200–1,
      203–6, 235, 285
Canada goose   103
carrion crow   235, 244, 245, 246, 251,
      253, 256
Casey, Edward   261
Castor Hanglands   199–201, 203–6
Celtic peoples and languages   13, 16,
      121, 148, 160–2, 185–6, 187, 234–5,
      244–5, 254, 288
Chaucer, Geoffrey
      'Manciple's Tale, The'   253
      'Parliament of Fowls, The'   189, 225
      'Sir Thopas, The Tale of'   225
      'Troilus and Criseyde'   220
      'Wife of Bath's Tale, The'   147
Chelmsford   260
Chester, Nicola   90–2, 97–100
      On Gallows Down   98
chough   237, 239, 287–88
Clare, John   97, 143–4, 190, 200, 203–4,
      205
Cleeve Hill   88, 100–1, 284
Cobham, David   227
Cocker, Mark
      Birds and People   281
      Crow Country   237, 241

Colwell, Mary   153–4
  Curlew Moon   153
Cnut, King   178
common crane   16, 19–39, 60, 282
common gull   160–1
common tern   178
cormorant   161
Cornwall   73, 164, 165, 179, 181, 285
corvids   16, 234–257
  carrion crow   235, 244, 245, 246,
    251, 253, 256
  chough   237, 239, 287–8
  hooded crow   287
  jackdaw   172, 234, 235, 238–9,
    242–3, 248–50, 251, 252, 256, 287
  jay   217, 236, 237, 252, 253, 287, 288
  magpie   90, 236, 252, 287, 288
  raven 96, 103, 167, 180, 234, 235, 236,
    237, 239, 244, 246, 251, 287, 288
  rook   90, 97, 234, 235, 237, 239–40,
    241, 242, 245, 249, 250, 250, 251,
    255–6, 288
Crackpot   233–4
Cranbrook   19–23, 25, 28, 107, 112,
    210, 212, 213, 214, 259, 289
Cranwich   31–2
Criseyde   220–1
crows; *see* corvids
cuckoo   16, 29, 41–63, 74, 90, 206
Cuckoo (Nick Davies)   50, 59
Cumbria   74–5, 77–85, 138, 179, 234,
    287
Cumbria Bird Club   79
curlew   81, 82, 150–5, 169, 175, 178,
    206, 286
Cuthbert, Saint   165, 167, 171, 172

Dál Riata, Kingdom of   163
darkness and night-time   111–2, 113,
    114–6, 117, 120, 122–3, 126–9, 149,
    155, 203, 204–6, 211, 242–3,
    247–8, 249–50, 254, 256–7
Dartmoor   44, 52, 59, 98, 119, 255, 256,
    283
Dengie peninsula   139, 141, 143, 166
Dering Woods   187–91, 194, 198, 200,
    206
deserted medieval villages   106–9
Devil's Dyke, The   243–5, 247
Devon   41–2, 44–5, 46, 47, 51–2, 59,
    62, 98, 119–21, 179, 181, 182, 246,
    254–7, 283, 288
Dícuill   178

Domesday Book   23, 31, 42, 107, 124,
    130, 212, 254, 281
ducks; *see* wildfowl
dunlin   134, 152, 153
dunnock   16, 50, 102, 105, 145

Eadwig, King   93
eagles   16, 28, 82, 167, 169, 176–7, 178,
    179–82, 209, 246, 289
Earnley   179–81
East Brabourne   108
*Ecclesiastical History of Orderic Vitalis,
    The*   124
Edwin, King   234
eider   103, 167
Ellah (goshawk)   224–7, 228, 230
English Hours (Henry James) 107
English Place-Name Society   281, 284
Escobar, Arturo   261
Essex   133–6, 138–43, 147, 150, 153,
    154, 155, 166, 177, 178, 259–60,
    283, 289
Exbourne   41–2, 44, 46, 51–2, 62, 254,
    282
Exeter   47, 51–2
Exeter Book, The   47, 48, 49, 51, 61, 77,
    151, 170, 179, 202, 252–3, 254
Exeter Book Riddles, The   47–52, 63,
    77, 202–3, 253, 288
extinction and loss   11, 17, 26, 33, 37,
    51–2, 56–7, 59–60, 61–2, 72, 73–4,
    82–5, 91, 97, 98, 104–5, 136, 138–9,
    153–5, 166, 177, 182, 183, 191,
    192–4, 196–7, 199, 201, 205, 218,
    228, 263–4, 266–9, 286; *see also*
    rewilding and recovery

falconry   224–30
Farne Islands   165–67, 171–3, 267
Fens, The   33, 54, 55–62, 71, 136, 143,
    147, 149, 266, 282, 285
fieldfare   76
Finan, Saint   164
finches   96, 102, 105
Fingringhoe   141
FitzOsbern, Osbern   179
Foulness   135–6, 138, 142
Frideswide, Saint   89, 100
Frilsham   89, 97

Gaelic place names   16, 104, 148,
    160–2, 185–6, 282, 285
gannet   161, 167, 169, 176, 177

Gerald of Wales
    History and Topography of Ireland,
        The   76–7
    Journey Through Wales, The   183, 193
geese; *see* wildfowl
Gildas   281
Ginny (author's husband)   19, 66–7, 70,
    72, 130, 140, 185, 255, 259
Gloucestershire   88–9, 100–2, 122
Glydwish   9–12, 17, 186
Godwinson, Harold   178
godwit   134
golden eagle   179
goldfinch   105
golden plover   84, 134, 150, 152
goshawk   210–32
Goshawk, The (T. H. White)   218, 227
Gotham   45, 62, 74
Gower, John (*Confessio Amantis*)   221,
    225
great black-backed gull   160
Great Expectations (Charles
    Dickens)   133
great grey shrike   76
great spotted woodpecker   102
greenshank   150
green woodpecker   102, 105, 236
grey heron   26
greylag goose   80
grey plover   134, 153
guillemot   103
gulls; *see* seabirds
Guthlac A (poem)   61
Guthlac, Saint   57, 59, 61

habitats and landscapes
    coast and islands   78–85, 133–43,
        150, 153, 154–5, 159–69, 171–4,
        176–82
    downland and valleys   65–7, 69–73,
        88, 100–2, 105–9, 119–21, 241–5,
        246, 247, 248–51, 254–7
    farmland   21–2, 41, 57, 109, 185,
        240
    upland   233–4
    wetland   25, 32–3, 34–5, 37–9,
        56–60, 79–85, 133–55, 177
    woodland   9–10, 21–2, 54, 112, 113,
        114, 115, 119, 122, 125, 186–91,
        198–9, 205–6, 210–13, 215, 216–8,
        221–4, 228, 229–32
Harriet (author's daughter)   188, 190–1,
    194, 206

hawks   16, 63, 209–12, 214–32, 288; *see*
    also goshawk, sparrowhawk *and*
    raptor
Hawkhurst   212–15
Hawkridge Wood   89–91, 92–4, 107,
    283
Headcorn   129–131, 186, 238–9, 240,
    259, 289
Heol-y-Cyw   184–6
Hickling Broad   33, 34–5, 37, 39
Hill of Summer, The (J. A. Baker)   127,
    260
H is for Hawk (Helen Macdonald)   219
History of the Countryside, The (Oliver
    Rackham)   136
hobby   29
Hodiford Farm (Hodoworth)   107, 108
Hodgson, Brian   79–85, 267
Holst, Gustav   149
hooded crow   287
Hooke, Della   91
Homer (*The Iliad*)   23, 28
Hopwood, Grahame   194–9, 201, 203,
    204, 205
Horsey   33, 34, 35, 37
Horsley, Dave   34, 35
Horsley, John William   108
Hoskins, W. G.
    Making of the English Landscape,
        The   87–8, 91, 92, 100
    Old Devon   254
Hughes, Ted   64

Inuit place names   103–4
Ireland   16, 22, 104, 136, 148, 153, 154,
    158, 161, 163, 164, 165, 177, 183,
    192, 193, 234, 263, 281, 286
Isidore of Seville (*Etymologies*)   67–8, 69,
    70, 174
Islay (author's daughter)   111–12, 114,
    116, 131, 210–11
Islay, Isle of   159–60, 163, 185
Isle of Wight   181, 209

jackdaw   172, 234, 235, 238–9, 242–3,
    248–50, 251, 252, 256, 287
Jansson, Jan   58
jay   217, 236, 237, 252, 253, 287, 288
Johns, C. A.   146
Johnson, Samuel   68

Kaber   234
Keats, John   191, 200

Kent   10, 15, 19–23, 25, 105–9, 111–2,
     114–6, 122, 129–31, 137, 138,
     186–91, 198, 210–5, 216–8, 221–4,
     228, 231–2, 238–41, 259, 284, 285,
     289
kestrel   214
kingfisher   96, 242
kings and other nobles
     Æthelred   108
     Æthelwold, Abbot   93
     Alfred   101
     Byrhtnoth, Ealdorman   139
     Cnut   178
     Eadwig   93
     Edwin   234
     FitzOsbern, Osbern   179
     Godwinson, Harold   178
     Leofric, Bishop   46–7, 77, 179, 254
     Offa   152

Landmarks (Robert Macfarlane)   103
Landscape of Place-Names, The (Margaret
     Gelling and Ann Cole)   286
Lapford   254–7, 288
lapwing   81, 84, 288
Leofric, Bishop (of Exeter)   46–7, 77,
     179, 254
Lévi-Strauss, Claude
     Savage Mind, The   23, 281
     Totemism   281
Life of Saint Guthlac, The (Felix of
     Crowland)   57, 58
Lincolnshire   25, 43, 56, 58, 106, 147,
     19–9, 200, 201, 285
Lindisfane   165, 168, 178
little grebe   29
little owl   130
long-eared owl   122
long-tailed tit   91, 100, 102, 105
Lossit Bay   160
Lundy Island   182

Macbeth (William Shakespeare)   251
Maldon   139, 140, 147, 260
magpie   90, 236, 252, 253, 287, 288
Marie de France   (Yonec)   225
marsh harrier   29, 140
Martial   252
Medieval Natural World, The (Richard
     Jones)   265
Mersea Island   139, 140, 141, 150
mistle thrush   102
Moby Dick (Herman Melville)   175

monastics and hermits (peregrini)   162–6,
     167, 168, 170, 174, 175, 178
Moorstock   107, 108
Moth Snowstorm, The (Michael
     McCarthy)   49
Mynott, Jeremy   140, 141, 143, 144,
     150, 153, 155

Natural History of Selbourne, The (Gilbert
     White)   68
Nature Cure (Richard Mabey)   38
Nature Near London (Richard
     Jefferies)   61, 137
night heron   284
nightingale   183–206
Norfolk   29–39, 42, 56, 181, 192, 201,
     237
Northumberland   165–7, 168, 171–3,
     176, 209

Offa, King   152
Oldberrow   122
Oldcotes   125
On the Nature of Things (Alexander
     Neckam)   193
Owl and the Nightingale, The   118, 127,
     189–90, 193, 201–2
owls   16, 109–31; see also Owl and the
     Nightingale
     barn owl   29, 109, 112–3, 122,
          130–1, 254
     little owl   130
     long-eared owl   122
     tawny owl   111–31
oystercatcher   134, 152
Oxfordshire   25, 73, 89, 192, 201, 207–8

Pang, River   91, 94, 98–99
peregrine   29, 82, 164, 227, 230
pheasant   90, 230
Philomela   221, 225
pink-footed goose   29, 82
place names, history of   10, 13–6, 23,
     24–5, 42, 54, 67, 88, 93, 103, 104,
     107–8, 120–2, 124, 125, 134, 135,
     136–7, 138, 141–2, 145, 148, 152,
     160, 161–2, 179, 185–6, 192,
     207–9, 212–3, 214, 233–4, 235–6,
     254, 280, 282, 283, 284, 285, 286,
     287, 288, 289
Place-Names in the Landscape (Margaret
     Gelling)   14, 284, 287
place, philosophy of   260–2, 263–4

Pliny the Elder (*Natural History*) 50, 63, 68
puffin 182
Purleigh 147

Rainham Marshes 139, 154
Raphael, Emma and Mike 224–30
raptors; *see also* hawks
   buzzard 82, 119, 208–10
   golden eagle 179
   goshawk 210–32
   gyrfalcon 225, 228, 230
   hobby 29
   kestrel 214
   marsh harrier 29, 140
   peregrine 29, 82, 164, 227, 230
   red kite 10–12, 17, 207, 210, 288
   sparrowhawk 214, 215–16, 220, 221
   white-tailed eagle 16, 28, 82, 167, 169, 176–7, 178, 179–82, 246, 289
Rautavaara, Einojuhani 149, 151
raven 96, 103, 167, 180, 234, 235, 236, 237, 239, 244, 246, 251, 287, 288
Ravenstonedale, 234
Rebirding (Benedict Macdonald) 52
Recovering Lost Species in the Modern Age (Dolly Jørgesen) 269
red kite 10–12, 17, 207, 210, 288
redshank 134, 150, 153, 155
reed warbler 60, 282, 283
Relph, Edward 268
rewilding and recovery 11, 31, 33–5, 37–9, 59–60, 134, 181–2, 199, 218, 229, 244, 265–6, 268–9; *see also* extinction and loss
Richard (author's brother) 74, 79–80, 81, 242–5, 247–50
robin 188
Rockcliffe Marshes 75, 79–85, 138
Romney Marshes 137
Ronan, Saint 167
rook 90, 97, 234, 235, 237, 239–40, 241, 242, 245, 249, 250, 250, 251, 255–6, 288
Rookby 234
RSPB 134, 135, 139, 194

saints
   Aidan 165
   Ambrose 117 and 122
   Brenhilda 167
   Cuthbert 165, 167, 171, 172
   Finan 164

   Frideswide 89, 100
   Guthlac 57, 59, 61
   Ronan 167
Sand County Almanac, A (Aldo Leopold) 26–7, 37, 38, 78
sandhill crane 27
sandpiper 102
Saxton, Christopher 228
Scotland 75, 104, 136, 159–62, 163, 164, 165, 174, 176, 177, 179, 181, 183, 193, 243, 263, 282, 286
Screaming Sky, The (Charles Foster) 73, 74
seabirds
   Arctic tern 103, 169, 171–74, 177
   black-headed gull 178
   common gull 160–1
   common tern 178
   cormorant 161
   gannet 161, 167, 169, 176, 177
   great black-backed gull 160
   guillemot 103
   gulls 81, 103, 160, 161, 163, 169, 171, 176, 177, 182, 288
   puffin 182
   shag 160, 161, 166–7
Seafarer, The 151–3, 168–70, 171, 172, 174–6, 177, 179, 182
Seafarers, The (Stephen Rutt) 172
Seahouses 166
Searoom, The (Adam Nicolson) 168
Sellindge 108–9, 241
shag 160, 161, 166–7
shelduck 134
Shepherd's Life, A (W. H. Hudson) 72, 137
Sherborne Missal, The 75–6
Sibelius, Jean 149
'Silence of the Lambswool Cardigan' (Rebecca Solnit) 264
Skellig Michael 164, 171
snipe 16, 144–6, 147–8, 149, 285
Solway Firth, The 74–5, 77–85, 267
song thrush 188
sparrow 102, 287
sparrowhawk 214, 215–16, 220, 221
Stephen (friend of author) 211, 216, 221–3, 232
Steyning 241, 248
St Peter-on-the-wall (chapel) 141, 166
Stubb Mill 35, 36, 38–9
Sula Sgeir 161, 167, 168
'Sumer is icumen in' 45–6, 49

Sussex   9–12, 17, 25, 137–8, 152,
        178–80, 186, 212, 213, 225–6, 229,
        235, 241–5, 246, 247–50, 256
Sussex (George Aitchison)   247
swallow   16, 65, 67, 68, 70–1, 72–3, 74,
        75, 78, 119, 185, 283
Swallowcliffe   65–6, 70, 71, 72, 74, 88
Swallowcliffe Down   67, 69–70, 71–3
Swallowcliffe Princess   66, 67, 70
swan   16, 158, 169, 176, 242
swift   64–5, 70, 73, 74, 283

tawny owl   111–31
Taylor, Christopher   92
teal   134, 150
Tereus   221, 225
Thomas, Edward   120
thrushes
    blackbird   44, 203
    fieldfare   76
    mistle thrush   102
    song thrush   188
tits
    long-tailed tit   91, 100, 102, 105
    willow tit   80
Topophilia (Yi-Fu Tuan)   261–2
Tottington Woods   248–50
*Tour Through the Whole Island of Great
        Britain, A* (Daniel Defoe)   139, 147
Troilus   220–1
Truleigh Hill   247, 250

Ulaham   106–9, 284
Ulcombe   122, 130
Ullenhall   122
Ulley   123–6, 128–9
Upper Beeding   241–3, 247

waders   134–5, 136
    curlew   81, 82, 150–5, 169, 175, 178,
        206, 286
    dunlin   134, 152, 153
    godwit   134
    golden plover   84, 134, 150, 152
    grey plover   134, 153
    lapwing   81, 84, 288
    redshank   134, 150, 153, 155
    snipe   16, 144–6, 147–8, 149, 285
    woodcock   96, 256
Wales   11, 88, 183–6, 243, 250, 281, 283
Wallasea Island   133–6, 138, 149, 154

Wanderer, The   157–8, 170, 172
Waterland (Graham Swift)   55
Wayfaring (Michael Bond)   105
Weald, of Kent   10, 21–2, 25, 36, 71,
        106, 112–6, 186–9, 190–1, 198,
        210–8, 221–4, 228, 231–2
Wensum, River   29, 30, 35, 98
Whisby   194–9, 201, 205
white stork   29, 289
white-tailed eagle   16, 28, 82, 167,
        169, 176–7, 178, 179–82, 246,
        288, 289
white-fronted goose   76
Wicken Fen   59–60, 266
wigeon   134, 150
wildfowl
    barnacle goose   75, 76–85, 267
    brent goose   134
    Canada goose   103
    eider   103, 167
    greenshank   150
    pink-footed goose   29, 82
    shelduck   134
    swan   16, 158, 169, 176, 242
    teal   134, 150
    white-fronted goose   76
    wigeon   134, 150
Wildlife Trusts   34, 35, 194
Wild Service (Nick Hayes and Jon
        Moses)   266
William the Conqueror   23, 124, 281
Williams, Ralph Vaughan   149
willow tit   80
Wiltshire   65–7, 69–73, 95, 179, 209
woodcock   96, 256
Woodland Trust   187
woodpeckers   16, 100
    great spotted woodpecker   102
    green woodpecker   102, 105, 236
Wordsworth, William   59
Worthing   137–8, 241
wren   96, 102, 188
Wroxton   207–9
Wulpenbek   152

Yaxley   52–6, 57, 58, 59, 60, 61, 62, 105,
        201, 207
yellowhammer   96, 102
Yeo Valley   254–7
Yorkshire   106, 123–6, 128–9, 179, 192,
        233–4